Vigilant Citizens

VIGILANT CITIZENS

Vigilantism and the State

RAY ABRAHAMS

Polity Press

First published in 1998 by Polity Press in association with Blackwell
Publishers Ltd.

Editorial Office:
Polity Press
65 Bridge Street
Cambridge CB2 1UR, UK

Marketing and Production:
Blackwell Publishers Ltd
108 Cowley Road
Oxford OX4 1JF, UK

Published in the USA by
Blackwell Publishers Inc.
Commerce Place
350 Main Street
Malden, MA 02148, USA

ISBN 0-7456-1637-2
ISBN 0-7456-1638-0 (pbk)

A catalogue record for this book is available from the British
Library and has been applied for by the Library of Congress.

Typeset in 10 on 12 pt Palatino
by Wearset, Boldon, Tyne and Wear.
Printed in Great Britain by TJ International, Padstow, Cornwall.

This book is printed on acid-free paper.

Contents

Acknowledgements

In assembling the material for this study, I have received much vital help from many people. Some, such as Ernest Gellner, Keith Hart, Warren Shapiro, Marilyn Strathern and Helen Watson, have given me encouragement to begin and complete the task. Several, such as André Czegledy, Suzanne Hoelgard and Stephen Hugh-Jones, have passed on valuable reports to me about vigilantes in different parts of the world. Library staff in Cambridge, London and Oxford have provided invaluable help in tracing and obtaining access to some of the less widely known material I have used, and I particularly wish to thank Aidan Baker and his staff in the Haddon Library, Mary Kendall in Churchill College, and Linda Williamson in Rhodes House, Oxford for their efforts and their patience in this context. David Anderson, Catriona Mirrlees-Black, my wife Eeva and my daughter Katherine, David Farrington, Leo Howe, Pauline Hunt, John Iliffe, Les Johnston, Italo Pardo and Garry Slapper have also variously helped me to gain access to useful out-of-the-way material. Heather Murphy in Churchill College has been helpful as ever with my efforts to make copies of material, and Paul Caldwell in the Department of Social Anthropology has provided useful technical advice. Ian Agnew, Owen Tucker and Mike Young gave help and advice with the map, and Gill Motley and her colleagues at Polity Press have provided friendly guidance on putting the manuscript into shape. Many people have also given me the benefit of their wisdom and advice in discussions about vigilantism. I am especially grateful for comments I received from Mike Rowlands and other participants in a recent conference at the University of Kent organized by Italo Pardo, and similarly for comments from Olivia Harris and others in Oslo in 1994. Matthew Kramer in Churchill College has also been kind enough to respond helpfully to questions on law both in general and in the United States, Loraine Gelsthorpe has been very helpful on the thorny question of gender and crime, and Sue Benson has given me useful advice on vigilantism and gender. In addition to such help from professional colleagues, I have also benefited from my role as a university teacher. Research is often said to enhance teaching, but the reverse is also true. The interest shown in vigilantism by my students, the need to present material in accessible form to them, and their power to ask disarmingly simple questions have all stimulated my thoughts on the subject. I owe a special debt of thanks to several people who have helped me in my Tanzanian work on Sungusungu. These include Per Brandström in Uppsala, my former students and now friends and colleagues Sufian Bukurura, Chris Lwoga and Martin Walsh, and also Liz Wiley. Lastly, I must take this opportunity to acknowledge once again my debt to all my Nyamwezi friends and former neighbours who turned my work among them into some of the happiest periods of my life. They are too many for me to list all of them individually, but I must make special mention of the late Julius Brush in Kahama and Nsabila Kitambi in Kakola, and my dear friends Kalugula, Ndulichimu and Tuli in Busangi. To them I send my thanks – *ng'wabeja* – and hope that my work has merited the help they have given me.

1
Vigilantes

Introduction

Vigilantes have arisen at many times in different regions of the world as defenders, often by force, of their view of the good life against those they see to be its enemies. Recent reports of their activities in Britain, Ireland, Italy, Mexico, South Africa and North America have appeared in the British and overseas press. Yet they have been relatively little studied outside the United States, where they hold a special, if at times romanticized, position in the nation's history. It may be that their common involvement in the defence of power, property and other 'bourgeois' interests has been less attractive to scholars than the more radical activities of bandits and revolutionaries. None the less, it is surprising that their often independent stance towards the state has not received more attention from both critical and friendly analysts of that institution.

Like many of my generation I first became aware of vigilantes as a young cinema-goer exposed to a large number of 'B Westerns', in my case on the silver screen of a small building in north Manchester known as 'the local' or 'the Mip' – an acronym for the undeservedly much grander title of Moston Imperial Palace. Vague memories of such films still occasionally surface when I read about Montana vigilantes of the 1860s and the wicked Sheriff Plummer, who immediately acquires the face of a minor 1940s Hollywood actor. So vigilantes were for me initially, and for some time to come, a phenomenon of the American Wild West, albeit dressed in powerful mythic imagery – as I later learned – by immigrant Hollywood moguls. While trying to do their bit to unify America, these middle-Europeans also strangely captured the imaginations of innumerable youngsters all over the world, and I look back with some astonishment at my own English childhood days of playing cowboys and Indians, with their 'goodies and baddies', and an adolescence captivated by the songs of the old West which I still find touching today.

Of course, vigilantes were only a small part of the epic, whose other characters were the men and women settlers, the cowboys, the railwaymen and businessmen, and the Indians through whose lives and deaths the history of America's emergence as a nation was scripted. But they were an integral part all the same, as the American historian Richard Maxwell Brown makes very clear. For the history in question was plausibly portrayed as a history of 'the frontier' of the nation state, and vigilantes are essentially a frontier phenomenon.

My next conscious encounters with them were East African, first when as a fledgling anthropologist I noticed that night-watchmen in Kampala in the 1950s were for hire from a self-styled 'vigilante' company, and later through preliminary reports of Suzette Heald's research in eastern Uganda. Then in the 1980s, I encountered grassroots village vigilante groups among the Nyamwezi and Sukuma in west-central Tanzania. These groups, widely known in Tanzania as Sungusungu (the word 'vigilante' is itself not often heard there) had arisen to combat locally unacceptable crime levels. At much the same time, vigilantes began to hit the newspapers in Kenya and, especially, in South Africa – where use of the name was typically restricted to 'right-wing' protectors of the local status quo as opposed to the 'comrade' supporters of the African National Congress.

Meanwhile in Britain, popular anxiety about crime has also increased noticeably in the last few years. Partly following the lead of similar developments in North America, vigilantism along with more peaceful forms of neighbourhood watch, street patrol and other comparable activity has featured prominently from time to time both in the media and on the streets.[1] Summer 1993 was a high point for press coverage. In addition to its front-page report of the August Gallup poll which it commissioned, the *Daily Telegraph* published a detailed summary of the poll's findings and an editorial on the issue. The *Independent* also ran an editorial and several features on the poll next day. It commented that, while public concern was clearly rising to new heights, 'the answer to the problem certainly does not lie with vigilantes'.

I mention all this not just for the sake of reminiscence, but also to draw attention to some of the many different times and places in which vigilantism has appeared as an idea, a reality or a threat – and to those already mentioned one may add the modern Philippines, contemporary North and South America and different phases of the history of China.[2] Also, I hope that this brief 'gazetteer' will begin to evoke some sense of the fundamental ambiguities in relations between people and the state that vigilantism reveals.

My own reactions to it are ambivalent. For the Tanzanians whose communities I studied, vigilantism has clearly been part of their efforts to make sense of their lives and maintain some sort of order in their world in the face of the state's apparent inability to deal effectively with increased cattle theft and other crime. Like many anthropologists who have worked in comparable settings, I have felt considerable sympathy in this and other contexts for such 'ordinary' villagers who are commonly situated on the edge of the state and at the bottom of the political heap. This has been an important part of the humanist tradition in social anthropology which I personally do not regret. The interests of such villagers often receive scant attention from the powers that be, and their voices all too frequently remain unheard outside the pages of the ethnographic monograph. Their knowledge, their capacity for sensitive and fruitful co-operation, and their deep insights into the enigmas of being human well deserve the place accorded to them in such work.

Yet I am also well aware of the warts on the face of such communities, their literal or figurative witch-hunts, and the oppressive social control which membership of a 'caring' group may sometimes entail.[3] Similarly, I am conscious that although they are not highly stratified or deeply divided along class or ethnic lines – as are communities in many other places – they are not simply homogeneous either, and elements within them and outside them may try to exploit 'community' institutions for their own ends.

The power of vigilantism to generate ambivalence goes well beyond such personal research experience of village life. Its chief attraction probably lies in the notion of decent, independent, law-abiding citizens, anxious to live and work in peace, and ready to defend their right to do so if the state fails them. At the same time, many people fear vigilantism's disturbing implications for the authority of the police and courts and other formal instruments of state authority. This is nicely brought out by the criminologist Les Johnston's recent (1992) characterization of vigilantism under the heading 'autonomous' as contrasted to 'responsible' citizenship. Again, the term often smacks of violent 'mob rule' and the Captain Lynches of this world, in contrast to 'the rule of law' and respect for due process. This point was strongly made by Caughey (1957) in his paper 'Their majesties the mob'.[4] He also reminds us sharply that vigilantism all too frequently carries 'the added onus of nativism, class prejudice, political motivation or personal ambition' – a point amply illustrated by the materials collected in his later book under the same title.[5]

Paradoxically, in contrast to repulsion by its threats to the established order, it is also likely to displease more radical critics of the state. For them, vigilantism can, by its nature, never go far enough. In spite of its potential for subversion, it commonly displays a non-revolutionary and even a reactionary character, and Maxwell Brown interestingly uses the term 'conservative mob' when discussing its practitioners. Rather than reject the state, vigilantism commonly thrives on the idea that the state's legitimacy at any point in time depends on its ability to provide citizens with the levels of law and order they demand. Its emergence is often a vote of no confidence in state efficiency rather than in the concept of the state itself. Moreover, vigilantism is not always what it claims to be. It may turn out on inspection to be an elitist weapon dressed in populist attire and more concerned with politics than law; and it is not unknown for its practitioners to be 'off-duty' members of the police or militia bypassing inconvenient formalities in their pursuit of political opponents and other 'undesirable' elements in their society.

What's in a name?

I use the terms 'vigilante' and 'vigilantism' partly because of, and partly in spite of, these mixed qualities. I have wanted neither to overemphasize nor to underplay their positive and negative connotations, since the phenomena they represent are multifaceted, emotionally highly charged and changeable.

Originally 'vigilante' was a Spanish word, from the same Latin roots as English 'vigil', 'vigilant' and 'vigilance'. In contemporary Spanish it is mainly used adjectivally to mean 'watchful' and as a noun simply to mean 'watchman' or 'guard'. It appears to have entered North American English from the south during the nineteenth century. The term 'Vigilance Committee', for a vigilante group, was also common in America at that time. Alternative cognate labels in America were 'Vigilant Societies' (a common term for associations formed to combat horse-thieves in New England), 'Vigilants' and

'Vigilanters'. Other early terms there for such groups included 'Regulators' and 'Moderators' and many other more specific titles, such as 'White Caps' and, of course, the Ku Klux Klan.

The emphasis on 'vigilance' in such contexts seems to have been predominantly American until relatively recently. The term 'Vigilance Committee' was also found in South African townships around the end of the nineteenth century, but its significance there was more akin to that of a 'board of guardians'. Apart from a brief 1839 reference to the encouragement of 'vigilance' in an official discussion of crime control in rural England, I have not consciously encountered this word and its cognates in such early British contexts. It has certainly not held the 'key word' status there which it acquired in America, and there has even been some recent effort on the part of British commentators to distinguish it, as a relatively unloaded term, from 'vigilantism'.

Another set of English words – 'wake', 'watch' and 'watchful(ness)' – covers much the same conceptual ground as 'vigil' and its cognates. These words are of Germanic origin, though they appear in fact to share ancient Indo-European roots with their Latin counterparts. However, the idea of 'neighbourhood watch', with its connotations of non-violence and collaboration with the police, is often contrasted with vigilantism in contemporary English usage.

The different shades of meaning of such terms reflect both the variety of forms of 'vigilance' in different times and places, and the wide range of attitudes they can elicit. The situation is, however, further complicated by the human capacity for deception, irony and metaphor. The term 'Regulators' appears to have been used in both England and America to denote both law enforcers and cynical lawbreakers intent on the 'regulation' of the wealth of others to their own advantage. Also, as if its diverse connotations when used literally were not enough, the term 'vigilante' has recently been used in a wide range of more figurative contexts. Almost any unofficial protesters, from animal rights supporters and hunt saboteurs to those opposed to the closure of a railway line, are likely to be described, at least by their opponents, as vigilantes. There are also 'cyber-vigilantes', including a self-styled 'vigilante moose', who monitor and in some cases delete material they do not like on the Internet. An article in *The Times* suggests that police action against members of ethnic minorities is likely to provoke accusations of racism from 'the vigilantes of the race relations lobby'. Another news item mentions 'the impatient monetary vigilantes' of the bond market, and yet another describes a well-known footballer, involved recently in a violent incident, as more like a thug than an avenging vigilante.

This last usage harks back to the many recent film portrayals of vengeance- and justice-seeking individuals, and the term is also often used in a comparable way to describe Batman and other popular film and comic book heroes. The name Vigilantes has been adopted by a number of American football teams and, apparently, one English Rugby team, and an American folk-rock and soul group call themselves 'Vigilantes of Love'.

Definition and comparison

As a concept for comparative study, vigilantism is not easy to define in rigorous authoritative terms even if one ignores more figurative uses of the term. There are several reasons for this, including some that derive from more general difficulties inherent in the process of sociocultural comparison itself. As students of other cultures and practitioners of a discipline that has sometimes been described as 'comparative sociology', social anthropologists have a long if not wholly successful history of trying to solve problems of this sort.

The labels that anthropologists attach to different features of society and culture fall into two broad groups. Some, like marriage, incest, politics, economics, religion and language, are generally treated as human universals to be found in all human societies. This creates particular constraints, since any definition must automatically be applicable to any society one happens to encounter. Others, such as unilineal descent groups, ceremonial exchange, age organization and ancestral cults, are more specific. Although there has been a great deal of argument about the nature and the incidence of such forms, it is not considered necessary to define them in such a way that every human group appears to have them. This provides some leeway to define them more pragmatically in a range of more or less inclusive terms, according to our perceptions of the relevance of a variety of similarities and differences between the patterns found in different places.

Vigilantism is a concept of this second kind. We may be interested in its distribution, but we do not expect to find it always and everywhere we look. We also have some choice about how narrowly or broadly we define it, and this will partly depend upon our research aims. This does not mean that we are free to act like some post-structuralist Humpty Dumpty, arbitrarily making words mean whatever we might happen to want. Rather it enables us to filter a variety of details in or out of our picture in our attempts to make what seems to us the best sense of our own and others' observations. However, it is never simple to decide that the details found in one particular historical and sociocultural setting are as significantly similar as we might wish to those recorded elsewhere and/or at another time.

In addition to such general issues, it is arguable that certain more specific qualities of vigilantism also create problems for its definition. It is not so much a thing in itself as a fundamentally relational phenomenon, which does not make much sense except in connection with and often in contrast to others. Like 'civil society', it is part of a broad zone in the world of law and politics, encapsulated within the state and yet conceptually and at times politically opposed to official governmental institutions. It is also in some ways comparable to the 'informal sector' in economics. It occupies an awkward borderland between law and illegality, and between public and more sectional interests, in what I have elsewhere (1987) called 'the shadows rather than the bright lights of legitimacy and consensus'. Again, despite some vigilantes' attempts to formulate strict constitutions for themselves, the secret and highly personalized nature of much of their activity also helps to make it rather labile. Many of its manifestations are relatively short-lived, and it is always capable of slipping and sliding in one direction or another. Also, as I noted earlier, vigilantism – like other forms and levels of political activity – is not always what it seems or claims to be. It is typical of vigilantes that they attempt to take the moral high ground, but they may also entertain or covertly develop other agendas.

As all this implies, any delineation of their general characteristics *must* be treated as an 'ideal type' which the phenomena one investigates may interestingly approximate to, or as likely as not depart from, to varying degrees. This said, it is possible to delineate some of the main features of this 'ideal type'. Richard Maxwell Brown has usefully described vigilante groups as 'organised extra-legal movements the members of which take the law into their own hands' and also as 'associations in which citizens have joined together for self-protection under conditions of disorder'.

A recent article by Johnston (1996) also helpfully explores a number of main vigilante characteristics. He sums up with the statement that

> vigilantism is a social movement giving rise to premeditated acts of force – or threatened force – by autonomous citizens. It arises as a reaction to the transgression of institutionalized norms by individuals or groups – or to their potential or imputed transgression. Such acts are focussed upon crime control and/or social control and aim to offer

1. CITIZENS, CRIMINALS AND THE STATE: NORMAL MODE

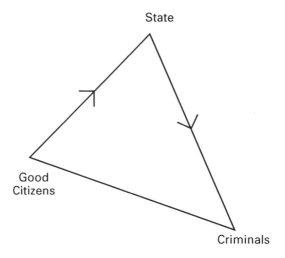

2. CITIZENS, CRIMINALS AND THE STATE: VIGILANTE MODE

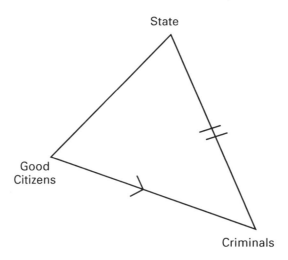

Figure 1 Structures of relations between 'good' citizens, criminals and the state

assurances (or 'guarantees') of security both to participants and to other members of a given established order.

This provides reasonably good coverage of the character of vigilantism, providing that one treats it as 'ideal' rather than 'substantive' and pays close attention to the implications of such phrases as 'potential or imputed' and 'crime . . . and/or social control'.

It may also be useful to state one or two points more explicitly at this juncture. Despite recent interest in lone armed figures like Bernard Goetz on the New York subway and in cinematic images of Charles Bronson or Clint Eastwood wreaking havoc in the city or on the High Plains, vigilantism is typically, as Johnston and Brown note, a group phenomenon both in America and elsewhere. Also, as Johnston's concept of 'autonomous citizens' implies, and as I have myself emphasized, vigilantism presumes the existence of the state, and of formal legal and other procedures involving the use of force over which the state normally claims a monopoly. Vigilantes typically lay claim, at least temporarily, to the state's own mantle of authority. If only for this reason, their relation to the state is bound to be awkward. Vigilantism typically emerges in 'frontier' zones where the state is viewed as ineffective or corrupt, and it often constitutes a criticism of the failure of state machinery to meet the felt needs of those who resort to it. It is a form of self-help, with varying degrees of violence, which is activated *instead* of such machinery, against criminals and others whom the actors perceive as undesirables, deviants and 'public enemies'.

At its most basic level, vigilantism thus appears, as in figure 1, as a particular form of a triangular structure of connections between 'good citizens, criminals and the state'. In what we might with caution label 'normal mode', this triangle involves good citizens successfully depending on the state to deal with criminals. In 'vigilante mode', the citizens are seen to bypass this procedure because, for one reason or another, the state does not deal to their satisfaction with their calls for help. They do not call upon the state, but simply try to deal directly with offenders. As I have already implied, however, it will become clear from the range of material dealt with in this book that reality may diverge from this basic ideal type in many different ways.

Vigilantism, at least as an ideal type, is thus conceptually very different from self-help of the simple oppositional kind – like feud, vendetta or simple revenge – between structurally equal individuals or groups, though it may sometimes tend in this direction. It also differs 'ideally' from local forms of dispute settlement and social control that are fundamentally rebellious against the state, or which, on the other hand, participate in a clearly recognized division of jurisdiction between state institutions and themselves. However, in this as in other contexts, the real social world is once again less rigorously structured than our conceptual frameworks, and the boundaries between actual forms of judicial and retributional behaviour are commonly less clearly marked than we might wish.

It will by now be clear that difficulties of boundary demarcation are endemic to phenomena like vigilantism, where actors' aims and motives are often mixed, disguised and contested, and constraints against changes in the character of behaviour itself are commonly weak. Here perhaps more than anywhere, the warning of Lucretius that 'nature does not make leaps' applies. In these circumstances, I have felt it sensible to include in my discussion some material, such as that on the Ku Klux Klan, which displays some but by no means all of the qualities of classic vigilantism, while also lending itself to other kinds of categorization. Apart from its own intrinsic interest, such material will I hope serve as a useful reminder of the fundamental 'fuzziness' and complexity of the world of law and politics and its boundaries.

The spontaneous, the traditional and the global

Despite its wide distribution, and although its functions are relatively well understood, the emergence of vigilante action in particular places at specific times is not altogether easy to explain. Can such developments be treated as spontaneous local reactions of 'human nature' to certain types of social circumstance and problem, or does their explanation demand a historical and perhaps even a 'global' approach?

In the early history of social anthropology, when Radcliffe-Brown and Malinowski led their functionalist crusades against the misguided worshippers of diffusion and historical conjecture, the issue seemed clear-cut. The functionalist message was that the origins of things mattered not a jot, or at most relatively little, compared to their place in a well-integrated and often small-scale social setting. Also, any local statements made about these origins were best understood as legitimating 'myths' and not as history.

Such functionalist fundamentalism could not hope to survive intact, even though paradoxically its allegations of the 'subjectivity' of history have flourished among some of its opponents and have even been expanded to include all forms of 'objective' knowledge. For some critics, social anthropology was not to be confined to a non-literate world, but had to come to terms with complex social systems with a 'history', such as those of the Islamic world and southern Asia. For others like Southall (1956), it also became clear that the past of many 'simpler' societies was neither uninteresting nor irretrievably lost. Later, the emergence of new independent nations tempted him and others to explore the extent to which old tribal divisions were convenient if not sinister creations of their former colonial masters. To this were added Marxist-oriented 'world-system' theories, ideas about 'cultural imperialism' and more recently – in the wake of studies of literacy and increasing awareness of the contemporary 'information explosion' – 'globalization'.

The study of social and religious movements has been an important part of such developments, though for a long time they attracted relatively little academic notice. Chinnery and Haddon's (1917) account of early 'cargo' cults and Engels' interesting paper (1894) on the early history of Christianity as a cult of the colonially oppressed did not at first receive the attention they deserved from anthropologists. It was only after World War II that one saw a mainstream interest in such movements, on the part of writers such as Worsley, Burridge, Lawrence, Mair and Jarvie, which is only partly explicable in terms of the emergence of new instances to study at that time.

Giddens (1984: 204) follows Blumer in his description of social movements as 'collective enterprises to establish a new order of life', and he adds that movements do not characteristically operate with fixed locales and well-defined role systems. His emphasis is clearly laid on fluid social change, though as another commentator notes, movements may emerge to either 'promote or resist change in the society of which [they form] a part' (Masanja). Such a concept immediately directs our attention to areas of society and culture which one might describe as 'less set in their ways'. A focus upon actors and their problems and ambitions becomes necessary, while at the same time these need to be placed within a wider context of personal experience, social history, cultural repertoire and social structural constraints.

The above rider on resistance to change resonates well with the inherent conservatism of much vigilante activity. It is also true that not all eruptions of such activity display sufficient coherence and organization even to qualify for Giddens' definition of a movement, while other forms of the phenomenon go beyond this to achieve a degree of structural definition and stability more akin to that of relatively established institutions. None the less, at one point or another in their history, most relatively persistent forms of vigilantism display some basic qualities and paradoxes of social movements generally.

An intriguing feature of such movements is that, despite their novelty and the possession of their own distinctive cultural and structural characteristics, they also exhibit recognizably similar features to developments occurring elsewhere and at other times. In fact, this mixed quality is largely shared by *all* social institutions, but it is particularly apparent in such 'new' developments.

There are three main potential sources of solution to the problem which such mixture poses. Firstly, there is the possibility of genuine spontaneity and independent invention. This in turn may be viewed more or less as pure chance or as resulting from a fairly predictable human response to a commonly recurring problem. In the case of vigilantism this problem could be defined as the failure of the state to provide the levels of order and social satisfaction that people would like to enjoy. The detailed differences between their responses can then be explained in terms of historical accident, individual quirks, cultural and social differences or a combination of some or all of these.

Secondly, the similarities may derive from experience or awareness of such action elsewhere and, thirdly, there is the possibility that they may represent the reuse of a pre-existing social and cultural template in the society itself.

My own strong inclination is not to see these different possibilities as mutually exclusive. Both freedom and constraint are of the essence of all human enterprise. Marx's well-known comment that men make their own history, but not just as they please and not in conditions of their own making, is as apt here as anywhere. The problem then becomes to understand the balance between the different factors in such situations. A long local tradition of particular patterns arising out of specific historical conditions may be crucial in some cases, while borrowing or spontaneous invention may loom larger in others. Yet all three seem likely to be found to some degree in every case, provided that sufficient data are available.

A brief discussion of the history of vigilantism in the United States may illustrate this point. Brown has attested to the presence there of a long-standing vigilante tradition, at least from the late eighteenth century to the present day, and he relates this to a number of key elements in American society and culture. These include the history and ideology of 'the frontier', the country's revolutionary origins, and the idea of 'popular sovereignty' that the state exists for and belongs to its members rather than vice versa. The asserted right of citizens to carry arms and to defend themselves, which has figured so strongly in recent 'militia' propaganda, is a further important element in this value system, and Brown also notes the post-colonial influence of inherited British law, which appeared to many citizens to be far removed from the actual conditions in which the new nation was being forged.

Brown argues, plausibly enough, that vigilantism arose in such conditions as a typically American phenomenon. The implication is that it was predominantly spontaneously generated initially, and that later examples were to be understood as the application of what had become well-known ideas and practices to local situations as and when they might arise. The San Francisco vigilantes of the 1850s and those of Montana in the 1860s were especially widely reported and were very influential in the middle period of this process of diffusion in North America, where Brown has documented over 300 separate groups between 1767 and 1904.

Brown also comments in this regard that there was no comparable vigilante tradition in Britain, although violent rioting was common there and in fact appears to have served as a model for riots in colonial America. Yet, as Philips and others have argued, some material suggests that it might be mistaken to draw too sharp a contrast between the two countries and also to discount the significance of a two-way traffic of ideas and 'know-how' between them.

I shall discuss some of the evidence for such traffic in chapter 5, where I examine the British situation in some detail, and I restrict myself here to a few brief comments. Firstly, a number of suggestions have been made of a connection between various forms of American vigilantism and the puritan traditions of the founding fathers, and E.P. Thompson has also speculated, light-heartedly but interestingly none the less, on the possibility of connection between lynchings and *charivari* in the American South. Also, as Brown notes, the term 'regulators' was used, albeit ambiguously, for a group of London 'thief-takers' in the early eighteenth century. This was the most common name for American vigilantes in the late eighteenth century, when America was still a British colony, and during the early nineteenth century. Moreover, at this time in Britain, we find a variety of local self-help associations for the prosecution of felons and for the repression of horse theft, and during the same period, American anti-horsethief groups, with similar names in some cases to their British counterparts, also began to flourish in New England.[6] As Philips and others have commented, and as Brown has stressed, the main difference between such societies and full-scale American vigilantes was the much greater use of and respect for the formal mechanisms of law and order in Britain and New England, and this in turn appears partly to connect to the readier availability of this machinery there.[7] The gap between the two forms of activity is not unbridgeable, however, either in imagination or in practice, though it may be viewed with strong emotion and is politically and legally of great significance. Indeed, one such old Horsethief Detection Society was resuscitated to provide support for Ku Klux Klan activities in 1920s Indiana (Wade 1987: 224–5). All this arguably suggests that American vigilantism was not so much a new invention as a step across a threshold of 'due process' within a framework common to both countries. There is good reason to assume that this threshold was clearly visible to actors on both sides of the Atlantic, and there is also evidence that it was occasionally crossed in Britain.

Support for southern lynchings and for vigilantes elsewhere in America was also sometimes voiced by English commentators. A tantalizing point to which Philips draws attention in this context is the fact that Thomas Josiah Dimsdale, the author of a well-known positive account of Montana vigilantism in the mid-nineteenth century, was a young Englishman who had settled there and was a close confidant of the men whose activities he describes. While this is interesting in itself, there is the further intriguing fact that one of the key early nineteenth-century activists in the organization of British anti-felon associations, and a strong advocate of local policing under their auspices, was another Thomas Dimsdale of Barnet.

It has not proved possible to demonstrate any clear family link between these two men, though some such connection – if only a very distant one – does seem likely. In any case, the present argument does not critically depend upon its presence or its absence. The early settlers, and the later highly mobile population of miners and others who went to California in the 1850s and to Montana in the 1860s, were drawn from a wide variety of backgrounds. Many, of course, were from Britain, including Ireland, and many of the Californian 'forty-niners' were from Australia (and before that, in many cases, Britain) in addition to those who moved west from the southern and eastern States. All must have had a mass of knowledge and ideas about different forms of unofficial crime control. and, as I will discuss in chapter 5, the flow of information through books, newspapers and, one may safely assume, letters and word of mouth was considerable even in these relatively early days. In these conditions, it makes little sense to see American vigilantism as a purely 'home-grown' product, however well it flourished in that country.

Evidence for an element of diffusion into other places and in later times is partly linguistic, but it is suggestive. The use of the term 'vigilante' on a global scale, which I have already touched upon, clearly testifies to American influence, given the word's first widespread use there. Again, the cinema has clearly been an important medium for the spread of such ideas from the beginning of the twentieth century, while more restricted local usage, such as the name 'A-team' for a South African vigilante group in the 1980s, testifies to the influence of American television. At the same time, modern media coverage of various sorts has ensured more or less worldwide knowledge of the activities of Guardian Angels, 'urban avengers' and many other forms of vigilantism. More generally, contemporary growth in worldwide information networks suggests that it would be foolhardy utterly to discount an element of diffusion in almost any context anywhere.

At the same time, however, there is also evidence in some cases for more narrowly localized vigilante development. The Tanzanian case of Sungusungu, which I discuss in chapter 2, seems genuinely to be of this sort – though it has roots in earlier forms of neighbourhood collaboration in the area – and it has also been suggested that recent northern Peruvian vigilantism (also discussed in chapter 2) has similarly been a mainly spontaneous development. In such cases, the recurrence of a problem seems to have been largely if not wholly sufficient in itself to generate similar solutions in different areas.

There is ultimately no real conflict here. The range of conditions under which vigilantism emerges is relatively narrow, and the idea of self-help in the face of state ineffectiveness is commonsensical. At the same time, knowledge of one's own or others' previous experience of such situations is unlikely to be wholly absent, and it seems likely to be especially important at the level of practical organization and of maintaining adequate control over the actions of participants.

Vigilantism, anarchy and the state

In spite of its conservative complexion, the ambiguities of vigilantism are reminiscent of some features of the much more radical idea of anarchy. As Woodcock (1986) has shown, this is fundamentally a double concept. For some it is synonymous with chaos, and as such to be deplored. For others it encapsulates an idea of good order without government and the state.

Like anarchists, vigilantes often see themselves as substituting for the state, if only for a time, in the pursuit of order. The state in turn commonly brands their activities as disorderly and illegitimate, and responds with firm assertions of its own monopoly in the use of force and the dispensation of justice.

From this perspective, anarchism and vigilantism each appear in contrast to and as a challenge to the state. Yet the fact that all three claim to provide order invites further thought concerning their comparability. It is already clear that anarchism is opposed to the principle of the state, while vigilantism tends mainly to bemoan its inefficiency. Yet it is also arguable that both anarchism and, at least, the modern state share certain concerns and dilemmas through their stress on values to which vigilantism often attaches relatively little weight.

One approach to this is through what some see as a fundamental flaw in anarchism. Every community, such critics argue, needs a series of conventions that individuals are not allowed to flout. Such a code of rules may claim to represent the will of the anarchist community as a self-conceived collection of free individuals, but it will in practice limit individual freedom and it is prone to reflect sectional interest.

At the same time, and from the opposite end of the political spectrum, modern western legal systems have, with variations, all incorporated and developed the liberal idea of individual freedom and rights, and these developments have also been quite influential outside Europe and America. In many areas of life, the range of these rights and the range of those deemed to possess them have expanded. Women's rights to their own property and the control of their own bodies, children's rights to care and even to 'divorce' from their parents, and legislation combating discrimination against individuals because of age, sex, colour or religion have been key areas of such expansion during the last century.

Most important in the present context are the rights of individuals suspected of or charged with criminal activity. Here too some recent expansion has been visible, as in the 1950s under Justice Warren's influence in the United States and in the constitutions of many newer nations, but the pattern tends to be less clear in this than in other areas. In Britain, many such rights have ancient roots, as in the well-known case of *habeas corpus*. Some enhancement of them has occurred, for example in the 1976 Bail Act, but their recent history mainly involves their clarification and delimitation rather then expansion.

The Police and Criminal Evidence Act (PACE) of 1984 provides a good example of this process. Its aim appears to have been to strike a balance both between conflicting values and between the ideal and the real. One aspect of the situation was anxiety about discrepancies between police practice and the rights of 'suspects'. In addition to its ethical desirability, the elimination of this problem also offered practical advantages. Police can arguably work more effectively if they are trusted by the public, and the collapse of prosecutions and the overturning of convictions because of police procedural irregularities are clearly best avoided. At the same time it was accepted that the police need substantial powers in the battle against crime. The Act set out to deal with these problems through the close specification of the rights and practices in question. The overall result appears to have been an increase in explicitly sanctioned police powers, tempered by the hope that their detailed definition in the Act will make it harder to exceed and abuse them.

A commonly heard argument is that the rights of suspects and their manipulation by skilled lawyers often make it difficult to convict the guilty, while those convicted are also often said to be given more help and comfort than a criminal deserves. A concerted government attack against this perceived trend began recently in Britain with considerable support from both police and public. This in turn heightened the anxiety of many legal and other professionals, whom Mr Howard, the former Home Secretary, has publicly dismissed as 'the woolly-headed brigade', that the state's commitment to the sanctity of individual rights within the judicial system is seriously under threat. At a more general level, the case for limitation of the rights of individuals in favour of those of 'the community' has been made by 'communitarian' writers like Etzioni.

It is clear that the debate about crime control, which vigilante activity both responds to and helps to generate, has to be seen not only as part of an argument about the functions of the state and its ability to fulfil them, but also in relation to the balance between state protection of the rights of individuals and the promotion of rights asserted to belong to the community or to society as a whole. Although vigilantism supports the rights of individuals to band together in the fight to maintain order, it very often involves repression of individual rights to due legal process as laid down by the state. In addition, it may also go beyond the boundaries of legally defined crime and demand adherence to some norms of good and bad behaviour about which the state prefers to leave individuals free to choose.

The search for order

Although contemplation and debate on social order are probably as old as humanity itself, the emergence of the state has posed special problems. Plato and a host of later writers have demonstrated that the balance between domination and the maintenance of order in the state is always likely to be questioned, and that it is also liable to be obscured by ambiguity and ideology.

Whatever one's political perspective, it is also clear that the development of the modern state – and with it capitalism, empire and bureaucracy – has generated much of the subject matter, stimulus and funding for the social sciences in general and the study of social order in particular. In the case of social anthropology, there is no need to cast it as the 'handmaid' of colonialism in order to acknowledge the connection between them. Empire made available for ethnographic study and comparison a treasure house of widely differing societies beyond the dreams of intellectual avarice. Contrasts and unanticipated similarities both between them and to 'home' were documented in profusion. Forms of order based on reciprocity and equilibrium were analysed in societies that seemed to manage reasonably well without the state, and a wide variety of forms of centralized control and legal institutions was explored.

Research in colonial and post-colonial Africa and elsewhere also presented anthropologists with a valuable opportunity to learn about the state itself. The relatively new national entities created out of nineteenth- and early twentieth-century international agreements, and inherited and modified by newly independent governments in the 1950s and 1960s, clearly displayed cracks which many older states had either filled or papered over. Cultural and linguistic diversity was commonplace, distances were great and communications relatively poor. Funds were scarce, and indigenous polities were subordinated to the overriding power of a state whose credentials were rarely well developed at the local level. All this drew attention to comparable problem areas of both historical and modern western European and other states whose frontier communities, ghettos and 'no-go' areas are the most obvious but not the only evidence that the power and authority of the state are not spread evenly throughout its territory.

Yet the problem of order remained – not simply for functionalist anthropologists and sociologists, but also for their various successors and not least for the communities they studied. Far more people than are dreamed of in more revolutionary philosophies place the quest for order and stability extremely high on their political agenda, and many in good Hobbesian fashion look to the state for help in this connection. Protestations that societies without the state are better thought of as 'societies against the state' are interesting but only partly true. People everywhere are thoughtful about their society and become aware, in personal experience, of its shortcomings. Problems of ineffective dispute settlement and crime control create anxiety and pain wherever they occur. As Elizabeth Colson (1975) notes, there is substantial evidence to show that many societies which lacked their own authoritative tribunals welcomed at least the courts of the colonial system if little else. Bohannan (1957) puts this strongly in the case of the Nigerian society he studied. Although he documents how the Tiv people had retained many of their traditional ideas about social order and still regularly made use of some of their own ways of resolving conflict, they were, he comments, 'for the most part, grateful for courts. Courts and administration have greatly increased the safety of the countryside'. Clearly, *Pax Britannica* was not always and everywhere an empty colonialist slogan, even though it could at times be tempered with Tacitus's comment – on a comparable Roman claim – that it 'created a wilderness and called it peace'.

In search of a comparative perspective

My main aim in this book is to provide a comparative and coherent picture of vigilantism that will bring out clearly both its general characteristics and the wide distribution and variety of its forms. Since vigilantes always operate on the edges of the power and authority of the state, and because fundamental questions of law and order lie at the heart of their activities, I hope that my discussion will also throw some useful light upon these broader issues.

This attempt to place my own research experience of vigilantism in a broader frame of reference has naturally led me to explore a wide variety of writings about other times and places. In choosing cases for discussion, I have tried to concentrate on those that seem to be both revealing and well documented. Others might well have chosen differently from the vast array of possibilities. The texts I have used will be acknowledged in the course of my discussion, but it is useful to outline their range and to note in advance the particular importance of some works. In the case of Sungusungu vigilantes in the Tanzanian countryside, I have made use of my own first-hand material and that

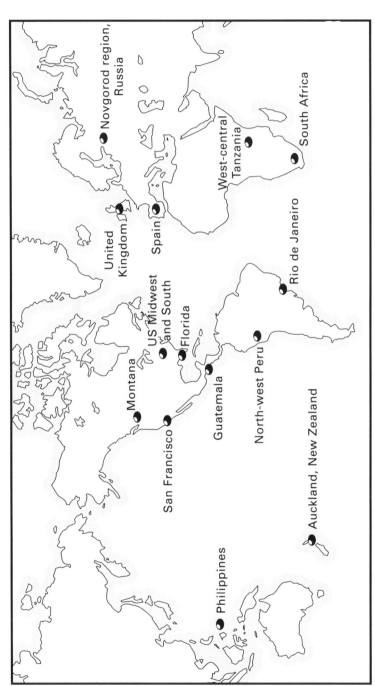

Figure 2 Locations of case materials discussed in the text

of my former student Sufian Bukurura, who conducted a full-scale study of the groups in the early 1990s. In other cases – mainly British and European, North and South American, Ugandan and South African, and Philippine material – I have naturally had to rely upon secondary sources. These include many books and articles, listed in the references, and a large number of newspaper reports, especially for Britain and eastern and southern Africa during the last decade. Where possible, I have consulted book reviews or other texts, and some specialists, to try to gain a picture of the status and reliability of such material. Even with such precautions, any comparative study that is not based simply on one's own research runs the risk of falling foul of local or historical specialists, who may well see as distortion what the author sees as distillation. This is ultimately an insoluble dilemma, and I can only plead that I have been quite painfully conscious of the difficulties of penetrating into the wide range of ethnographic settings that I attempt to deal with.

Two books have proved especially valuable for the study. The first is Richard Maxwell Brown's outstanding monograph *Strain of Violence* (1975), which examines the history of vigilantism in North America and places it squarely in the wider history of the United States.[8] Brown's delineation of the main features of the phenomenon and his analysis of the sometimes tenuous relation between crime control and due legal process is of classical status in this area. His argument, anticipated in his title, that a detailed understanding of American vigilantism demands recognition of particular attitudes to violence rooted in the history of the frontier and revolution also provokes thought about the possibilities and limits of comparison in this field.

The second text, to which Brown also contributes, is quite different. Rosenbaum and Sederberg's edited volume, *Vigilante Politics* (1976), covers a wide range of material from many different countries. The editors adopted a potentially risky policy of allowing their contributors a relatively free hand in the content of their papers, but the result has been an interesting collection that highlights the genuine difficulties of pinning down the subject within rigid definitional boundaries. This is in keeping with both the informality and instability of much vigilante organization and activity. The authors also make a useful contribution towards a typology of vigilante forms.

My references above to ambiguity, ambivalence and instability immediately suggest that this is not an easy task. In any sociological or historical investigation, one is likely to encounter uncertainties about who did what and why, and confident assertions about these may tell us less about 'the truth' than about the investigator's prejudices or lack of energy to pursue matters further. A study of vigilantism poses these problems in an acute form. The polarized views that it tends to arouse in its supporters and opponents make it more difficult to portray in an objective way than less heatedly debated forms of social action. Its labile nature and the secrecy that commonly surrounds it make it hard to grasp and hard to document in detail. Its tendency to arise in real or alleged social and political crises provides it with special opportunities to conceal a variety of purposes behind assertions of public spirit, moral rectitude and the need for desperate measures in a desperate situation.

The book contains eight chapters. Chapter 2 explores the 'frontier' quality of vigilantism in more detail. I examine the relatively straightforward case of village vigilantism directed against cattle thieves and other 'public enemies' in Tanzania, and I also cast a side-glance at some interestingly comparable material from Uganda, Peru and rural Tsarist Russia. Chapter 3 extends the discussion of such attempts at crime and deviance control to the well-documented North American examples of San Francisco in 1851 and Montana in the 1860s.

Chapter 4 focuses more sharply on the significance for vigilantism of boundaries within communities themselves. These may mark divisions based on class, ethnicity, age and gender, and they may sometimes involve factions struggling for political hegemony. Who claims the right to define public enemies is an important question in this context, as both American and southern African material reveals. Chapter 5 examines a variety of forms of vigilante and related patterns of activity in Britain both historically and at the present day.

Chapter 6 returns to the question of relations between vigilantes and the state. Although reactions from the police, courts and politicians are often hostile, more complex relations between vigilante activity and the state and its officials also occur. Politically motivated state encouragement of vigilante 'counter-insurgency' groups has been recorded in the Philippines and elsewhere, while 'death squad' vigilantism in South America and elsewhere involves the covert participation of officers of the state in attacks on political opponents and other claimed 'public enemies', ranging from criminals to street children.

Chapter 7 explores some aspects of the fact that most vigilantism appears to be male activity directed against other males. At the same time it reviews the varying roles of women in different vigilante settings, and considers the possibility of the development of more active parts for them in such activity. To close the book, chapter 8 discusses some conceptual issues in the relation between vigilantism and the law. The idea of law as a dual system of rules about behaviour and rules about the rules themselves is discussed, in the context of the state's claims to a monopoly of rights in legislation, jurisdiction and the definition of due process. This helps to clarify vigilantism's ambiguous position as a form of crime control which is itself criminal. I also pay attention here to the search for justice and security that underlies archetypal vigilante behaviour, and I examine some of the paradoxes crystallized in Brown's evocative characterization of vigilantes as 'conservative mob'. Lastly, I extend my discussion to consider similarities and contrasts between vigilantes and mafias, bandits, resistance movements and guerrilla groups. While all these are part of an 'informal political and legal sector', it is clear that distinctions between them are also important and enlightening.

2

On the Frontiers of the State

Vigilantism is a frontier phenomenon, but the frontiers in question are not always those marked by lines on maps as the official, if at times contested, boundaries of states. Indeed, as Kopytoff has noted (1987: 9), the term 'frontier' may refer both to a boundary and to a frontier 'zone'. The effectiveness of state power is typically spread unevenly over the state's territory, and the legitimacy of its authority is recognized more clearly in some places than in others. The long arm of the law does not stretch everywhere with equal force, and areas where its power is significantly diluted or resisted have a frontier quality.

The simplest model of such frontiers or edges of state power is a spatial one of centre and periphery. Especially when distances are great, communications poor and population thin, the state tends to operate much more effectively at or near the centre of its power base. Regional sub-centres of state authority may of course be established, but the capital may find it difficult to control them, and they are liable to experience similar problems at their own peripheries. The expanding western frontier of the United States during the nineteenth century, and the shifting frontier zones of China over several millennia, provide numerous examples of these problems.[1] Southall's (1956) concept of the 'segmentary state' usefully encapsulates some of the main features of this situation. Originally developed to deal with indigenous chiefdom states of north-west Uganda, its depiction of political centres with increasingly autonomous sub-centres and a great deal of political and legal self-help on the edge of state and regional authority is widely applicable in its most general form.

A second model is that of the 'no go area', though this term is commonly reserved for more extreme examples of this type. Here we find a social island that may be spatially quite close to the centres of state power and authority, but which is not easily accessible to state representatives. Some inner city areas are of this kind. Police, and even fire and other public services, may be unable to penetrate effectively into such enclaves. Their presence may be actively resisted in some cases, or lack of co-operation may seriously impede their work at least in some contexts. A significant section of the population of such areas typically feels alienated from the state and sees its personnel as enemies. High levels of political and, sometimes, racial tension are often characteristic features of the more extreme forms of this kind of frontier zone.

Such inner frontiers can also be cultural. The state may include subgroups that do not share all the main ideas and values of the centre. Sometimes, though not always, such cultural division follows ethnic and religious lines. In the present context, 'cultural distance' of this sort may pose problems for the state if it involves sharp differences of attitude to the definition of 'acceptable' behaviour, and it seems likely to cause special difficulties when it is combined with 'spatial distance' and inaccessibility. In the context of vigilantism, such a combination may result in the state's double failure in local eyes to deal with 'criminals'. The state may not only find it difficult to reach the offenders in question, but it may also fail or even refuse to recognize that their behaviour constitutes a serious offence by local standards. Indeed, the state may well appear in such cases as the passive or active friend of the locally defined public enemy. Many African villagers are said to have seen the colonial state, and some of its successors, in this light as the 'friend' of witches owing to its unsympathetic legislative stance towards witchcraft accusations. In a very extreme case, such as that of Ku Klux Klan hostility to the federal imposition of black emancipation in the post-bellum southern American states, vigilantism and rebellion start to merge together. The attacks on former slaves and their supporters were in many ways a continuation of the Civil War by other means and, as such, more than simply a stop-gap measure to make up for central government deficiencies.[2]

In addition, one may note that at least one writer also makes a case for 'temporal' frontiers.[3] Melbin (1978) argues that mainstream social life not only is localized but also has its 'place' in time. For him, night constitutes a natural frontier zone which, like many spatial frontier areas, has been rolled back and increasingly 'settled' as a variety of social and economic activities among different sections of the population have spilled over from the daylight hours with the help of artificial light and improved transport and communications.

The argument is too complex to treat in detail here, but two points may be noted. Firstly, Melbin interestingly treats at face value a distinction that has sometimes been used metaphorically to characterize social distance. Hobsbawm and Rudé, for example, write of farm labourers and the village poor in early nineteenth-century England as leading hidden lives in 'the dark village', which remained largely unknown to the local gentry and others of their 'betters' who nominally lived in the same community (1969: 62). Also, as with spatial frontier zones, nocturnal social control is often weaker than in 'normal' working hours and criminality more frequent, though Melbin argues that both kinds of zone also tend to generate high levels of helpfulness and co-operation.

As all this implies, not all frontiers are the same, and we may find complex mixtures of different kinds in particular situations. Urban frontier zones are likely to be densely settled, while some spatial peripheries are only sparsely populated. Again, although there is a tendency for criminals to be attracted to those areas that the state finds hard to police, the presence or absence of local forms of social organization and control varies. Vigilantism, of course, implies that some such forms exist, at least in the mind but probably more tangibly as well, both as a contrast to the crime and deviance that rouses vigilante action and as a partial basis for its own extra-legal response. In such cases, then, one may have to deal with frontiers on the edge of what are commonly seen themselves as frontier communities.

Autonomous villagers

My main focus in this chapter is on forms of vigilante action in rural communities where remoteness from the centres of state power – often exacerbated by poor communications and relatively weak administrative structures – is commonly combined with some degree of cultural distinctiveness. In many cases, this distinctiveness is seen, at least from the centre, as a failure of villagers to adopt the 'civilized' ideas and standards of behaviour of 'mainstream' high culture. At the same time, their independent treatment of offences in the absence of state help may also appear as a challenge to the state's political authority.

I will begin more detailed treatment of such rural vigilantism with an account of developments in Tanzania that I have studied at first hand. As I indicated in the previous chapter, it is not surprising if such issues emerge in particularly clear form in some parts of Africa. Most modern African states are large and not especially densely populated, and communications within them are subject to both technical and economic constraints. Their identities as independent nation states are relatively new, and they often contain a variety of groups with different local languages and cultures. The villagers who commonly comprise these groups subscribe to some of the main aims of the modern state, but they also often have their own priorities which complexly reflect both their political and economic situation in the state and their own local value system.

Out of Africa

In 1983 I received a letter in the comfort of my college room from an old friend in a Tanzanian village. The village, called Busangi, is in the Nyamwezi area of the country, and it was there, in 1957, that I began postgraduate study with two years of field research. At that time the country was still a United Nations Trust Territory under British rule and it became independent in 1961.

Since then, Busangi and other villages have experienced many political and economic changes, which I have witnessed during an extended return visit during 1974–5 and on several subsequent occasions. Shortly after independence, local 'traditional' chiefship was replaced by new forms of local government. Grass-roots patterns of village-level co-operation in agricultural work, house building, dispute settlement and the punishment of some minor offences, which were still present in some communities during the colonial period, also began to wane and to give way to new official forms of co-operative and collective organization under the country's single-party socialist regime.[4]

The letter-writer, who had helped me in my field research, informed me that a new system for protecting property had been adopted in the village. Every man, young or old, had to be equipped with bow and arrows, and with a gourd-stem whistle that was to be blown only in emergencies. If a theft was committed, a hue and cry was raised and the thieves were to be followed by the young men of the village concerned. The whistles would alert the members of neighbouring villages, who would in turn forewarn others in the same way to look out for and try to intercept the criminals. There was a special village fund to which all contributed, and this was used to support the young men on such forays.

The system was still in action when I revisited the area in early 1986, and it had by then become the subject of Tanzanian newspaper reports and academic discussion. It became in fact a lively talking point throughout the country, though its spread was interestingly confined initially to the Nyamwezi and the related neighbouring Sukuma region, whose four to five million inhabitants constitute about one-sixth of the Tanzanian population. It spread very rapidly throughout this region from its area of origin on the borders of three administrative Districts. Its brief history has already sharply highlighted a number of aspects of relations between local communities and the state, and it seems likely that its future development will do the same.

This system of village vigilante groups is variously known as Sungusungu or as Busalama.[5] The latter term is a Nyamwezi form of the Swahili word *usalama*, which means peace, safety and security, and it is commonly used by the villagers themselves along with a cognate term *basalama* (singular *msalama*, literally 'person of peace') for the groups and their members. The name Sungusungu is more problematic. It is widely used both within and outside the region, and it is a common idea in Tanzania as a whole that it is derived simply from the Swahili word *sungusungu*, which denotes a species of large, black biting ants. I have also heard suggestions of this derivation among Nyamwezi themselves, and it is possible that the obvious connotations of 'biting power' are combined with a reference to black cloths with which Sukuma cattle-herders sometimes drape themselves. Others derive the name from a Nyamwezi and Sukuma word *busungu* meaning poison, and connect it with the use of arrow poison by the groups concerned.

Sungusungu is not a single organized group with branches in different villages. At least at the start, each village had its own leadership and organization, and villages collaborated with each other without co-ordination from above. More recently, several wider committees have been set up, and they have been able to exert some political influence especially at Administrative District level, but mostly each village still deals with its own affairs, collaborating as and when necessary with other neighbouring communities. In this and some other respects, Sungusungu is quite similar to a variety of other forms of Nyamwezi and Sukuma social organization, a point to which I will return later.

According to some sources, the first group was formed some time in 1982 in an area called Kahama ya Nhalanga, near the Kahama, Nzega and Shinyanga District boundaries, and they name as its founder a man called Kishosha Mang'ombe, which means 'the returner of cattle'. He is said to have been given this name following his successful activities in earlier years against Maasai cattle-raiders in the Shinyanga area. He is reputed to have possessed effective medicines against raiders and to have had powers as a seer. Others name a different founder or founders and a different though neighbouring location. Which village was in fact the first, however, seems less important than their shared peripheral position in a zone with many cattle-owners close to Regional and District boundaries.

Each village group has its own body of officers. There is a chief, *ntemi* (plural *batemi*), at the top, who is supported by a second-in-command known as *ntwale*. Such leaders are often diviners and medicinal experts. A main reason for this is the need to prepare medicines to protect members from attack when they go after thieves. Below these leaders there are six or so *makamanda* (cf. English 'commander') who organize the main body of ordinary members. In addition, there are a few named officers whose job it is to summon people to assemblies, and there is also a secretary, *katibu*, who should keep records of proceedings and issue receipts for subscriptions. The fund made up of these is looked after by the officers and some 'elders of the chief'. In addition, the 'chief' may also look after arrow poison for use in hunting cattle thieves, though some individuals may possess such poison of their own. Ordinary members, and especially younger ones, are simply called *askari*, the Swahili word for soldiers or other armed staff.

The organization is primarily a male one. Unmarried women took part in some areas in 1986 and had their own 'commanders', but Bukurura (1994a: 68) found little active participation by women a few years later. Special songs assert the loyalty of members to the groups and their dependence upon the system. Both male and female members often have a feather or similar head-dress that they wear when undertaking Sungusungu business. The men are also typically stripped to the waist when in action, and were keen to take off their shirts before being photographed. This contrasts sharply with their behaviour in other situations – for example, when they are working in the fields they may well ask a photographer to wait while they put on their shirts.

The system spread directly from one village to another. In Busangi village, for example, the organization was established in 1983 when the chief of a neighbouring group came with some of his subordinates. A meeting was held at which leaders were chosen by the villagers. The visitors explained their role in catching thieves and restoring stolen property, and admonished the new leaders to perform these duties properly. A feast was provided by Busangi villagers for the occasion. The rank and file each brought a chicken and the new chief and his second-in-command each gave a goat. The Busangi leaders not long after went to a few neighbouring areas to start up the system there.

When Sungusungu began, some governmental and party officials feared that it was an attempt to resuscitate traditional chiefship in the area. This fear stemmed partly from the use of the title *ntemi* – which was also the title of the traditional chiefs – but it has now largely been dispelled. It is a long-standing practice of neighbourhood groupings and other associations in the area to take the titles of their offices from the system of traditional chiefship and from other hierarchies which simply provide them with a convenient terminology of ranks and offices.

A further source of anxiety for the authorities was a tendency for early groups to describe themselves by the Swahili word *chama*. Although this term has a wide range of referents, and is likely to be used for any form of club or association, it is also the standard Swahili word for a political party, as in the name of the ruling Chama cha Mapinduzi (CCM), or Revolutionary Party. Tanzania was till very recently a one-party state, and the public use of the word *chama* for Sungusungu was soon dropped under pressure from officials who saw it as threat to the hegemony of the party.

These official fears about names and titles are reminiscent of colonial government anxieties about some earlier grass-roots groupings, including even dance societies. In the present case, however, the specific misconceptions that were voiced were symptomatic of a more general and relatively well-grounded perception that, whatever its explicit aims, Sungusungu posed some awkward questions for the state.

Sungusungu began quite specifically as a defence against crime. Armed cattle theft in particular caused a great deal of anxiety among villagers in the region, but there were also fears of other forms of theft and brigandage, including highway robbery. This was part of a more widespread set of worries about law and order among ordinary Tanzanian citizens both in the rural areas and in the towns. Villagers were deeply concerned about issues of security and the failure of government and police to combat crime effectively. Some commented relatively charitably about the police, pointing to the shortages of vehicles and fuel, which are essential for dealing with mobile rural criminals. Other comments were more critical, and ranged from the suggestion that the police were often uninterested in dealing with offences to insinuations that they have at times been in league with the criminals. Similar accusations have also been made against some village officials.

The establishment of Sungusungu groups in villages can be seen as a vote of no confidence in the state's ability to maintain security, and this in itself has clearly been something for officialdom to ponder over. At the same time, the fact that villagers have set up their own apparatus for solving their problems reflects the further worrying possibility that the state's failure, as Hyden (1980) puts it, to 'capture' the rural areas economically may be accompanied by a failure to maintain a hold on them politically.

In addition to this element of competition, it appears that the way Sungusungu groups have dealt with known or suspected criminals has sometimes fallen short of governmental aspirations to see justice done through due process. Armed rustlers have been killed, as have some Sungusungu members in their confrontations with them. It is probable that some such deaths were unavoidable, and it seems clear that many villagers have shown great courage in the face of often desperate and well-armed opposition. There are, however, also stories of failure to hand over captured criminals to the police and courts for trial, and in some cases this has involved the violent treatment, and even the alleged torture, of those apprehended.

Witch hunting

Sometimes the Sungusungu groups have concerned themselves with hunting out suspected witches, and some of these are said to have been killed. Suspected witches have often simply been expelled from their villages, but occasionally villagers have 'seen them off' (a similar idiom is used in the local language) in more ways than one. Young men are sometimes instructed by the village elders to escort such exiled suspects on their way, and their charges are afterwards reported to have disappeared without trace.

A belief in witchcraft is still strong in this and many other areas of Tanzania, and witches are seen by many people as a major public enemy. One old village friend directly compared Sungusungu with the Mchapi witch-finding movement of the 1930s, even though he did not see Sungusungu as itself mainly directed against witches.[6] I should add also that there has been a more general spate of witch killing in the Sukuma area dating back to the 1970s, and that the government has tried to quell this. An official inquiry into it was conducted in the early 1980s, and later a ban was placed upon the activities of witch-finding diviners in the Shinyanga Region, where the police commander was reported to have claimed that an average of nineteen people per month were being killed on suspicion that they were witches.[7] Even in more recent cases, Sungusungu groups do not seem to have been the only agents involved in such killings, and it appears that even the police themselves have not always been blameless in the treatment of suspects.

Like many others who do not believe in witchcraft, I am personally appalled by such events, but as an anthropologist I am also conscious that they need to be reviewed in a comparative context. This does not diminish their significance as an example of the dark side of life in small communities, but it does help us, albeit somewhat depressingly, to avoid dismissing such activities as simply an alien aberration that has nothing to do with our experience 'nearer home'.

Many Tanzanian villagers and urban dwellers consider witchcraft to be a dangerous reality which they would like to see controlled and if possible eradicated in one way or another. Some others, while less convinced of this reality, are none the less disturbed by the potential of beliefs and accusations to generate violence and other forms of harassment. I should also stress that Tanzania clearly is, in many senses of the term, a modern and not simply a 'contemporary' country, and this may involve a paradox for some readers. The country is very much part of the modern international community, and since its independence in 1961, it has made substantial efforts to enhance the levels of social justice among its citizens, while pursuing a foreign policy marked by a morality that has at times put many wealthier countries to shame. For me and many others, who have enjoyed the privilege and pleasure of living for long periods among its villagers, it has offered a wealth of humane hospitality, and it has been the source of a substantial part of any social wisdom we have managed to acquire.

At the same time, in the eyes of many members of the modern world, and especially in the so-called West, belief in witchcraft appears as an archaic phenomenon that is expected to survive only in odd pockets among countryfolk and some eccentric urban mystics. It is thought of as something that Europe and America have in general long since shed, although the reasons for such shedding, and indeed the extent to which it has in fact occurred, are by no means clear. In fact such beliefs are surprisingly widespread in many countries both within and outside Africa (cf. Luhrmann 1989; and Favret-Saada 1980).

The paradox in the Tanzanian situation can partly be resolved by a wider contextualization of the beliefs and practices involved, and with it a recognition of the ethnocentricity that simplistically equates their decline with moral progress. Witchcraft is only one of a number of conceptions of the human capacity for evil and for doing harm to others. The word 'evil' is a complex one, and it is said to have largely fallen into disuse in Britain, though it has in fact begun to re-emerge quite strongly in recent discussions about particular local tragedies – such as the massacre of five- and six-year-olds at Dunblane school – and the moral state of the nation more generally. The word 'harm' is more straightforward. Both of them, however, make a great deal of immediate sense to English speakers, even if neither immediately evokes the idea of witchcraft in their minds.

It has been remarked that in some societies 'evil is attributed ultimately to monsters that cannot exist', whereas in contemporary Britain and the West it is attributed to monsters that do (Pocock 1985: 56). It is hard to know how true this is and which, in any case, of these conditions should be thought the more regrettable. Certainly, recent rumours and anxieties in Britain about satanic ritual, the sexual abuse of children and a more general state of moral malaise suggest that such a hard-and-fast distinction is difficult to maintain. Some of the accusations of child sexual abuse that shattered the calm of Cleveland a few years ago had much in common with accusations of witchcraft. It seems that there was a less clear nexus than one might expect between some of the diagnostic techniques employed by 'scientific experts' and the assumptions of actual abuse. The accusations themselves were also evocative, at least for an anthropologist, of the common belief that witches engage in incest and other sins committed against those for whom they have the strongest moral responsibilities; and like witchcraft accusations they were deeply damaging to the moral reputations of those accused. More generally, it also seems quite probable that some recent fears and anxieties – for example, with regard to the morality of youngsters in the aftermath of a child's recent murder in Liverpool – could, without police presence, easily have led to lynchings.[8] Moreover, the capacity of modern Europeans to consider whole communities as intrinsically evil and legitimate targets for attack is all too painfully obvious from a cursory glance at the horrors of the Holocaust, 'ethnic cleansing' in the Balkans and sectarian violence in Ulster. Nor is it surprising that a whole range of activities involving systematic discrimination and often enough lethal violence against ethnic and other minorities in the West is also commonly subsumed under the term 'witch-hunt'.

A satisfying explanation of this general human propensity to such opinions and activities is elusive for those who seek more than a pious statement about our inherent sinfulness. Perhaps the most promising line of inquiry is that initiated by Edmund Leach (1977) in his discussions of the human capacity for language and classification, a theme also taken up by Michael Herzfeld (1992) in his study of bureaucracy. Given the common tendency to distinguish not simply between words and things but also between words and deeds, this may seem surprising. Yet we are also used to the role of language, especially in the form of rhetoric, as an important stimulus to action. Also, linguistic pronouncements such as declarations of war and sentencing of criminals have long been recognized as a highly significant form of action in themselves.

Leach's argument connects two characteristics of language. One is linguistic diversity, which becomes one of a number of bases on which people can decide to treat others as if they belonged to different species, as an 'enemy without'. The second and partly related feature is the gap between linguistic classification and the reality it is supposed to represent. Our tendency to classify is clearly of enormous value in our attempts to make sense of the world around us. Yet the same capacity also allows us to define the world in many contexts as we like, and this may include the depersonalizing, or the demonizing and bestializing, of others through powerful labels which often sanction harsh and sometimes lethal action against them. The victims of such labelling may be outside our society, but often too they become 'enemies within' – Jews, blacks, witches, communists or the 'undeserving' poor or rich. The ascription of evil to others in the guise of witches thus appears as a special cultural variant of a much more widespread phenomenon in which a stigmatizing label is attached to others and transforms them from our fellow human beings into legitimate victims of our own inhuman behaviour. This theme recurs in several contexts of vigilante activity.

The role of Sungusungu

However this may be, villagers with whom I and other researchers have discussed Sungusungu activities are almost unanimous in their praise for the groups and their activities. They argue that, since Sungusungu started, violent crime has noticeably decreased in the rural areas. There is no comprehensive evidence of past and present

Table 1 Offences dealt with in Busangi in the early 1980s

Offence	Offenders	Penalty
Cattle theft	5 (all men)	1 head of cattle
Highway robbery	3 (2 men and 1 youth)	1–2 head of cattle
Fraud	1 (a man)	1 head of cattle
Other theft	8 (3 men, 3 youths and 2 women)	1 head of cattle
Alcohol offences	3 (all women)	1 goat – 1,000 shillings
Fraternizing with ostracized villagers	8 (all women, attending a wedding there)	1 chicken
Quarrels and abuse	5 (3 men and 2 youths)	1 goat
Blowing whistle in false alarm	1 (a man)	1 head of cattle

crime rates to support or oppose this commonly heard claim, though the few data I possess lend it some credence. Newspaper reports have quoted both government and party leaders as well as Sungusungu representatives themselves to the effect that violent deaths, armed robbery and cattle rustling have been substantially reduced. In some cases, it appears that thieves have been caught with substantial numbers of stolen cattle or with money, and large quantities of weapons are reported to have been captured. It is also argued that the mere creation of the Sungusungu groups has acted as a strong deterrent. I do not have details of the situation prior to Sungusungu in Busangi village, but it seems that, although the group there has been active, it has not had to deal with much serious violent crime.[9] According to the material at my disposal, the group dealt with thirty-four offenders in the first three years of operation, and the maximum penalty imposed was a fine of two head of cattle. The cases involved are shown in table 1. All the offenders listed in the table were from Busangi and immediately adjoining areas.

I was told that people are usually dealt with by the Sungusungu groups themselves if police fail to prosecute or a court cannot convict because of a shortage of hard evidence. It is also clear, however, that some of the offences shown in table 1, such as those concerned with going to a wedding, did not in any case involve a breach of law. The broadening of the Busangi Sungusungu's remit to include such issues is fairly typical. Bukurura has noted that the groups have more generally taken it upon themselves to deal with a wide range of matters, including the enforced return of women who have left their husbands.

It has also been reported to me that a background motive for originally establishing Sungusungu, in addition to anxieties about rustling and witchcraft, was elders' dissatisfaction with the lack of discipline and respect displayed by some younger village men. The issue of law and order and community well-being has thus, apparently, been partly seen in terms of the authority of senior men over their juniors and over women. Moreover, although accusations against men also occur, older women are, in Nyamwezi and Sukuma thought, prime suspects as witches, and many of them have suffered harassment and worse on these grounds in recent years.

It seems clear that in some cases people have been dealt with largely on the basis of their reputation. Unlike the official courts, the groups are also said to be ready to rely on divination as a source of vital clues to people's guilt. One case I encountered during a visit to the area illustrates some of the problems this may cause. It was discovered that some village funds were missing, and village officials agreed with Sungusungu to summon a diviner. The diviner identified three culprits, including the Village Secretary, who was one of the officials who had agreed to summon him. The Secretary was outraged, and higher-level party officials were called in. In the end the Secretary was exculpated at a meeting between these officials and the villagers, and one of the other two suspects – a watchman – was eventually convicted in court. The case was further complicated by the fact that the diviner was the Secretary's father-in-law and may have had some animus against him, and it was more generally a most unwelcome embarrassment for the higher-level officials who were called in to mediate. Further friction was avoided by a party decision to transfer the Secretary to its town headquarters.

The groups typically follow regular procedures in the handling of cases. Suspects are summoned to a meeting and are first subjected to a simple but effective discourse of questions and greetings. They are asked if they are 'people of peace' (*basalama*), and after agreeing that they are, they are told to greet the assembled elders. They are expected to respond with some of the slogans about peace and prosperity which Sungusungu has adopted. They are then asked why they are there and are expected to confess to their offence. They are then told to 'stab themselves', a metaphor for pronouncing sentence on themselves, and they should then volunteer to pay a penalty. If the offer is considered insufficient, the assembled Sungusungu simply remain silent. A higher offer is then usually made, and if this is acceptable the assembly applauds.

Suspects who refuse to confess or who fail to propose a satisfactory penalty for their offence are ostracized by fellow villagers. The above case of eight wedding-goers involved a breach of ostracism of this sort. Ostracism is brought to an end when the suspect calls another meeting at which he or she agrees to the offence and offers to make suitable amends. Such ostracism has a long history as a sanction against recalcitrant neighbours in the area. It involves a refusal to co-operate in any way, rather than simply a refusal to communicate. Its effectiveness is evidence of villagers' continuing dependence on each other for a wide variety of help, though it has also been felt necessary in recent years to reinforce it by extending recognition of it to neighbouring villages in addition to the miscreant's own.

The above procedures of confession and self-imposition of a penalty were adopted partly through fear that offenders would complain to the authorities if they were more simply tried and convicted by their neighbours. As it is, Sungusungu argue that offenders both convict and sentence themselves in such gatherings, and that they therefore have no grounds for such complaints. Some appeals to the authorities have occurred, however, even against ostracism, and some Sungusungu leaders have been ordered to withdraw this sanction and have also been fined in some cases.

Because most villagers consider this unjust, they have not always been willing to resume connections with offenders and they have sometimes clubbed together to pay leaders' fines. People sometimes remark that the police appear to be more active in such cases than in dealing with more obvious crimes. Moreover, their procedures have a rationale beyond the mere avoidance of police intervention, and they feel that this is not always well understood.

Villagers consider that both ostracism and the system of confession and self-punishment will normally provide offenders with the opportunity to admit the errors of their ways and return to the fold of the community. This strategy of reinstatement is also visible in the way that fines are used. As with earlier forms of neighbourhood court in the area, the fines which offenders pay in kind are typically consumed communally by the villagers. Monetary fines are put into local Sungusungu funds and often used for a feast at a later date. An important feature of such feasting is that it ideally brings the whole community together, including the offenders, who provide the meat while other local households contribute the usual staple of stiff porridge.

Many government and party officials have argued that such feasting is a wasteful use of valuable resources. This 'puritanical' view partly reflects Tanzanian socialist ideals, but it also seems to stem from a resentment of the economic freedom that the groups enjoy.

Government and party reaction[10]

It is not surprising that government and party have been keenly interested in Sungusungu. From the start, the groups and their leaders
were extremely influential in the villages. They had substantial funds
at their disposal that were free from state and local government control, and even the names and titles they adopted caused anxiety, as we
have seen. It seems likely that the groups and their activities were also
at first formally illegal, and there was naturally deep concern that
their activities could easily get out of hand. This danger was particularly manifest in witch hunting and the violent treatment of some
criminals, and there were also some less serious issues such as government's desire to prevent the groups from dealing with adultery cases.
More positively, it was clear that such groups were able to provide an
effective mechanism of crime control, and this was obviously valuable
to the state if it could be suitably harnessed.

Official reaction has been predictably mixed in these circumstances,
though the character of Tanzanian socialism has also influenced patterns of response. Socialism, of course, has many faces. At the ideological level, it is clearly a system for the sharing of control and
ownership of a society's resources, and this is commonly taken also to
imply a substantial degree of sharing in policy making and the management of public affairs. At the level of action, this ideal of popular
participation has been often tempered by a number of real or asserted
practical constraints. In many socialist regimes, 'socialism from
above', sometimes in quite oppressive forms, has been deemed necessary for the sake of efficiency and, at least temporarily, for the control
and re-education of recalcitrant and unenthusiastic groups still bur-
dened by their bourgeois aspirations.

Governmental structure under such regimes frequently involves a
readily recognizable combination of institutions. Commonly, there is a
single party, which may be varyingly populist or elitist, a governmental and bureaucratic structure, and an elected chamber. There is also
typically a military, whose role varies greatly from one period and one
country to another. There is often a substantial overlap between the
party leadership and that of other institutions, and this can sometimes
make it difficult to distinguish them in practice, but there are also tendencies to divisions of interest and struggles for power between them.
The party tends to assert the ideology of the system, and demand its
dominance in the formulation and implementation of policy.
Governmental staff and bureaucrats are likely to be much more

sensitive to practicalities of administration and to the demands of their own inherited norms and *modus operandi*. They are also likely to be the most highly educated element in the system. An elected chamber may perhaps be expected to exhibit a special respect for the demands of an electorate, but this is not always the case, and such a chamber rarely has the same amount of power and influence as the other major structures I have mentioned. Of course, the ideals of the system stress that all the organs we have mentioned should work together for the enhancement of the interests of the people as a whole, but just as this does not prevent their quarrelling among themselves, it also often fails to stop them using domination and control as the main media of public service.

Much of this general picture of a socialist regime fits the Tanzanian case. Tanzania was a single-party state until the 1995 elections, and its stated aim has been the development of socialism and participatory democracy. The party leadership has strongly asserted its constitutional predominance, often at the expense of the elected Parliament. Early military unrest was suppressed, and since then there has been little overt trouble from that quarter. Relations between party and bureaucracy have been complex and uneasy.

In the present context, an important special element in the Tanzanian situation was the vision of an African socialism developed by the country's first President, Julius Nyerere. Although this vision involved a substantial misreading of many features of traditional African society, it was not simply a 'mystifying' charter for manipulation and control. It served, not always successfully, to support the view that socialism could be achieved in Tanzania without violent imposition from above or violent revolution from below. It also stressed the idea – which both government and party have at times ignored – that the country's villagers possess a range of social and cultural resources which the state should treat with respect.

Initial complaints and court action against Sungusungu were in fact quickly followed by positive comments from the President himself, who saw the groups as a grass-roots attempt to deal with serious problems. He described them as a revolutionary force within the villages that ought to be encouraged, rather than harassed by bureaucracy, and he said that all who had been arrested for such activities should be released. This support continued, and in 1986, as Chairman of the party though no longer President, he roundly condemned continuing attempts to prosecute them. At that time there were still some cases in which Sungusungu members were accused of wrongly seizing cattle from suspected rustlers and returning them to their assumed rightful owners. Nyerere was reported to have said that the law under which they were charged was a bad law because it worked against the people's interests and was creating conflict between people and the state. He is said to have added that Sungusungu were in a better position than the police and courts to know who thieves and rustlers were.

Rashidi Kawawa, the party's Secretary General, also spoke warmly of the groups in 1983, and again in early 1984 at a national youth rally. Like Nyerere, he described them as a revolutionary force working for the safety and security of their communities. He stressed how violent crime and corruption had been stemmed by the groups' activities, and he noted that their members were public-spirited and unpaid volunteers. Their only enemies were the 'enemies of the revolution', and young people everywhere should follow their example. Kawawa significantly described Sungusungu in this speech as working under party guidance and he claimed that 'Sungusungu are young CCM members fulfilling the party's call for mass action to maintain security'. He also described them as a front-line force in the struggle to build socialism.

Such rhetoric could also be encountered at the local level. I was told by a divisional party officer that Sungusungu were party men and that CCM was the party of Busalama. This partly harks back to the naming problem noted earlier, but it also involved an attempt to incorporate Sungusungu within the party, rather than to draw a line between the two. In fact, party membership was much less widespread than such pronouncements asserted, and many villagers clearly saw Sungusungu as something quite distinct from CCM.

As some of Nyerere's comments suggest, the idea of a clash between the ideology of the party, stressing popular participation in political life, and the interests of a powerful officialdom, keen to maintain the system and its own special status in it, is no stranger to the Tanzanian socialist scene. Some of the most overt hostility to the groups was initially displayed by police and magistrates, who were, of course, extremely likely to see Sungusungu as unwelcome competition in the field of crime control. Many group members were zealously prosecuted in the early years, and some of the most violent received death sentences that were mostly later commuted, some under the influence of the President himself.

The groups were clearly seen both by some party officers and by the law-enforcing agencies as competition to themselves and to the formal structures of the state. The threat to the police and the judiciary was most immediate and obvious, since it highlighted their failure to solve a series of pressing law and order problems which had been a major stimulus to establishment of the groups.

At the same time it is arguable that the threat to the party was also serious, though less immediately critical. This was most clear at the ward and village levels, where local party leaders complained from an early date that the groups were undermining their authority. Also the use of the word *chama* for the groups, as noted earlier, caused much anxiety for party leaders at local and higher levels. Party membership was much less widespread than leaders' rhetoric suggested, and Sungusungu – with its inclusive and enthusiastic membership – seemed in danger of providing an enriched sense of community sentiment and commitment from below that the party had tried but failed to generate from above. One interesting aspect of this was the wildfire success of Sungusungu, as opposed to the earlier failure of party-led 'people's militia' units, in engendering popular participation and support.

Yet fear of competition and a bureaucratic mentality can only go some way towards an explanation of official attitudes towards the groups, if only because these also partly reflect the legitimate concerns of any government – socialist or otherwise – about law and order and its own role in their maintenance. Early police statements stressed that Sungusungu was unlawful and was bent on harassing and torturing people, and it should be recalled here that a number of people seem to have died violently at the groups' hands, and that only some of these were cattle-rustlers caught red-handed. Others included individuals suspected of such thievery, and also some suspected witches.

It makes more sense, despite the party's aspirations to the ideological 'high ground', to see that both the party and the police and courts were faced with issues both of values and of interests. A genuine respect for due legal process was undoubtedly significant for a wide range of officials, including many party leaders, who seem to have been much less willing than their chairman to cast this to the winds in their positive pronouncements on the groups. Many urged Sungusungu to co-operate with police and the courts, and especially to hand over offenders rather than take the law into their own hands. Similarly, as one might expect, many members of the legal profession and at least some of the police were also committed to the maintenance of such norms in themselves, rather than simply as a source of their own power and authority. The roots of such commitment are at least in part 'colonial', and it is arguable that for better or for worse this is part of a more general link that persists between the post-colonial legal worlds of Tanzania and Britain.

The attitudes in question are interestingly apparent in a student dissertation on the Sungusungu groups, written by two Tanzanian lawyers (Sabasaba and Rweyemamu 1984). Their main focus is simply the formal legality or illegality of the groups' activities. They argue, plausibly enough, that the groups were in fact illegal at the time of writing, and they are highly critical on these grounds of party support for them. They also express strong disapproval of the methods used by groups to detect and interrogate their suspects. At the same time, they show little interest in the more practical issues of effective crime prevention, which gave rise to the groups' establishment, and they are not fired with any enthusiasm for the element of grass-roots initiative that clearly caught Nyerere's imagination, and which fitted well with party guidelines on security.

Before moving away from the question of the ideological components in the situation, one should also take into account the value system of the Sungusungu members in the villages. The existence of a gap between such local interests and values and those of the state extends well beyond the setting of a socialist Tanzania, and I have argued elsewhere (1989) that, in one form or another, such a gap has been a persistent feature of relations between Nyamwezi villagers and all their various pre-colonial, colonial and post-colonial rulers. The world of Nyamwezi villagers has, of course, been deeply influenced by government and the state, but it also has its own internal driving force. It is a world of 'ordinary' people concerned to secure the health, and the moral and material prosperity of themselves, their families and at times their neighbours, against real and culturally constructed enemies. For them, all governments, despite variations, tend to be above and outside many of their everyday concerns, and the legitimacy of government is to a considerable degree dependent upon its ability to satisfy their needs. This ability is, moreover, typically measured against the substantial fund of organizational skills that the people themselves possess in many different spheres of life, including that of law and order maintenance.

From villagers' response to national institution

Sungusungu still persists in its home area, and it has developed well beyond this into a legally recognized organization that has spread to several other areas, including major towns. Legislation, passed in 1989, recognized the groups and conferred on them powers of arrest similar to those of the police. The law provides for compensation for injury that members suffer in the course of duty, and the Minister of Home Affairs has formal powers to ensure the proper functioning of the system. These developments have brought new problems. In Dar es Salaam, for example, regular night-watches were established and members were recruited from all households on a rota basis. Some people have complained that it is difficult to carry out such duties and follow them with a hard day's work. Others have complained of harassment by Sungusungu groups when moving after dark on perfectly legitimate business. However, the groups, both rural and urban, are supposed to receive training and they are also supposed to collaborate fully with the police and courts. It is hoped that this will permit them to work effectively while limiting the damage that can all too easily arise through over-enthusiasm. More recently I have heard that their activities have slackened off, at least in the capital.

In addition, government has from the start gone beyond a simple attempt to encourage the groups and keep them under control. For there has also been a substantial attempt to use them for a range of tasks which they themselves did not apparently envisage in their own original 'terms of reference'. This involves a sort of hijacking of the groups' time and energy for governmental purposes. In October 1983, for example, the Prime Minister, Edward Sokoine, addressed a rally of 6,000 Sungusungu in Kasamwa in Geita District. He praised them for their 'revolutionary' activity, and warned them to stay within the law. He also publicly urged the Mwanza Region authorities to deploy about 1,000 Sungusungu members from the villages to weed out racketeers and loiterers in Mwanza Town, which had so far failed to implement the national campaign against racketeering and economic sabotage. At the same time he promised a sum of 200,000 shillings for the Geita District groups, which they should be allowed to spend as they wished. During the Mwanza exercise they would be allowed to use their traditional weapons and wear their usual outfits. In 1986 I myself encountered Sungusungu in Tabora District preparing to round up tax defaulters, and I was told that those in Kahama had been instructed to do the same in due course. When I asked people in Busangi how they would respond to this directive, I was told that they could not really refuse. At the same time, it appears that comparable locally generated activities can arise. Thus the recent purchase of a lorry for Busangi village was financed by the sale of produce of a village field whose cultivation was 'policed' by the Basalama.

The world of political motivation is, of course, notoriously uncertain, and it would be naive to see the process of legalization of

Sungusungu as simply the realization of a populist ideal. Government and party officials, for example, clearly wished to take pragmatic advantage of the new development and there is no doubt that both party and bureaucracy were anxious ultimately to bring it under their control. It would be too cynical to suggest a conspiracy between them, of a 'hard' and 'soft' policeman kind, but it is clear that once assimilation rather than abolition began to emerge as the most practical possibility for control, all sides began to move to implement that aim.

The particular and the general

It is difficult to determine the extent to which Sungusungu should be seen as a specifically Nyamwezi and Sukuma or even Tanzanian development. Vigilantism is a widespread phenomenon both spatially and historically, and milder cognate forms of organization – of suburban neighbourhood watch or rural farm watch – coexist reasonably amicably with the police and courts in Britain and elsewhere. The problems of political control from above, and the potential for conflict between 'due process' and effective 'crime prevention', emerge in a wide range of political and social settings. Moreover, the kind of cultural diversity and local-level specificity of Tanzania is a common feature of all sorts of 'new nations'.

None the less, some special features seem important. I have mentioned that the development of Sungusungu has largely been confined to the Nyamwezi and Sukuma area of Tanzania. Yet the problems that the groups set out to combat have by no means been confined only to that area of the country, and there have been suggestions that similar groups be set up elsewhere. Thus there has been widespread violent cattle rustling in the Tarime area to the north-east, but, despite some official encouragement, villagers there seem to have done no more than sporadically take the law into their own hands when police action has failed. It is, of course, possible that positive governmental stimulus to start up such a system is off-putting, and there may be other reasons why the system has not spread, such as the existence of alternative arrangements in other regions.

However this may be, there are some reasons why I have not been surprised to witness the development of Sungusungu among the Nyamwezi and Sukuma in particular. I am thinking here especially of the many pre-existing forms of village-level groupings and associations that have been common in the area. These include dance societies, cultivating teams, spirit possession and other ritual associations, hunting groups, threshing teams and more general forms of neighbourhood association, including informal courts.[11] These have provided individuals and households with many different forms of interaction and support additional to those of kinship, and complementary to and at times in conflict with the formal political institutions of traditional chiefship and its post-colonial replacements. They have also helped to ensure that villagers possess a continuous fund of organizational skills that have served them well in this and many other contexts.

Given this start, some elements of Tanzanian socialism also appear to have facilitated the development of Sungusungu. Some writers, such as Campbell, have attempted to explain the system in Marxist terms as part of an emergent class struggle, arising out of colonial and post-colonial features of the political economy of the country and its rural areas. There is little evidence to support this view, and I would hesitate to go much further in this context than my previous analysis (1981) of custom in the area, as a creation and possession of the people which has been a source of power and identity for them in a wider world where they in general occupy a relatively humble status. It is true and important that Sungusungu seems to be a truly grass-roots development, and I have no evidence of any control or manipulation of it by better-off or other sectional elements in society, which appears to have marked vigilantism in many other areas of the world.

If there is a 'class' element in the situation, it is perhaps most clearly visible in the idea, to some extent implicit in Nyerere's support, that the rise of Sungusungu partly involves a recapture of village-level organization by villagers themselves in the face of increased state influence and, especially, the creation of new compact villages by the state in the 1970s as formal corporate units from which many villagers could easily feel alienated. The role of the new villages in the rise of Sungusungu may in fact be quite complicated. It is possible that they contributed to the problems that Sungusungu sets out to solve, not only as a government imposition but also through their nucleated settlement patterns, which created substantial space between villages into which both human and animal predators could move relatively freely. At the same time, however, it is arguable that such compact settlement has itself facilitated the rapid creation and mobilization of Sungusungu groups through the improved communication that it affords between neighbours.

A further factor within Tanzanian socialism was the influential positive reaction of ex-President Nyerere and his close party associates to the groups' emergence. There was nothing automatic about the persistence of the system through the 1980s, and without this intervention, the chances of violent confrontation and the ultimate suppression of the groups would probably have been much greater. In this case at least, the dominant position of the party in the Tanzanian system was confirmed. It is interesting that such a possibility was foreseen for the Tanzanian system in more general terms by Ghai (1976: 80), who noted that a broad ideological orientation may be more adaptive in situations of rapid change than a rigid and narrowly defined rule structure.

At the same time, the groups also benefited from the Tanzanian state's interest in indigenous culture. Some early commentators saw them – mistakenly, I think – as an echo of the former regiments of 'royal guards', called *rugaruga*, which chiefs used to recruit in precolonial days. The tendency of newspapers to call the groups 'traditional' (*wa jadi* in Swahili) partly stems from this conflation, though their bows and arrows and their head-dresses were also probably important here. The question of their choice of weapons is intriguing. Some say that it stems from a vision of their founder, Kishosha, that it was only through a return to these traditional weapons that the people could free themselves from the attacks of cattle thieves, even though the latter might be armed with modern guns. It is not clear to what extent the choice represents a 'nativistic' vision. Certainly, bows and arrows have a number of important resonances in local culture, where they serve as major symbols of paternal ancestry and male identity. At the same time, one must note such practical considerations as the ready availability of such weapons and the fact that government would not have tolerated the widespread use of guns by groups of this sort. Certainly their supporters cited their use of these weapons when resisting claims that the groups were in competition with the state, and this helped to blur the debate about their legal status until legislation clarified the issue.

Some further features of the situation also deserve mention here, though it is difficult to pronounce authoritatively on them. No evidence exists at present to suggest that Sungusungu activities represent the kinds of political or economic faction and division with which vigilantism seems to be connected in South Africa or in some of its American manifestations. I have noted differences of interest and issues of authority between men and women and between older and younger men, but at least originally the main cleavage seems to have been between ordinary law-abiding villagers and actual or perceived violent criminals.

Too little is known about the background of the rustlers and brigands to pronounce upon the social and economic roots of their activities. There is little to suggest at present that they fit easily within the category of 'social bandit'. Some of them seem likely to be veterans of the Uganda war, and others have almost certainly obtained firearms from such veterans, but detailed life histories are not yet available. One hypothesis might be that they represent the extreme edge of Tanzanian criminality of the 1970s – whose milder forms consisted of black-marketeering, smuggling and the like – which appears to have been partly generated by attempts to maintain a centrally controlled economy in unfavourable conditions both internal and external to the country. If this is the case, it becomes conceivable that, in addition to the positive response that Sungusungu groups have received from party leaders, both their broad popular base and the cattle thieves and brigands whom they arose to combat have been to some degree a product of the same 'socialist' system.

I have concentrated so far on some of the more particular aspects of Sungusungu as a Nyamwezi/Sukuma and Tanzanian phenomenon. Yet many generalities remain. Perceptions of state ineffectiveness in dealing with serious crime, the concern with victims, and more general issues of authority, respect and morality are, singly or jointly, commonly recurring elements in such contexts, as too is the general popularity of much vigilante activity.

Examples abound, particularly in North America. As Maxwell Brown has amply documented, the history of the western frontier, with its problems of horse thieving, cattle rustling and counterfeiting, provides hundreds of cases of vigilante responses to crime on the edge or beyond the reach of state control, though the situation there is marked by the particularities of class and status differences within the communities concerned. Some recent material from elsewhere in east Africa and also data on some other and quite different areas of the world – modern northern Peru and nineteenth-century Russia – also reveal interesting similarities with Sungusungu.

The Banalukoosi of eastern Uganda

During the late 1960s, local vigilante groups became common in the rural areas of Bugisu on the slopes of Mt Elgon in eastern Uganda (Heald 1982, 1986a and b, 1989). The groups formed one wing of a two-pronged attack on problems of order in the villages. The other was the foundation of a series of drinking clubs or 'companies', which also acted as rotating credit groups. The 'companies' imposed strict rules of etiquette and decorum on their members when they got together for social drinking.

The vigilante groups had much in common with the Tanzanian Sungusungu groups of the 1980s, and like them they seem to fit quite closely the basic ideal type of vigilantism outlined in chapter 1. The chief focus of their attention were thieves (typically younger men) and witches (usually elders), who were said to be unprecedentedly rampant in the area at this time. The groups were usually known as Banalukoosi – 'the people of peace, order and respect' – and as 'Bugisu government'.

As this latter term implies, the groups were perceived essentially as an alternative source of law and order to that of the wider state. People felt that the courts could no longer be relied upon for justice. Thus Heald describes how one group was founded after some villagers tracked down two cattle thieves and handed them over to the police, only to find themselves arrested and imprisoned for assault after the thieves had bribed the magistrate and been released. She notes, however, that the groups were typically not revolutionary in their intent, though a few early ones sometimes persecuted local dignitaries and wealthy men. Rather they saw themselves as filling a gap created by post-independence local government reforms and by the increase in political disorder that preceded and then followed in the wake of Amin's coup.

Like Sungusungu, the groups spread from one locality to the next. Leaders from villages where a group had been established would travel to neighbouring communities and help to start groups there. The groups commanded a high level of support in many villages, though Heald notes that some villagers were worried about their activities. This seems largely to have arisen from the fact that some early groups consisted largely of unemployed young men, who disdained agricultural work and were themselves considered likely to be thieves. Some such groups apparently operated flourishing protection rackets, and were a source more of harassment than security for their neighbours.

In spite of such cases, the groups clearly satisfied a felt need in the villages, and they were also encouraged by some local chiefs whose power had been seriously curtailed after independence. The groups continued to be active during the 1970s and early 1980s despite attempts by the police to crush them. At least initially, they organized regular night patrols, in which all local men had to participate in turn, and they arrested and punished suspected thieves and witches. In some cases they are said to have executed their suspects, especially if they were deemed to have continued in their evil ways after a warning. The groups do not appear to have resorted to divination as an aid to the identification of their targets, but relied instead on local consensus and confession in the face of threats of retribution.

Northern Peruvian Rondas Campesinas

In April 1990 a large gathering of peasants converged on the north Peruvian town of Chota to complain about a rise in interest rates charged by the government's agrarian bank. In the midst of the protest, a further group of about 200 peasants suddenly appeared and paraded two young cattle rustlers whom they had captured. They then proceeded to the Provincial Prosecutor's office, and the Prosecutor, protected only by a small police squad, rapidly agreed to their demand to bring immediate charges against the two rustlers. The peasants were members of a widespread and well-established vigilante movement known as Rondas Campesinas.[12]

Despite such confrontation with authority, however, the vigilante groups in question for the most part conform very closely to the classic formula of a grass-roots response to a rise in crime in an area where state reaction fails to satisfy the felt needs of the local population. Naturally, they display some special features, which are readily explicable in terms of the particular cultural and political history of the area. Yet the patterns described for them in the literature have much in common with my own and others' findings in Tanzania. In the face of rising crime against property – especially cattle rustling – and in an atmosphere of economic insecurity, groups of villagers began to come together in 1976 to form armed *rondas campesinas* (peasant patrols), which kept watch in the countryside at night and challenged those whom they encountered on their rounds. As with Sungusungu, the groups began in a particular locale and then quickly spread to other villages. They appear to have been successful in containing rustling and other crime in the area, and they have now turned their attention to other matters, including dispute settlement. Various forms of overarching organization have also begun to emerge. The formation of the groups was the result of dissatisfaction with the police's failure to deal with rising criminality and a suspicion that police were sometimes in league with the criminals. They are described as being specially interested in the restoration of security and the maintenance of law and order. Their relations with government have been predictably ambivalent. This is due partly to the threat they seem to pose to the authority of governmental institutions, and partly to their penchant for rough justice when they capture suspects. At the same time, some officials and politicians appreciate the usefulness of their activities in stemming crime. Among other points of similarity to Sungusungu is the predominance of males in the groups and with it some tendency to perpetuate and reinforce the subordinate status of women. None the less, some women – as with Sungusungu – have been engaged in their own supporting activities.

Among the special features of the situation, as compared at least to that in Tanzania, are attempts by politically radical individuals and groups to use the *rondas* as a medium of revolutionary change. Despite the establishment of some connections between such activists and the groups, however, these attempts have been largely unsuccessful, and – as in Tanzania – it appears to be mistaken to see the groups as vanguards of revolutionary class struggle (Starn 1992: 103–4; Gitlitz and Rojas 1983: 196).

A further point of difference is that the *rondas* seem to have been formed initially on the basis of the 'know-how' of their leaders, some of whom have had considerable experience in the wider world. This is in some contrast to the Sungusungu groups, whose local leaders are not particularly more educated or widely travelled than their fellow members, who themselves have a long experience of established patterns of neighbourhood collaboration in dispute settlement and other fields of social and economic activity.

Russian Peasant *Samosud*

In an article on 'Popular justice, community and culture among the Russian peasantry, 1870–1900', Stephen Frank (1990) has documented a wide range of villagers' extra-legal responses to offences including theft, witchcraft and breaches of sexual morality. It is clear from their behaviour, including attempts to bribe locally based representatives of the state, that they were well aware of the serious illegality of some of their activities – for instance, when they burned a witch to death or tortured and killed a horse thief. In cases against witches, they took independent action mainly because the state largely refused to recognize the existence of witchcraft as a legally indictable offence. In the case of horse theft and other forms of banditry, which posed a serious threat to the economic viability of family and community, they felt that the police were often corrupt and in league with the thieves, and that even when they were honest, they were overworked and ineffi- cient. They also felt that, if a case came to court, the penalty imposed did not take full cognizance of the seriousness of the crime.

This part of Frank's account is reminiscent of material from many other places, including the American West, though Russian peasant treatment of such criminals when captured was particularly savage. He describes how horse thieves often operated in gangs, sometimes containing several hundred members spread over a wide area, and enjoying the illicit support of many members of the rural police force. In one area, a gang of highwaymen also harassed villagers until they finally selected some of their number to hunt them down and kill them. If a horse thief was caught, village reaction was often violent in the extreme, and included many different forms of ultimately lethal torture.

Frank notes that the concept of *samosud*, which literally means 'self- adjudication', included both the violent punishment and ultimate exe- cution of horse thieves and witches and also rather different penalties imposed on fellow villagers for relatively minor offences. As he him- self is clearly aware, peasants resorted in such minor cases to a form of 'rough music' or *charivari*, which seems clearly to belong to the wide- spread European (and later North American) tradition of such prac- tices.[13] As in western Europe, the offenders were paraded around by their fellow villagers to the accompaniment of much noise and hilar- ity, while children often pelted them with clods. In Russian villages the din was made by banging heavily on oven doors with sticks. The most common forms of offence seem to have been petty thefts, often of cloth, and the punishment was known as *vozhdenie vora*, or 'leading the thief', who was typically pulled along with a horse collar, and sometimes also the object of his or her greed, around their neck. Women offenders were often stripped for the parade. There was com- monly an attempt to 'rehabilitate' offenders into the community through insisting upon their providing vodka for their neighbours, but it is also clear that such demands were sometimes punitive and, at least in the recipient's eyes, excessive. It is also clear that the punish- ment caused deep distress to many who experienced it. Some sexual offences were also punished in this way, though much less than in western Europe. Errant wives were typically expected to be punished, often violently, by their husbands, with moral, and if need be physi- cal, support from the community. Unlike the torture and murder of horse thieves and witches, *charivari* appears to have been seen by villagers as a form of discipline internal to the community. They appear to have resented attempts by those subjected to it to seek redress for it through the authorities. In one such case, which led to the arrest of the village elder, the woman who complained was subjected to a flogging after his return and, finding life increasingly impossible within the village, ultimately left for the city.

Given the disparities of culture, history and political setting, the parallels between such material from rural Russia, Peru and East Africa is interesting. It draws attention to the fundamental nature of the problems of relations between ordinary villagers, criminals and government, in state systems where official forces prove unable to satisfy local demands for law and order. It also offers some support to the view that vigilantism is a 'natural', or at least predictable, response to such problems in a wide range of cultural settings, while at the same time drawing attention to links with related historical traditions. In the case of Sungusungu, these links are mainly to the villagers' own past forms of independent action, whereas in Russia there is clear evidence, at least with *vozhdenie*, of connection to a much wider European tradition of *charivari*. In Peru, links to other times and places appear to be present but are hard to specify, and access to them seems to have been mainly through the medium of local leaders' knowledge of the wider world.

3
Early San Francisco and Montana

The Tanzanian and other cases discussed in the previous chapter are relatively straightforward examples of a community resort to vigilante action where the state has not proved able to provide the levels of personal security and property protection desired by its subjects. I turn now to two classic cases from the American West – the San Francisco Vigilance Committee of 1851 (and its predecessor of 1849) and the Montana vigilantes of the early 1860s (and the early 1880s) – which have commonly been described as archetypical cases of this kind.

I do this with some hesitation. In both cases there is a great deal of material long since published on these cases, though it is better known and more accessible in the United States than in Britain and elsewhere. Much of this material was written by participants in the events or by contemporaries who knew them well. Thomas Dimsdale and Nathaniel Langford were both intimately involved in the formation of the Montana vigilante group and its destruction of the notorious gang of road agents that had begun to rob and kill at will in the area around the first mining settlements. Another well-known author, Granville Stuart, was also active then and was the leader of the later movement against rustlers and horse thieves in the 1880s. The best-known text on San Francisco vigilantism in 1851 (and also on the larger outbreak in 1856) is that of the American historian Hubert Bancroft, who moved to the city in the 1850s and was well acquainted with the main characters involved, in addition to employing a small army of assistants to amass monumental quantities of data.[1] Despite some rehearsal of opposing viewpoints and some moments of anxiety about particular events, these writers portrayed the movements in question in positive terms as fundamentally the cool-headed response of public-spirited citizens to an emergency in which life and property had become dangerously insecure.

In addition to those who have been content to turn out a variety of paler or, sometimes, more florid versions of these engaging classic texts, a number of more recent scholars have explored these and other cases with more care. Although Brown largely accepts the claims that both developments (as against some later ones) were fundamentally concerned with law and order problems that the state could not yet solve, his work has been justly praised for the model he develops of the patterns of stratification marking these and other early cases of North American vigilantism. Other writers have attempted to take this further and to explore the idea that religious and ethnic divisions may have also played some part in the events. Certainly it appears that the persuasive accounts of the actors and their friends raise several questions that are not yet clearly answered.

For obvious reasons, I am not in a position to resolve such issues here in an authoritative way. The specialist historiography of the events in question is voluminous and I am not an expert in it. Beyond this, even a cursory examination of the cases clearly shows that several levels of analysis – from the global to the local – are ultimately needed to make proper sense of them, and the material lends immediate support to Marilyn Strathern's assertion that all such levels are, on close examination, likely to prove equally complex.

In this respect one must recall that America as a whole was very much in flux at this period. The expansion west and the destruction of Indian society had long since begun. Moreover, while the new gold miners of Montana were staking their claims, the eastern part of the country was racked by the bitterness and bloodshed of the Civil War, on which opinion in the West was divided. At the time of their first vigilante movements, both California and Montana had only very recently attracted floods of 'gold rush' migrants from a wide variety of backgrounds. This was especially true of San Francisco and surrounding areas, where South Americans, Australians, Mexicans, Chinese and Irish were all suddenly brought together with a mixed bag of migrants from eastern and southern states. A dozen or so years later, migrants to Montana included veterans of the Civil War's early campaigns and the California rush. In both regions, new settlements sprang up almost over night and many rapidly became communities.

Many of the migrants were young and most of them were males. Many, though by no means all, arrived with empty pockets, but not, of course, with empty heads. Some hoped simply to make a fortune quickly out of mining or from business and depart for more salubrious surroundings, though many went back empty-handed. Others were attracted by the opportunities for profitable crime, while some just drifted into criminality. Others again were attracted by the possibilities of building a new life in the West, and some simply did not have the wherewithal to leave. Yet, despite the newness and excitement of it all, those who typically became the civic leaders of the new communities they helped to found were looking not for something really new, but for the reconstruction of the best parts of the world they left behind. In their travels also, many of them already had experience or hearsay knowledge of vigilante activity elsewhere.

In such conditions, the problems of spontaneity that I raised earlier, and problems of cause and effect more generally, are particularly thorny.

San Francisco, 1849 and 1851

By 1851, as Brown has clearly shown, there was already a strong American vigilante tradition. Starting in the 1760s in the 'back country' South Carolina settlements established after the carnage of the Cherokee Wars, vigilante action became common and followed the expanding frontier south and west. Brown lists substantial numbers of Regulator and other vigilante groups for the 1830s and 1840s in Alabama, Arkansas, Georgia, Illinois, Indiana, Iowa, Kentucky, Mississippi, Missouri, Ohio, Tennessee and Texas.

San Francisco, originally called Yerba Buena, was from the start a trading centre with good access both to sea and hinterland. It experienced an enormous rate of population increase – from an estimated 200 in 1846 to 5,000 in the gold rush year of 1849, and to over 35,000 by 1852. The sense of growth, pace and excitement that its new citizens enjoyed is nicely summed up by a letter-writer of the day, who wrote in 1854, 'I feel that I am in the Center of the world'.[2]

The problems of maintaining law and order under such conditions were clearly very great. Theft and assault were commonplace and so too, at least in the minds of many citizens, were homicide and arson. The thrill of adventure no doubt coexisted with and gave way to a fear of anarchy for many residents. This led, in the simplest versions of the story, to the establishment in June 1851 of a Vigilance Committee, which hanged four men and summarily deported many others before adjourning its activities some three months later.

The 1851 committee was not quite the first of its kind in San Francisco. In 1849 respectable citizens had got together to break up a disreputable and troublesome contingent of the population, commonly known as the Hounds, but also operating somewhat cynically under the name of Regulators. Among them were disbanded veterans of Stevenson's Regiment of the New York Volunteers. Bancroft (1887, vol. I: 79) writes of their headquarters as the 'Tent of Tammany', and describes how they moved arrogantly around the city, harassing local merchants and others, and ultimately taking over a variety of public offices including that of Sheriff. Lotchin (1974: 190–1) reports that they were said to work as agents for some local businessmen who were anxious to catch 'runaway sailors', and that they also worked for the government but got out of control. In this they are a little reminiscent of the original London 'Regulator', Jonathan Wild. Governmental institutions at this time were in an awkward transitional condition, with an Alcalde (T.M. Leavenworth) and council still technically in power while new arrangements were awaited. The official police force in the city stood at thirty men in summer 1849.

Matters came to a head in July that year. According to Bancroft (1887, vol. I: 92–102), a local businessman had asked the Sheriff, first in his official capacity and then – when this failed – as a leading Regulator, to help collect a debt that he claimed he was owed by a Chilean. In Bancroft's words, when the Chilean refused to pay, 'the Regulators proceeded to the avenging of justice in their own fashion'. That evening, after violently demanding free drinks and cigars in several bars, they decided to 'avenge' an earlier accidental killing of an American bystander by a 'Chileno' who had been resisting their activities at the time. Asked what they were going to do, the Regulators reportedly replied, 'We are going to whip and drive out every damned Chileno in town.' About a hundred of them, armed with pistols, knives and clubs, then began a massive riotous attack on a tented colony of Latin American 'Chilenos', in which one person was killed, many others were badly hurt and robbed, and a great deal of property was destroyed.

More reputable citizens were appalled and decided that they had to 'regulate the Regulators'. Bancroft's account is worth quotation here, as he weaves his way by the light of his own conservative political perspective through the ethical minefield of the situation. He notes (p. 97) that 'Fear took hold on the money-makers, and indignation . . .'. He goes on to comment (pp. 101–2) that 'Under the existing laws of the United States, foreigners had the same rights in California as American citizens, and wantonly to injure them was in the highest degree criminal.' But he also tells us that no 'special sympathy is due the class' against whom the Regulators' wrath was kindled.

> The Chileans and Peruvians who infested the towns and rifled the Foothills of their treasures were low enough in the scale of humanity; by instinct and association they were lazy, ignorant and deceitful, and they seldom scrupled at any crime they might with certainty cover.

If the Regulators had 'extirpated them, and had then themselves been hanged for it, society would have been the gainer'. But they were human beings and 'the persecution of a class was a very different matter from the punishment of criminals'. 'Right nobly', he concludes of the strong reaction of the citizens to the atrocity, 'did the people of San Francisco thus early vindicate their integrity and fair fame, rallying to the help of down-trodden justice.'

A meeting was called in which the raid on the Chilenos was denounced in the face of threats of violent Regulator retribution against their critics. Four groups were organized, each of 100 men, which were to take turns to keep watch and hunt out the miscreants. A public meeting was also held to discuss the problems of restoring peace, and 230 men enrolled themselves to act in the emergency as extra police. Nineteen of the Regulators were arrested and arraigned before a grand jury of twenty-four citizens. They were then tried in official court, and their leader, Sam Roberts, and eight others were convicted on one or more counts. Various suggestions for their punishment were voiced, including hanging, whipping and banishment, but prison sentences and fines were imposed. Imprisonment was difficult to effect in the absence of a local gaol, and some were simply shipped away while others were discharged. Their power was, however, broken.

By early 1851, fears about the level of violent crime, including arson, in the city had once again become acute, and comparable anxieties were developing in Sacramento and elsewhere in the new state. By the end of the year, Vigilance Committees to combat crime and restore order had been established in San Francisco and another dozen towns and settlements, including Monterey and Sacramento, and several were created in the following year in Los Angeles, San Diego, Santa Cruz and other communities. The formation of the San Francisco committee appears to have played a central role in this process, serving as example and encouragement for similar developments in other parts of the state.

In February 1851, a merchant called Jansen was beaten and robbed in his store by two men. Next day the police picked up two Australians who fitted the descriptions of the robbers, and one of these, who said his name was Berdue, looked very like a well-known criminal called James Stuart and nicknamed 'English Jim'. The thought that Stuart was in custody caused some local excitement, and the press began to demand strong action with references to Lynch Law if the authorities did not give satisfaction. An unsuccessful attempt by a crowd to seize the prisoners was followed by a promise of an early trial and a request that those who wanted justice should enrol as jurors. William Tell Coleman, a young merchant who was to become the leading figure in San Francisco vigilantism right up to the 1870s, denounced the courts as inefficient and demanded an immediate trial by the people. The prisoners were taken by the crowd and the trial was set up. Coleman was appointed prosecutor, when no professional lawyer would agree to serve, but the prisoners were allowed the use of lawyers who had volunteered to defend them. The trial was inconclusive since the jury failed to achieve unanimity, and the prisoners were returned to the authorities who in fact convicted them. Later that year, Berdue was accused of another of Stuart's offences in Marysville, but he was released when news was sent that the real Stuart had at last been captured by the San Francisco vigilantes.

Anxiety about crime had risen once again by June 1851, and meetings were held to discuss the situation. At one of these, the Reverend Samuel Willey is reported to have told his congregation that such trouble was to be expected in a new city in which little interest was shown in public welfare.[3] This 'sociological' analysis proved much less attractive than the claims made at a second meeting that Australian immigrants – the so-called 'Sydney Ducks' – were the main problem, along with the inefficiency of the courts and the niceties of lawyers. It was resolved to set up a Committee of Vigilance to deal with the 'Ducks' and circumvent the vagaries of the law.

The constitution of the committee, dated 9 June 1851, is quoted in full by Bancroft (1887, Vol. I: 211–13), and is worth reproducing in some detail.

WHEREAS, It has become apparent to the citizens of San Francisco that there is no security for life and property, either under the regulations of society as it at present exists, or under the law as now administered; therefore, the citizens whose names are hereunto attached do unite themselves into an association for the maintenance of the peace and good order of society, and the preservation of the lives and property of the citizens of San Francisco, and do bind ourselves, each unto the other, to do and perform every lawful act for the maintenance of law and order, and to sustain the laws when faithfully and properly administered; but we are determined that no thief, burglar, incendiary or assassin shall escape punishment, either by the quibbles of the law, the insecurity of prisons, the carelessness or corruption of the police, or the laxity of those who pretend to administer justice.

The document then specifies the organization's name as the Committee of Vigilance, for the protection of the citizens and residents of the city of San Francisco, and lays down a variety of rules. These include the establishment of a committee room, at which a series of designated members will be present day and night to receive reports of crime and if necessary summon the committee by sounding the alarm bell. Majority votes are to prevail at meetings, and officers will be elected monthly.

Two hundred signatures were appended to the document. At its peak there were over 500 Vigilance Committee members, and there was a rather smaller Executive Committee whose composition is not clearly documented, but which seems to have had twenty or more members. It seems clear that these were leading merchants, the 'most intelligent, best educated, and property owning classes of the city', as one vigilante put it.[4] Men of commerce also formed a large proportion of the wider general committee, as opposed to lawyers, who were very few. Working men are said to have been generally excluded, and considerable care was taken over the enrolment of new members. Members could be assigned special policing duties, and the committee also employed its own city and water police.

The original document also stated that secrecy would be observed only when necessary for the success of their actions. Bancroft notes, however, that while arrests, hangings and banishment were public enough, the deliberations of the Executive Committee were confidential to themselves. Ordinary members knew no more than non-members. This secrecy was maintained for many years afterwards, and Bancroft reports that he was granted access to Executive Committee archives only after many years of trying.[5] He describes admission to a meeting of the Executive Committee meeting as 'much the same as at a freemason's lodge' (p. 219), with passwords and other security checks. Members had numbers by which they were known to others. Bancroft largely accepts the need for such long-term secrecy in terms of the fact that their behaviour had been, strictly speaking, criminal, and there had been considerable opposition to them both from lawyers and from state officials. In addition to arrests, hangings and deportations, there were also some illegal searches without warrants.

A few days after its foundation, the Vigilance Committee gained the custody of an Australian called Jenkins, who had stolen a safe. The small group of merchants who had captured him intended at first to deliver him to the police, but one of them – a member of the new association – suggested taking him to the committee's headquarters and this was agreed. There he was tried and convicted, behind closed doors and without a defence counsel, and he was publicly hanged late that night before a crowd, after separate attempts to rescue him by police and by some of his associates had been held off. The body was left hanging under guard until the following morning, when it was at last consigned to the authorities.

A coroner's inquest reported that Jenkins had been hanged by the Vigilance Committee and named seven of its members as directly implicated in the act. The committee next day boldly published a reply, signed by 180 of its members, regretting the 'invidious verdict' and asserting that they were all equally implicated and responsible. The committee also successfully resisted opposition from the State Governor and from the Mayor of San Francisco, finding strength both in its numbers and in popular and press support.

The following month, the notorious James Stuart was captured and handed over to the Vigilance Committee for trial. A lawyer, Pixley, who had often defended him in earlier encounters with the law, made several attempts to have him removed from their custody, but the committee kept him hidden and denied all knowledge of his whereabouts. The immediate offence in question was the theft of a trunk, but he was widely reputed to have committed many others. He at first denied that he was Stuart, but after careful questioning he eventually confessed both to his identity and to a long history of criminal activity, including the Jansen robbery. He said that he was born in England in 1820 and transported at the age of sixteen to Australia for life after a conviction for forgery. There he was emancipated with the help of friends, and he came to San Francisco in 1850. In addition to listing his robberies, the confession also tells (without denial of the charge) how he had been identified on an earlier occasion as the killer of two men, but had managed to escape from custody. The confession also suggests that Stuart's lawyer, Pixley, had few scruples about using legal technicalities to get him and other criminals off the hook.

On the afternoon of 11 July, Stuart was escorted by an armed guard of vigilantes to a waiting derrick on one of the wharfs. There he was hanged before a silent crowd and to the sound of cannon fired by flagged vessels in the harbour.

July proved to be 'a busy month', as Bancroft puts it. Other committees were already operating elsewhere in the state, and there was a great deal of communication between them about suspects. Stuart's confession had also listed several individuals who were now being sought. New arrivals in the city were routinely vetted, and some were not allowed to land. Some of those arrested in the city were deported at the committee's expense. Early in the month, the committee also agreed to collect the $15,000 needed for the completion of the city's gaol, with each of its by now 500 members pledging to collect ten subscriptions of three dollars.

Meanwhile, the 'law and order' opponents of the committee were also extremely active. Meetings were held to protest against the actions of the vigilantes, and writs of *habeas corpus* were brought against them. One of their main opponents was David Broderick, a budding politician whose power in the city became very strong during the next few years. His political machine was destroyed in 1856, when the Vigilance Committee was re-formed with a revised constitution under the leadership of William Coleman.

The attacks of their opponents were successfully resisted and two further men were hanged in August. These men, Whittaker and McKenzie, had been named by Stuart as accomplices in some of his activities. Whittaker was a cool and clever man, whom one witness described as 'the smartest thief in the gang'. The leading vigilante, Ryckman, who obtained his confession, said, 'he was the only man whose execution I regretted; he exhibited so much manliness that he won my admiration'. In his confession Whittaker told how he was transported from England to Australia in 1836, and arrived in California in 1849 after receiving 'a conditional pardon' from the Governor. He confessed to a large number of robberies, but not to killing or other violence. He admitted that his real name was not Whittaker, which he had assumed at the time of his transportation to protect his family.

McKenzie, who had also come from Australia, was a very different character. He seems to have been of relatively low intelligence, and Stuart described how he had bungled an attempted robbery by giving the wrong signals. Ryckman called him 'a miserable specimen'. He seems mainly to have taken part in robberies, but was not accused of killing anyone.

On 14 August, the Vigilance Committee sentenced the two men to hang, and the State Governor made an attempt to rescue them through a writ of *habeas corpus*. This was delivered to the Sheriff, a former Texas Ranger, who broke into the committee's headquarters and took the prisoners to gaol. On 24 August, the vigilantes retaliated by breaking into the gaol and taking and hanging the two men.

After this, the activities of the committee began to wane, partly because of the long hours of work they required. By the autumn it had ceased to operate, although it never formally disbanded.

Montana, 1863–1865 and 1884

Like their predecessors in San Francisco, the Montana vigilantes of the early 1860s were extremely influential upon subsequent developments elsewhere. Information on their activities quickly spread, and they are probably the best-known early group today. Thomas Dimsdale wrote contemporary reports about them in a local newspaper, the *Montana Post*, and his colourful book, *The Vigilantes of Montana*, was published shortly afterwards in 1866 and soon became, in Brown's words, a 'veritable textbook on the vigilante method'. Langford waited until 1890 to publish his own *Vigilante Days and Ways*, which generally supports but also usefully supplements Dimsdale's account. Granville Stuart's *Forty Years on the Frontier* was published posthumously in 1925. In addition to its diary entries for the 1860s, it contains a quite detailed account of the events of 1884. Other texts and memoirs abound. Several later writers have provided further analyses and recastings of events, and some discussion of neglected issues, including information about women of the period.

The region that became Montana came into the United States' possession during the first decades of the nineteenth century. Following Jefferson's 'Louisiana Purchase' from Napoleon in 1803, Lewis and Clark were the first white Americans to penetrate the area, though parts of it had earlier been seen and visited by Canadians and others. White activity during the first half of the century was largely confined to the fur trade and some missionary endeavours. A missionary, de Smet, discovered gold in the mid-1840s, but kept silent, fearing that a gold rush would be harmful to the Indians. In the 1850s, a few miners made good money from prospecting, but it was not until 1862 and 1863 that gold was discovered in sufficient quantities to attract several thousand prospectors and others to the region. The rush never took on the scale and pace of those in California, Colorado and Nevada, but there were still many men who had failed to get a good stake in those regions and were keen to try their luck elsewhere. Despite obvious differences of scale and density of settlement, the situation in the camps and new towns of Montana and the rapidly growing city of San Francisco in its early days had much in common. Opportunities for making money through work, trading and crime were plentiful, and both places attracted many immigrants from a wide range of backgrounds. Most of them were younger men, and some of these, such as Granville Stuart, married local Indian wives.

The development of vigilantism in reaction to crime in Montana was not surprising, since such activity was already quite widespread and some of those involved had experience of Vigilance Committees in San Francisco, Colorado and elsewhere. Levels of crime in and around the new towns of the region soon began to worry several citizens. In December 1863, twelve of them got together in Virginia City, took an oath of secrecy, and discussed a plan of action. The next day twenty-four men in Nevada City signed the following declaration:

> We the undersigned uniting ourselves in a party for the laudable purposes of arresting thieves & murderers and recovering stollen [*sic*] property do pledge ourselves upon our sacred honour each to all others & solemnly swear that we will reveal no secrets, violate no laws of right & never desert each other or our standard of justice so help us God as witness our hand and seal this 23 of December AD 1863.

Membership grew quickly, and units were established in the other settlements. According to one estimate, as many as 1,500 members were probably enrolled in different groups in the first week.[6] A carefully constructed set of regulations and by-laws was also agreed at this time. These specified that an Executive Committee was to be established with the power and duty to legislate and try all criminals who were arrested. The rules also state that 'The only punishment that shall be inflicted by this Committee is DEATH.' The vigilantes did in fact hang about thirty men in the space of two or three years. Many of these were members of a gang of 'road agents' (a local term for highwaymen) whose reputed leader, Henry Plummer, had become the Sheriff of two of the main towns.

Dimsdale presents an overwhelmingly positive account of vigilante action. A well-educated Englishman and in his thirties at the time, he is said to have sought the Rocky Mountain air to combat consumption. He arrived in Virginia City in mid-1863 and died there in 1866. In addition to his work as editor for the *Montana Post*, he taught in a small private school and held singing classes. He was also appointed as first superintendent of instruction for the newly constituted Montana Territory in 1864.

Dimsdale himself was not, apparently, a vigilante, but he knew their leading members well and he is said to have checked his text carefully with at least one of these. He became an active member of the local Freemason lodge in Virginia City, to which many leading vigilantes belonged.

Dimsdale's tale is stirring stuff. Plummer is portrayed as a daring man, a born leader with great powers of organization, a deadly shot and a superficially fine character, who in fact ran a powerful gang of violent highwaymen and thieves who ranged widely over the area. Hold-ups and even murder were becoming commonplace, and some of the more respectable citizens began to talk of the need for a Vigilance Committee. Two violent robberies among the several Dimsdale describes appear to have been particularly significant in local eyes. One was the killing of Lloyd Magruder, a popular merchant who was travelling back east with some of his profits. The second was the brutal robbery and killing of a young man called Tiebault, who seems to have been foolish enough to let it out that he was carrying the proceeds from a livestock sale. This murder, for a relatively small sum, seems to have been the last straw. Swift counteraction followed, and Plummer's gang was smashed by a rapid series of vigilante raids, trials and hangings which were facilitated by a detailed confession by one of the group's associates.

Dimsdale also describes other vigilante 'executions'. The most controversial was that of Joseph Slade, who was himself a member of the vigilantes. Slade was born in Illinois in 1829 and came from a highly respectable family. His father was elected to the United States Congress in that year, but died in 1833, leaving a wife and five young children. In 1847 Slade volunteered for service in the Mexican War, and he returned home the following year with an honourable discharge as a private and a reputation for courage and effective action.

A few years later he got involved in a quarrel that turned into a fight, in which his opponent died, apparently after being struck with a rock. Although he might well have been acquitted even of a charge of manslaughter, Slade fled west and was employed as an overseer of freighting and stage-coaching on a long and dangerous section of the Oregon trail. There he developed a reputation as a tough and effective organizer with a penchant for rough justice. He was involved in further violent altercations and some shootings, and he often went on drunken sprees in which he would ride into a saloon or store and wreck the place. When sober, however, he was a man of great personal warmth and charm, and he made many friends as well as enemies. It is also clear that he never engaged in common criminality of robbery or murder for personal gain.

His employers eventually dismissed him, under pressure from the army when he violently damaged some of their property, and he eventually arrived in Virginia City in 1863 and began a transport business of his own. Although he made a great deal of money from this, he was a profligate spender – not least on sober compensation for his drunken violence – and he died in debt.

The circumstances of his death have been described by Dimsdale and others. A typical drunken rampage with some of his companions in March 1864 led to a meeting of the local vigilante Executive Committee and the issue of stern warnings, which he did not heed, to go home before the situation became irretrievable. This committee was still reluctant to pass sentence on him and decided to summon a general meeting of vigilantes, in which several hundred members voted clearly for his execution. Despite pleas for clemency from some leading citizens, and his own request for forgiveness and permission at least to see his wife before he died, he was quickly hanged.

Dimsdale also records the hanging of a man called Rawley in September of that year, and it is interesting that there appear to be no other references to this case in the major texts. Rawley was a well-educated man, and a merchant in his earlier days, but had sunk down, in Dimsdale's words, to the 'character and standard of a "bummer"'. He had hung around the road agents, though he does not seem to have been closely connected with them. He left town when the vigilante hangings started, but he returned in a destitute state after the gang had been destroyed, and took work nearby. He often uttered drunken threats against the vigilante Executive Committee and expressed sympathy for those they had hanged. The committee decided to examine his history, and Dimsdale says that they found clear evidence of criminal connection with the road rangers and also expected that he would join up with a new gang which they thought was likely to be formed. They decided 'to put a sudden end to all such doings, by making an example of Rawley', and they secretly arrested him at night and hanged him.

One final case mentioned by Dimsdale is worth noting, though one has to turn to Langford and to Bancroft for more details.[7] James Daniels had already killed someone in California by the time he came to Helena, Montana. Shortly after his arrival, he stabbed and killed a man following a quarrel over cards. He was arrested by the vigilantes and then handed over to the new civil authorities. At his trial, the court considered that there were mitigating circumstances and he was convicted of manslaughter and sentenced to three years in prison. A petition for pardon, signed by thirty-two respectable citizens, was presented to the acting Governor of the Territory, who ordered his release. This was in fact illegal, since only the President could issue pardons, and the judge demanded his rearrest. Meanwhile Daniels returned to Helena, letting it be known on the way that he had a score to settle with some of the witnesses at his trial. On arrival, he sensed that he was himself in danger, and he asked the local Marshal for protection. A place was found for him to sleep, but in the Marshal's temporary absence he was snatched away by the vigilantes and hanged. Dimsdale comments that this was 'not because he was pardoned, but because he was unfit to live in the community'.

Despite the development of an official justice system, short spates of vigilante activity continued for some time in Montana, and there was a further serious recurrence in the 1880s. This was led by Granville Stuart and other larger ranchers, and was fired by anxiety about increasing rustling and horse theft. Many, including the future President Theodore Roosevelt, were keen to organize swift and large-scale violent reprisals, but Stuart was sharply aware of the need to proceed cautiously, since he realized that vigilante action could easily be interpreted as simply criminal by the authorities and others. Divisions were developing in Montana and elsewhere between larger 'outfits' and small-holders and 'sheep men', and the term 'rustler' was very loosely used by the 'cattle kings' to include many smaller farmers who sometimes filched stray animals. A Vigilance Committee of fourteen ranchers was formed, and raids were directed against some of the more active horse thieves. Some were shot in the ensuing gun fights and some were captured and then hanged. More than 280 stolen horses were recovered. In spite of the careful organization of the raids, Stuart notes that 'there arose a great hue and cry in certain localities over what was termed the arrogance of the "cattle kings". The cattlemen were accused of hiring "gunmen" to raid the country and drive the small ranchers and sheepmen off the range' (1925, vol. II: 209). He goes on to deny this accusation, arguing that all their efforts were directed against hardened criminals and that relations with the smallholders were generally good. The good sense of his anxiety about the dangers of more widespread action was clearly demonstrated some years later in the 'Johnson County War' of 1892 in Wyoming. A trainload of armed large ranchers and their men set off to wipe out 'rustling', but met strong small-holder resistance and received short shrift from the military.[8]

It seems to have been typical of this period that criminals and others hostile to the vigilantes referred to them derogatorily as 'stranglers', though the term was also used in this way in the 1860s.[9]

True to type?

It will be clear that Bancroft, Dimsdale and Stuart set out to provide a very positive portrayal of the early San Francisco and Montana vigilantes. The vigilantes were decent men, anxious to stem lawlessness in their communities, and unable to turn to effective legal institutions for the purpose. They would have much preferred not to have been forced to do what they did, but the command 'Men, do your duty', which signalled that a man was at once to be hanged, had to be issued and obeyed for the sake of public order.

Langford is also commonly included in the list of key 'apologists', and one of the sharpest critics of the first Montana vigilantes, J. W. Smurr, at times simply writes of Dimsdale-Langford. At least in print, however, and with hindsight, Langford presents a more discriminating account than Dimsdale. It is true that he fully supports the actions against Plummer and his gang. Yet his account of Plummer is less self-confidently damning than Dimsdale's, and he expresses uncertainty about whether the man was genuinely keen at one time to get back into decent society or was merely feigning. In his Introduction he sets out the conditions that he considers to have justified the vigilante action, but he adds that his remarks are a vindication not

> of all the acts of the Vigilantes, but of so many of them as were necessary to establish the safety and protection of the people. The reader will find among the later acts of some of the individuals claiming to have exercised the authority of the Vigilantes, some executions of which he cannot approve. For these persons I can offer no apology. Many of these were worse men than those they executed.

Later, in his brief chapter on the Daniels case, he remarks that the vigilantes 'committed an irreparable error in the hanging of this man'. He could easily have been arrested and kept under guard, and this 'at least was one case where the Vigilantes exceeded the boundaries of right and justice, and became themselves the violators of law and propriety'. He asserts that the hanging did not have the approval of the Executive Committee, which disavowed all responsibility for it, and he describes it as 'the unauthorised act of certain irresponsible members of the organization'. Nor, he says, was this an isolated case.

> Under the pretence of Vigilante justice, after the establishment of the
> courts of justice in Montana, and when many of the respectable citizens
> of the Territory had virtually abandoned the order, a few vicious men
> continued occasionally to enforce its summary discipline.

He adds that several men were hanged for horse theft and for threats,
or simply on suspicion of some crime, and that the perpetrators of
these hangings were in due course told that any further action of this
sort would lead to similar retribution for themselves. Here he seems to
be referring to an incident of 1867, later reported by Bancroft (1887,
vol. I: 704) and discussed by Smurr (1958), when the following notice
was published in the *Montana Post* in response to recent secret hangings.

> We now, as a sworn band of law abiding citizens, do hereby solemnly
> swear that the first man that is hanged by the Vigilantes of this place,
> we will retaliate five for one unless it be done in broad daylight, so that
> all may know what it is for. We are all well satisfied that in times past
> you did do some glorious work, but the time has come when law
> should be enforced. Old fellow-members, the time is not like it was. We
> had good men with us, but now there is a great change. There is not a
> thief comes to this country but what 'rings' himself into the present
> Committee. We know you all. You must not think you can do as you
> please. We are American citizens, and you shall not drive and hang
> whom you please.

It is not clear which cases are referred to here.

Langford's criticism of excesses, while not necessarily insincere, is
arguably quite selective. The comments on Daniels' execution also
seem applicable to Slade's, and were indeed applied to it by others,
but Langford ultimately defends it as a stern necessity when the man
refused to heed to reason. Similarly, the charges in the 1867 notice
could reasonably have been voiced against the earlier hanging of the
'bummer' Rawley, which Langford does not mention, and for which
Dimsdale's apologia is quite feeble.

Langford's arguments are, of course, designed to reinforce, by contrast, what he sees as the impeccability of mainstream Montana vigilantism in the early 1860s. In his eyes the problem was the penetration
of the movement by less noble-hearted individuals and, one suspects,
an inability to keep the numerous lower ranks under complete
control. For critics like Smurr, however, these were fundamental

structural problems of such a powerful, private and highly personalized organization.

Like its counterpart in San Francisco and elsewhere in America, the Executive Committee in Montana was an elitist group. In words reminiscent of those of the San Francisco vigilante quoted earlier, Langford claims in the introduction to his book that 'the early vigilantes were the best and most intelligent men in the mining regions'.[10] His text is also well known for its unusually explicit discussion of the connection between the movement and the spirit of Freemasonry. He describes how, at the time when citizens were becoming deeply anxious about crime, a man called Bell had asked on his deathbed for a Masonic funeral. Langford says he was surprised how many members of the order there turned out to be in the locality, and how the many non-Masons at the ceremony stood and watched in awe as these good men averred their fellowship with each other. Subsequently, the group met regularly and applied for separate lodge status. At the same time, and under cover of its other business, the group also secretly explored the possibilities of setting up a Vigilance Committee. In fact, eleven of the first twelve members in Virginia City were Freemasons. Langford claims that their membership of the fraternity frightened the 'roughs', and deterred them from attacking individual members. He also notes with pride that not a single Mason in the area turned to crime. Both Smurr and Brown have noted that such connections between Freemasonry and vigilantism were in fact quite common, and we have seen hints of such a link in San Francisco.[11]

As in San Francisco, several of the Montana vigilante leaders were also businessmen. Some were merchants or traders, and men like Stuart became rich ranchers. Senkewicz and others have explored the role of business in the 1851 San Francisco movement. His argument, to which I shall return, is that business was depressed, and merchants were looking for scapegoats. The slack in trading also gave them time to set up the committee and organize its activities.

The situation in Montana was rather different, since business was apparently booming. Businessmen were, of course, likely to be interested in stable 'market peace' as an environment for making money, and they often had considerable wealth and property to protect. So too, however, did many of the miners and prospectors, who were also members of at least the wider vigilante groups. Two recent critics of the Montana movement, Mather and Boswell, have attempted to go further than this. Their book, *Hanging the Sheriff*, is an attempt to redeem the reputation of Henry Plummer and to portray him as an ill-starred, tragic figure rather than a scheming master-criminal. In the course of their discussion, they note that the vigilantes' policy of impounding the possessions of their victims laid them open to suspicion of acting upon baser motives than the noble ones they claimed. The authors quote a rumour that huge profits accrued after the impounding of Plummer's wealth, but rumours of course tend to abound in a world of secrecy.[12]

It is probably not sensible, however, to attempt a rigorous separation of the money making of the leading pioneer merchants, ranchers and prospectors from their aspirations for a civilized community in the western wilderness, though it is also sensible to bear in mind that life for them, as for the criminals, had a material base. Even the scholarly schoolmaster and reporter/editor Dimsdale, who managed to postpone a local prize-fight set to take place on a Sunday, had material needs which led him to quarrel with one of the leading vigilantes from whom he had requested a subvention for his book.

Brown's general picture (1975: 104–5) of 'the typical American community of the eighteenth and nineteenth century' provides a more realistic model, though not all the elements that he identifies are clearly visible, at least in early Montana. The model he presents is that of a stratified community in which the upper level includes 'well-to-do businessmen, the most eminent professional men, affluent farmers and planters, and prominent men of whatever occupation. This was the local elite'. Then there is a second level of industrious and honest men of average means, 'the legendary but real American yeoman'. Thirdly, there are the honest poor and also more marginal characters – the 'ne'er-do-well, shiftless poor whites' – whom he describes as 'in but not really *of* the community' and as 'viewed with contempt and loathing by the members of the upper and middle levels'. Lastly there were the outlaws, living on the fringes of the community and denying its values, though not necessarily permanently excluded from it.

'Lifestyle' as well as more material 'life chances', in Weberian terms, constitutes an important element in this model. Brown's picture also helps to clarify the apparent savagery of the 'bummer' Rawley's death, and the ultimate abandonment of Slade by his former friends. These were failed members of the elite, ultimately traitors to their status-group, who also failed to treat it with the respect it demanded – Rawley, the educated man and former merchant, and Slade, the former vigilante and freighter whose wild ways led him into debt and violent confrontations with local leaders, some of whom he saw as sanctimoniously going beyond their brief of protecting life and property against murderers and thieves. Callaway mentions in this context how, in his final fling, Slade sang a ribald song about some of them and later cited an association between two of them and 'a woman not unknown to fame'. He notes 'a silly story' that the song played a part in sealing Slade's fate, but adds that the 'high-minded and distinguished men' concerned were 'above any such puerile thought'.[13]

The most serious criticisms of the early San Francisco and Montana movements focus on the basic claim that they were necessary to deal with a severe rise in violent crime when other mechanisms, including police and courts, were unavailable or quite ineffective. For San Francisco, Senkewicz and others, such as Lotchin, have been sceptical about the extent of criminal activity in 1851 and the effectiveness of the movement in stemming it. Senkewicz notes that the San Francisco movement was not sparked off by any spectacular outbreak of crime, and he stresses the frustrations of the business depression and a 'nativist' American hostility towards Australian and other immigrants as crucial elements in the situation. The 'Australians' were branded as a whole as a convict class, despite the fact that most of them were simply family men and women trying to scrape an honest living. To add to their problems, many of the immigrants had gone originally to Australia from Ireland. Hostility to the Irish and Catholicism, which was already strong in New York in the 1840s, was apparently an exacerbating factor, though not as strong as in the later vigilantism of 1856.

Comparable claims have been voiced for Montana. Mather and Boswell (1987: 99ff) argue that the numbers of murders and robberies attributed to Plummer's 'reign of terror' were much exaggerated. Smurr suggests that political issues were a further factor in the situation. He notes that some of the literature implies that many of the 'roughs' were southerners and possibly secessionists, though he adds that a sifting of the evidence does not wholly support this. He also quotes material suggesting that the vigilantes were effectively the government as well as the 'judicial' power in the territory. In addition, he claims that a substantial proportion of the miners were of Irish Catholic origin, and he argues tentatively that this may have been a significant factor in the situation, given the long-standing hostility between Catholicism and Freemasonry.[14]

Smurr's comment about Irish Catholic miners relates not so much to criminals as to the courts. He argues that the Montana Executive Committee could and should have made more use of, and in a police capacity given more support to, the available miners' and, later, people's courts in the new settlements, and he sees their disdain for these as part of an arrogant elitism on their part. Langford and Dimsdale stress the ineffectiveness of such arrangements, and they provide some evidence to support this view, but it is also true that even some of their own material shows such courts to have been capable of acting quite effectively when given popular support. A number of features of such courts underlay the Dimsdale and Langford view. One was the by no means wholly irrational fear of individuals of serving on juries in the people's courts, because of threats to their lives made by accomplices and friends of criminals who came before them. A second was the chicanery of the lawyers who defended some such criminals. Thirdly, in the case of the miners' courts, where the accused were arraigned before the community of miners as a whole, there is an elitist suspicion of the reliability of judgement and the steadfastness of purpose of such a group and of what Bancroft later calls 'mobocracy' (1887, vol. I: 8–15).

In San Francisco, there were also courts of different sorts, and there a main consideration of the vigilantes was their unreliability as instruments of conviction. The tricks and, in some cases, the dishonesty of lawyers were felt to be particularly troublesome, and there was evidence to support this. Also, police provision was, at least initially, quite insufficient for the city's needs. None the less it has been argued, to some extent along the lines of the Reverend Willey's strictures, that the city's elite got the policing and the courts that they deserved. Many were reluctant to serve on juries, and some seem to have felt that a full-blown legal and police system was an expensive luxury. As Brown has argued, one appealing feature of vigilantism in many American communities has been its relatively low monetary cost to the taxpayer, even though this may have been counterbalanced there and elsewhere by its demands on both the time and energy of those engaging in it.

As I noted earlier, the provision of clear answers to such questions and criticisms is not possible here. Assertions and counter-assertions abound in the voluminous and at times arcane literature on the movement. Some general reflections are, however, possible. Firstly, although some criticisms made are tentative and others are tendentious, it is clearly valuable to be reminded of the need for extreme caution when dealing with a 'local law and order problem' in as complex and mobile a society as mid-nineteenth-century America. Secondly, secretive activities of an elite are by definition open to questioning and doubt, and are, as I have noted, liable to generate a mass of rumour. Thirdly, it seems clear from this material, as from current problems in Britain and elsewhere, that anxiety about crime is not necessarily well correlated with crime rates and may stem from a variety of sources, some but not all of which may still arouse our sympathy for those experiencing such worries.

Lastly, there is clearly something highly paradoxical about the combination of elitism and democracy which this kind of vigilantism seems bound to entail. 'The great and the good', who organize such actions, speak up for themselves and through the pens of Bancroft and others, asserting the fundamental tenets of American democracy. The state and its laws and instruments exist for the people, and the people have the right to replace them with their own direct action if the state lets them down through corruption or inefficiency. Yet, it is typically an elite with some tendencies towards autocracy which decides for itself that it can speak and act in such circumstances for the people as a whole, a stance that smacks rather more of Plato's Republic than of democracy.

The cases viewed here appear to occupy a middle ground between two poles, and indeed to share some of the qualities of both. At one extreme, there are the kinds of case discussed in the previous chapter – such as Sungusungu and the Peruvian *rondas* – which arise in relatively undifferentiated rural communities, and which appear genuinely to be concerned with problems of crime control in remote parts of an inefficient state. Even in such cases, however, we have to rely largely on the reports of the actors and their supporters for evidence of the crime-waves they oppose, and we find a kind of 'proto-elitism', if only that associated with the patriarchal aspirations of male elders. We also find some tendency to broaden the group's agenda to encompass more general questions of social order and morality.

In the San Francisco and Montana cases discussed here, the elitism and the questionable status of the arrogation of representative power to themselves by vigilantes are more marked and more complex, as one might expect with the increased diversity and stratification of the communities in question. At the same time, the case for the need for vigilante action in the face of crime, crooked lawyers and an inefficient legal system retains some plausibility, even when critical scrutiny reveals a possibly much wider set of aims than that to which the vigilantes might care to confess.

Towards the opposite extreme are cases such as those described for southern Africa, San Francisco in 1856, and Florida and other southern states, where group and regime control, in Rosenbaum and Sederberg's terms, are more clearly visible. The boundary between such cases and those considered so far is not always quite as sharp as taxonomic exercises might tempt us to believe, but the explicitness with which blacks, trade unionists or political opponents are branded as public enemies by such movements gives them, none the less, a special character.

4
Vigilante Politics

Introduction – politics, community and state

What is political? There are all too many answers to this question. For some, politics begins and ends with the state. For others, it embraces everything from sex to scientific claims to objectivity. The first view tells us far too little, and the second – unless further qualified – too much. There is also a great deal of room for argument in the middle ground between these two extremes. Some commentators focus mainly upon power and competition to acquire it. Others, harking back to the word's roots in the Greek city state or *polis*, stress the element of public affairs and their management.

The difference between strong versions of this last pair of perspectives emerges clearly with respect to law. To those who concentrate on power, law is likely to appear as a relatively subtle way in which the sectional interests of the powerful are supported and imposed on others. The powerful may be the rich and privileged or, in a simpler society, they may simply be older men. In a relatively gentle critique of the British legal system, John Griffith (1977) notes the influence of political and class interests in the recruitment and behaviour of the judiciary. For the more radical position of Marx and Engels, the legal system itself was essentially part of the ideological superstructure based on the material forces and relations of production. Although liable to disruption by change in its base, this superstructure worked under capitalism to maintain, in albeit complex ways and imperfect ways, the control of property in the hands of the relatively small proportion of the population who possessed it.[1]

The more functionalist 'public affairs' approach tends to assume a set of common interests of all 'good citizens', while regretfully asserting that society cannot survive if we rely solely upon the good will and moral conscience of its members. There have to be rules that people follow in the conduct of their affairs, and these rules must be enforced if society is not to degenerate into a 'jungle'. Law is also essentially political in such a view, but in the sense that politics is fundamentally concerned with the orderly conduct of life in society.

There are good reasons to suggest that these two perspectives are not simply alternatives to each other, if only because administrative systems are always at the same time power systems. Also, not all such systems are marked to the same degree by cleavage and the exploitation of the weak by the strong. Thirdly, within any system of control there is likely to be ambiguity and doubt. Concern for effective administration and for social order in general is often linked to support for one or other form of social order in particular, and those in power are rarely ready to abandon it to others or to a new system altogether. Again, the concept of 'the public interest' is notoriously adaptable as a flag in which to drape individual or sectional ambitions, and it can be difficult to penetrate beneath its folds.

The prime focus of arguments of this sort has been the state, which forms an essential background to the subject matter of this study. The state normally claims for itself a monopoly or at least a large proportion of legitimate control over both political and legal processes, and especially the use of force, within its territory. This control is exercised through a variety of formal institutions such as parliament, the courts, a civil service, local government, the armed forces and the police. The state's legitimacy, as Max Weber classically set out, may rest on a variety of bases, including tradition, a formal legal constitution and the individual charisma of a leader. He also notes that its ability to provide expected services for its subjects is a further if unstable basis of acceptance by them. At the same time, in a relatively large-scale unit of this kind, the common interests and mutual commitment of citizens in general and of rulers and their subjects in particular cannot easily be taken for granted. They appear all too often as key terms of ideological rhetoric rather than as palpable realities, and one need not be a revolutionary or an anarchist to appreciate the need for checks on the abuse of power by those wielding it.

Within the state one typically finds a variety of smaller-scale groupings and organizations. Some of these, such as larger companies and local government bureaucracies, have closely defined functions and operate under strict rules of procedure which are both internally and

externally controlled. Many others are communities whose membership is based upon personal ties of kinship, neighbourhood or friend-
ship. For many citizens of modern states, the 'village' forms the
archetypal case of such 'communities'.

The personalized nature of relations within small communities contrasts sharply with the impersonality of bureaucratic systems. This
contrast is often expressed in terms of an opposition between formal-
ity and informality, but there are problems with this formulation.
Some relations within small communities may be highly formalized.
Strict rules of etiquette may apply between masters and servants or,
more symmetrically, between neighbours or some categories of kin.
Also, there is another version of the contrast between formal and
informal, encapsulated in the term 'informal sector', which was first
used by Keith Hart. This is also relevant in the present context, but it
focuses as much on the locus and the content of behaviour as on style.

The concept of the 'informal sector' was initially developed in the
field of economics. It relates to fields of economic activity outside the
'formal' structures of the market, treasury, banks, registered companies and, usually, the tax system. As is now well known, the high volume and wide range of such activity, which ranges from
'moonlighting' in strongly industrialized societies to small-scale rural
and urban production and services in developing countries, may be
easily missed if one concentrates only upon officially recognized channels of production and distribution.

In much the same way, it is also possible to think of an informal
'political sector'. This consists of a wide range of political activity outside the formal structures of the state outlined above. Sometimes this
may involve the exertion of political influence outside the 'normal
channels' of the ballot box and the strict limits of bureaucratic regulations – for example, through patron–client links. Sometimes too it may
appear as a challenge to the state itself. Given the state's typical aver-
sion to competition in legal, fiscal and governmental affairs, and more
generally in the use of force, there is a tendency for 'informal sector'
involvement in these areas to be treated very seriously as a threat to
the 'rule of law'. Vigilantism is one form of such activity, while others
include certain forms of banditry and outlawry, and some of the activities of mafia-type organizations.

The term 'community' immediately suggests common interests and
shared understandings, although contemporary usage has become so
loose that one might not be too surprised to encounter a well-meaning
reference to 'the individualist – or even the hermit – community'. Yet
the implication of intrinsic mutuality can also be more seriously

deceptive. As I have indicated, 'caring communities' may exercise oppressive control over the behaviour of their members, and sectional interests of both individuals and groups may masquerade as those of 'the community'.

Such comments are particularly applicable to vigilantism. In its attack on crime and in its search for justice and security, it affirms 'obvious' common interests to which decent folk should all subscribe. In the case of Sungusungu, described in chapter 2, the political aspects of vigilantism are mainly restricted to this sphere of order maintenance. For many Nyamwezi and Sukuma villagers, insecurity had reached unacceptable levels. The state had failed to cope with this problem to the villagers' satisfaction, and they decided to deal with it for themselves. Despite fears that the groups were trying to reintroduce traditional chiefship and to usurp the hegemony of the ruling party and official law enforcement agencies, they did not in fact set out deliberately to compete for power with anyone. It has also been suggested that the system constitutes a protest against growing class divisions in the Tanzanian state, but this view also seems to be mistaken.

At the same time, however, we have seen that the system has arguably been one in which the power and influence of middle-aged men have been, to some degree at least, asserted over women and young men. The groups' attack on witchcraft, whose main practitioners are felt to be older women, and their keenness to return errant wives to husbands smack of sexual politics. Young men were also said to have become disrespectful and undisciplined in some villages before Sungusungu assigned them responsible tasks in crime control under the guiding hand of village elders.

It clearly becomes important in such contexts to cast a dispassionate eye on such communities and at the same time to recognize that not all 'communities' are the same. In the Nyamwezi case, despite the disruptions of the 1970s villagization process, village communities were relatively homogeneous, both economically and culturally, and most if not all of their members knew each other well. Elsewhere, however, the situation may be very different. The inhabitants of an English suburb are likely to be far more mixed than Nyamwezi villagers in their class status, political ideals and personal interests. Relations between many of them may amount to little more than a nod and a 'Good morning', and many more will probably not know each other at all. For many, connections outside the locality may be more significant than those within it.

In many places – for example, in the Philippines and in the

Americas – vigilantism has served a variety of clearly sectional interests. In the Philippines a variety of local groups, often sponsored by
the state, and in collaboration with the police and the armed forces,
have been engaged since at least the days of the Marcos regime in
counter-insurgent activities against communists and other enemies. In
North America, local vigilante activities have been pursued at different times in support of white supremacy, as in the case of Ku Klux
Klan and similar groups, and against political rivals. In Latin America,
a variety of groups including death squads have attacked a range of
locally defined 'undesirables', including socialists and street children.

It can be hard to say where law and order, power struggles and
vigilantism itself begin and end in situations of this sort. Rosenbaum
and Sederberg helpfully suggest a conceptual distinction between
three ideal types of vigilante action distinguished by the goals that
they pursue. These are control of crime, control of sub-groups in society, and regime-control. They note that these goals may not be clearly
separable in all cases, but they hope that they may none the less provide useful points of reference for analysis.

Crime control vigilantism is the classic type, to which Sungusungu
and similar cases largely conform, and which Brown (1975: 118) char-
acterizes as 'socially constructive'. Here there is a high degree of consensus in the fight against crime and the basic aim is to compensate
for state weakness in this field by citizens' direct action. Social group
control is directed not so much at ordinary criminality as at sub-
groups in society that are seen as threatening to the social, cultural
and economic status quo. Vigilante violence directed against ethnic or
religious groups – blacks, gypsies or Jews, for instance – or at Indian
untouchables or at political dissidents is of this kind. The reactionary
quality of many such cases is shared also by 'regime-control'. Here
Rosenbaum and Sederberg have in mind a variety of organizations, in
Latin America and elsewhere, whose members are determined to prevent existing or future regimes from dismantling the ordered world of
values and of privileges that they aspire to achieve or to preserve. The
authors also suggest that each of these forms may have a private and a
public face, depending on the extent to which private citizens or the
state and officialdom are the prime actors.

I find these distinctions useful, providing one remembers clearly the
overarching principle that the enemies of vigilantes are either seen by
them as 'deviant' and threatening to the public good, or at least
claimed to be so. In other words, despite the sometimes lethal violence
to which they may resort, vigilantes typically lay claim to the moral
high ground as the guardians of society. Their enemies are not simply

rivals; they are also evil. In addition, just as politicians may claim to uphold the public interest when less charitable views might see their actions as self-seeking, not all that goes under the name of vigilantism deserves the term. Here a concept of 'pseudo-vigilantism' might also be useful. Let us consider some examples.

San Francisco, 1856

As I noted earlier, the San Francisco Vigilance Committee of 1851 did not formally disband, but rather went into abeyance. On 15 May 1856, a notice headed 'The Vigilance Committee' appeared in a number of newspapers. It requested that 'The members of the Vigilance Committee, in good standing, will please meet at No. 105 1/2 Sacramento Street, this day, Thursday, 15th instant, at nine o'clock A.M. By order of the Committee of Thirteen'.

The events leading to this request, and the tumultuous activities that followed it, have been described and dissected at considerable length in several well-known publications, including Brown's general study, *Strain of Violence*. Most of the 748 pages of Bancroft's *Popular Tribunals*, vol. II, are devoted to the episode, and Senkewicz accompanies his own detailed analysis with an enlightening review of the literature.

At the same time, because of its scale and significance, no account of vigilantism in North America or more generally can justifiably ignore the 1856 committee. It attracted an enormous membership, estimated at around 7,000 at its peak, and despite the short span of its 'official' activities – it disbanded with a grand parade on 18 August – it exercised decisive influence on the political complexion of the city for some time to come.

I confine myself here to a brief outline of the main events and to what appear to be the main features of the movement. The immediate spark which lit the fire on 15 May was the shooting of a flamboyant newspaper editor, known at his own request by the exotic name James King of William. A member of the 1851 committee, and keen to see its resurrection, King had used his paper, the *Daily Evening Bulletin*, to launch a series of sensational attacks against crime and corruption in the city. An issue that particularly incensed him was the jury's failure, in January 1856, to convict a gambler, Charles Cora, of the murder of the United States Marshal, William Richardson. Cora's culpability appears genuinely to have been quite unclear, since evidence suggested serious and intemperate provocation on Richardson's part. None the less, King fulminated on the case. He also regularly and violently attacked the administration of the city under the Democrats and their leader, David Broderick, whom he described as 'unblushing and determined as the dark fiend' Satan himself.

A week before his death, King became publicly embroiled in a personal controversy with James Casey, the editor of the *Sunday Times*, who had a reputation for both violence and political corruption. In a controversy over patronage in the hiring of port workers, King had expressed uncharacteristic support to Milton Latham, the accused Port Collector, and a letter in the *Sunday Times*, signed 'Caliban', suggested that his motives for this were dishonourable. King launched a counter-attack against Casey himself, highlighting his unsavoury past, which had included a spell in Sing Sing prison. After an enraged confrontation in King's office on 14 May, Casey shot him in the street as he was walking home from work.

The shooting triggered off the notice and the meeting the next day. Within a short period of the re-establishment of the committee and the recruitment of large numbers of new members, Cora and Casey were seized while in official custody and hanged by the vigilantes. Two months later, two further men were seized, tried and hanged by them for alleged murders. In addition, twenty-eight men were tried and banished – typically put on ships for eastern ports or other destinations. Significantly, those believed to be involved in political corruption and electoral malpractice on behalf of the Democrat administration were the chief targets of attention. Many, including Casey, were Irish Catholics, and this went hand in hand with a wider set of anti-Catholic fears and prejudices which were already well established further east.

Both Brown and Bancroft have, each in his own way, stressed the special features of the movement. Brown writes of it as the 'pivot of American vigilantism', marking a transition 'from a rural to an urban America'. In contrast to the maintenance of law and order on the frontier, this 'neo-vigilantism' used the old methods of hanging and banishment against new victims whom it found among 'Catholics, Jews, immigrants, blacks, labouring men and labor leaders, radicals, free thinkers and defenders of civil liberties'.[2] Bancroft, while placing the movement generally within the context of crime and justice, makes a similar point. 'The crimes committed by the victims of the first tribunal were', he tells us, 'against property and life, while those by the second were strongly tinctured by political morality.'[3] In addition, he emphasizes the high levels of organizational skill and military-style precision exhibited by the 1856 committee's leaders, whom he sees as generally a more able and more statesman-like group than their 1851 counterparts. He is particularly fulsome in his praise of the committee's President, William Tell Coleman, whose coolness, strength of character and purity of purpose he extols at length. He also tells us that the '*personnel* of the Executive Committee of 1856 was quite different from that of the Executive Committee of 1851'.[4]

The organizational scale and the clear political focus of the 1856 vigilantes cannot be denied, and it is also true that an official system of policing and the administration of justice were relatively well established in the city at this time. Coupled with this, the 'law and order' opposition to the movement was itself more formidable than in 1851, and the clash between them took the vigilantes almost to the brink of a potentially disastrous major insurrection, from which they seem to have been relieved to be able to withdraw without loss of face.

I am somewhat less convinced, however, that the movement marked quite as radical a change from earlier forms as Brown and Bancroft claim. Brown's list of victims appears far from wholly without precedent. As he himself describes in his study, the lynching of blacks and their white protagonists in the southern States has a long history going back much earlier than 1856. Even Bancroft notes that 'the expatriated of 1851 were mostly convicts from Sydney; those of 1856 were Irish, and other foreigners of low origin', and Senkewicz has stressed the scapegoating of Australian immigrants in the earlier episode.[5] As we have also seen, Senkewicz and others have also cast some doubt on the genuine existence of a crime wave in 1851. Moreover, although it is true that many members of the 1856 Executive Committee were apparently not members of its 1851 predecessor, at least nine of them were, including Coleman and a number of other leading figures. More generally, both movements were predominantly led by city merchants, most of whom were relatively young.

Although it is clear that the 1856 vigilantes were keen to destroy Broderick's political machine, and indeed succeeded in this task, Senkewicz has suggested that the levels of political corruption and electoral malpractice were not as high as King and the vigilantes claimed. A careful analysis of municipal and other elections in preceding years shows considerable swings from one party and party caucus to another, and does not wholly support the allegations of extensive 'ballot stuffing' that were rife.

Senkewicz at the same time pays a great deal of attention to the economic aspects of the situation, and he in fact links each of the two movements to contemporary problems in the business life of the community. Despite public protestations to the contrary, California was not the land of milk and honey many hoped it would be, and many businessmen and others found prosperity elusive. Scapegoating in 1851 and 1856 seems to have been at least in part a reaction to such troubles. A key issue in 1856 was the high level of public spending of the Broderick administration, which many merchants saw as serving mainly to line individual officials' pockets. There was also fear of municipal bankruptcy and the threat that this would constitute to vital credit from the East. Such arguments against 'high-spending and high-taxing' councils from those, typically wealthier, citizens who support 'fiscal discipline' are of course commonplace in the United States and Britain today. Some critics of the vigilantes were not slow, however, to assert other, and less noble, economic motives of the movement. Accusations, which appear difficult to confirm or refute, point to the existence of overstocked warehouses and the notion that the hangings and expulsions, and the accompanying atmosphere of instability, would inhibit the delivery of further imports. This in turn would permit a rapid shift from surplus to manipulated scarcity and higher prices. Such manipulation of the flour market had already been known earlier in the decade.

After the destruction of the Broderick administration, the new vigilante-sponsored city government temporarily achieved sharp reductions in public spending, but many of the problems of the city were structural, rather than resulting simply from the wickedness or inefficiency of individuals. Brown comments in this context that

> the vigilantes of 1856 were on the right track when they abandoned the rope for the ballot box, but their People's party reform movement was much too narrowly concerned with fiscal matters to achieve any lasting solution to San Francisco's problems. The vigilantes never had a real understanding of the fundamental issues involved.

None the less, vigilante action did not altogether die away there, and in 1877 Coleman was once again active in this field, leading a 2,000-strong 'Safety Committee', in collaboration with the police, against violent elements in the labour movement.[6] Part of the problem here was workers' opposition to the use of cheap Chinese and convict labour.

Tampa, Florida

A recent book by Robert Ingalls, *Urban Vigilantes in the New South: Tampa 1882–1936*, interestingly documents several episodes of 'neo-vigilantism' in Tampa, Florida, which were characterized by complex mixtures of politics, ethnicity and economics. As in 1877 San Francisco, clashes between capital and labour leading to strike action were a central issue in a number of these cases.

The history of Tampa vigilantism dates back to its early urban days in the late 1850s, when Vigilance Committee members lynched a number of accused criminals who were said to plague the city in the wake of Florida's last Indian war. The outbreak seems to have fallen into the more widespread pattern of anxiety about a crime wave, and support for vigilante action from at least some segments of the press. An anonymous letter to the *Florida Peninsular* of the day notes opposition to the vigilantes, but adds that 'some of our best Citizens have adopted this plan of ridding the state of an alarming increased number of murderers, gamblers, horse thieves, robbers, petty thieves, swindlers and counterfeiters', having little faith in the effectiveness of the formal legal system.[7] At least some of the accused criminals seem to have been killed. In language similar to the Sungusungu idioms of the 1980s, an editorial in the *Peninsular* describes how one 'prisoner disappeared, and it is whispered, by knowing ones, will *never steal again*'.

In 1882 a white itinerant of about thirty years of age was hanged by a large crowd, after being seized from official custody. He had been arrested and was awaiting trial for sexually assaulting a young white woman in the course of a burglary in the house of a prominent local businessman. The hanging was defended locally in terms of the southern code 'of "honour" and the "sanctity of the fairer sex"', which sanctioned summary justice of this sort even in the eyes of many southern professional lawyers. A leading figure in this hanging was in fact a Tampa lawyer and an established public figure, Joseph Wall, whose legal career appears to have continued relatively unhindered by a formal disbarment by a federal judge following the event.

In 1887 Wall was also the leader of a citizens' Committee of Fifteen which engaged in vigilante action. This time, however, despite old-fashioned protestations that the aim was the protection of their families and their homes, the objects of their attention were no ordinary criminals. They were Cuban workers in the Tampan cigar industry, who were guilty of no legally indictable offence.

The details of the case are complex. Ethnicity was a factor in the situation, but it was one of many, and the case was certainly not simply one of conflict between American white capital and immigrant Cuban workers. Rather, competition between different sections of the labour force and different unions was the chief focus of the conflict.

The establishment of the cigar-making industry in Tampa in the 1880s was a result of earlier political and economic difficulties, first in Cuba in the 1860s and then in Key West, Florida, to which several manufacturers had moved. In 1885–6 two Spanish-born entrepreneurs established a new base for their activities on the edge of Tampa, and this contributed to an economic boom in the city. Industrial unrest, however, which had driven them to Tampa, travelled with them. The first conflicts arose after some Cuban and Spanish workers joined a local branch of the American union, Knights of Labour, which had earlier operated in Key West. In December 1886 other Cubans formed a rival branch of the Cuban Federation of Cigar Makers, based in New York. They were then accused by the Knights of being predominantly politically motivated and fomenting hatred against Spaniards, who still ruled Cuba. This was denied. The group insisted that they were a 'trade union' and that their opposition to the Spaniards was directed purely against their attempts to control an industry whose development in Florida had depended upon Cuban efforts. This in turn reflected a high level of self-monitoring and autonomy of workers in the then current production process.

There was a strike with some accompanying violence in early 1887. Knights workers walked out of their factory and demanded the dismissal of a Cuban foreman, who was said to have dismissed a Spanish worker simply because of his nationality. The manager refused to act without support against the foreman from other workers. Shooting broke out at a meeting and four Knights supporters were hit, including one fatally. Two Cubans were arrested and remanded for trial. A few days later, the Knights returned to work and the foreman was dismissed. The Cuban workers then walked out, demanding he be reinstated, but they returned to work when the foreman himself decided to leave the city.

The situation remained tense, however, and local businessmen refused to see the problem in its wider context of previous disputes in the industry. In his newspaper, the *Journal*, William Coneley, a founding member of the local Board of Trade, denounced the leaders as 'evil ... agitators, revolutionists and agitated patriots'. He added that a continuation of 'the unsettled state of affairs' was sure to damage social and business interests' in the city. The newspaper also noted that 'terrorism' would be dealt with promptly by whatever means were necessary.

Some weeks later, the Spanish factory owners complained to the Board of Trade, asking for help to get rid of 'obnoxious characters'. The Committee of Fifteen, composed of the by now familiar 'best and most responsible business men', was then established, and a list of eleven Cuban trouble-makers was drawn up. The committee ordered the listed men to leave on the next boat for Key West. Eight Cubans sailed immediately, and two more who were on bail for the earlier killing were ordered back into custody. Fearing for their lives, the Sheriff transferred them to prison in Key West. The eleventh man was National Secretary of the Cuban union, and had only recently come to Tampa in an attempt to sort out the problems in the local industry. He demanded that the committee reconsider their decision, which they appear to have done without changing it. He too left the city.

The fact that a majority of the workforce in the industry were foreign 'outsiders', living and working in a 'factory town' on the edge of the city, no doubt contributed to the intolerance of their activities among Tampa's businessmen. They were welcome as long as their presence brought money to the city's businesses and encouraged building and industrial development. On the other hand, the 'best and most responsible' citizens resented the capacity of such workers, by prolonged industrial action, to damage business and possibly deter further outside capital investment. These concerns quickly led to the establishment of further links between the city and the Spanish factory owners. Some of the leading owners were admitted to the Board of Trade, and one of them was made Vice-president of the Board. The factory settlement of Ybor City – named after the leading Spanish entrepreneurial family – was also formally incorporated into the city, which potentially increased control over the workers. Yet the desired expansion of the tobacco industry simply helped the area to retain its character as a distinct community of Cuban and Spanish workers, with its own social centre and newspapers, and important links to Key West and Havana. Support for Cuban independence, and for socialist and anarchist political ideas, was widespread. At the same time, class solidarity was still cross-cut by tensions and some outbreaks of violence between Cuban and Spanish workers and organizations.

Further conflict, including strikes, group rivalries and violent clashes between individuals, brought new threats of vigilante action in the early 1890s. A new committee, first of five and then of twenty-five, was formed to help employers deal with what was seen as a largely anarchist threat to industrial and public peace. Although the committee did not actually resort to violence against strikers, its presence and support helped the factory owners to resist the strike, which petered out without further serious trouble.

This pattern of Vigilance Committee support for factory owners against workers continued in the growing city, and Ingalls analyses two further major episodes of such activities. In 1901 a complex series of strikes involving different unions led to the secret vigilante arrest and expulsion of several 'agitators'. Later, in 1910, a further disruptive strike, involving issues of wage levels and of union recognition, once again brought vigilantes to the fore. Reports of the 'attempted murder' of a factory owner and a foreman by some strikers, and of the violent treatment of a 'black-leg' worker, led to renewed threats of vigilante reaction. Then a factory book-keeper, a native American called Easterling, was shot and seriously wounded. Two Italian immigrants were arrested by the police and charged with attempted murder, but they were shortly afterwards seized from official custody by a group of men and hanged. A notice pinned to the body of one of them warned others to beware of suffering a similar fate. The members of the group were never identified. The hanging was justified, at least among the leading businessmen, by claims that the victims were professional killers and further assertions that, although they were not directly involved in the strike, they had been hired by a 'certain element of the strikers'.

Despite protests from some quarters, official reaction to the hangings was slow and indifferent, and a new large Citizens' Committee was actually formed in their wake. The membership of the committee was drawn predominantly from the local business 'establishment' and also included the Mayor and Chief of Police and some lawyers. Several hundred members were enrolled at the committee's peak. Armed patrols broke up meetings, intimidated workers and kept the factories open. They were granted powers of arrest and used these to bring strike leaders into custody, where they were charged with conspiring to incite riots and – in some cases – to kill Easterling. Those arrested were warned that seeking bail could be unhealthy for them.

Socialist and union protests went unheeded. The Mayor stressed the legality of the action taken, and state and federal authorities refused to intervene. Heavy penalties were imposed on those charged, and when one visiting union leader was acquitted, members of the committee told him that they could not guarantee his safety and advised him to leave town. A Governor's investigation produced a 'whitewash' of the whole affair, and despite further resistance the strike was eventually broken. The Citizens' Committee, rather than disbanding, was transformed into a new Citizens' Association, whose constitution openly admitted to its anti-union stance. The dependence of the city's prosperity on an industrial sector untroubled by unions and strikes was stressed.

As Ingalls notes, the use of the term 'citizens' allowed Tampan businessmen and their supporters to pursue their sectional interests while claiming to be representative protectors of the community at large. The ethnic origins and outside interests of many of the workers clearly gave some credence to this claim, but Ingalls also emphasizes the significance for local actors of the class dimension in the situation. This of course fits well with Brown's wider assertions of the role of 'the elite' in American vigilantism, which we have seen in different guises in Montana and in San Francisco, and especially with his discussion of the emergence of anti-labour vigilantism as one of several forms of political and economic neo-vigilante action.

The final episode discussed by Ingalls took place in 1935 and was even more overtly political. It involved Ku Klux Klan activity against political 'radicals', one of whom, Joseph Shoemaker, died after being flogged and tarred and feathered. The second Ku Klux Klan – the first had flourished in the Reconstruction period after the Civil War – was founded in Atlanta in 1915 and spread widely throughout the United States during the 1920s and 1930s.[8] Its violence was aimed less specifically against blacks than either its predecessor or its later forms of the decades following the Second World War. Its victims included blacks, Jews and Catholics, but many were also 'Anglo-Saxon Protestants' who were seen as traitors to what Brown refers to as 'the Bible Belt morality'.[9] In some areas, there appears to have been a strong overlap of membership between the Klan and Freemasons' lodges, though many lodge leaders expressed disapproval of this.[10]

It appears that Klan and comparable violence in the Tampa area in the 1920s and 1930s was also directed mainly at varieties of immorality. In 1920 a Spanish immigrant was tarred and feathered after allegedly exposing himself in a park, and three men accused of illegal trade in alcohol were seized and beaten. In 1935 an attorney was castrated for 'fooling around with the wrong person'.[11]

The Shoemaker case emerged out of factional politics in the city and accompanying accusations of electoral malpractice. Control over the city's administration went hand in hand with control over the profits from the city's highly organized illegal gambling industry. Shoemaker had recently come to Tampa from the north and was living with his brother, who had been there for several years. He was employed as a 'poll-watcher' in the municipal primary elections, which had been marked by intense competition, violence and accusations of false counting. Shoemaker noted a discrepancy at the station he was watching – over a hundred more votes were recorded than appeared to have been cast – but the police on duty simply told him to recast his count. This led him to try to organize an electoral reform group, which he called the Modern Democrats, in the city.

Shoemaker had been a member of the Socialist Party in Vermont, but had been expelled for supporting the New Deal and Democrat candidates in the 1934 elections. He was opposed both to capitalism and to revolutionary communism. In the general election of November 1935, his Modern Democrats supported independent candidates in Tampa, and also collaborated with local Socialists. Although their candidates were not elected, the Modern Democrats kept up their activities, and Shoemaker wrote about his ideas for political and economic reform in the local press. On 30 November, the police arrested him and four members of the Socialist Party at a house where they were meeting. The police claimed that they were looking for communists, but showed little interest when told that there were none present. After being questioned at the police station, the men were released one at a time, and Shoemaker and two others were pushed into cars and driven off. All three were flogged extremely violently and then tarred and feathered. They were told to leave town within twenty-four hours or be killed.

Shoemaker died of his wounds, and his death led to a campaign to unmask and convict his killers. Eleven men, including the police chief, were arrested and charged, but despite some apparent progress, the attempt ultimately failed. Two potential witnesses, one of whom had probably participated in the flogging, died suspiciously before they could give evidence. Both were said to have committed suicide. Apart from the police chief, those accused were not local leading figures, but they were defended by one of the city's main political bosses, and several prosperous businessmen raised bail for them. It was clear that the Ku Klux Klan had been involved and also that several of the assailants were not only Klansmen but also police officers. The final failure to bring the men to justice created an enormous scandal, and although the city's leaders retained local popularity, the Klan is said to have refrained from violence in the area after 1936.

Vigilantism in South Africa

Over the last fifteen years, South Africa has been the scene of many different forms of vigilantism within a wider framework of political and social violence. Some recently reported vigilante action seems close to the classic formula of 'crime control', being chiefly concerned with offences by alleged thieves, rapists and witches.

An article by David Beresford in the *Guardian* (29 September 1995) is headlined 'Law moves into vigilantes' hands'. It describes a scene in Kwazulu-Natal in which two young men hanged themselves before a crowd of about 500 people, after being caught allegedly trying to rob a home. It appears that the 'local tribal leader' refused to be involved and that the people themselves tried the men, since there are no police in the area. It was stressed that no one acted as judge, and that the group made a joint decision. This and the self-infliction of the penalty seem intriguingly reminiscent of Sungusungu attempts, described in chapter 2, to limit the risk of official reprisals. Comparable cases are said to be common, though some 'convicted' criminals have been stoned or burned to death, rather than hanged. A macabre twist in this last context is the reported use of the name Operation Nandos by some groups – apparently taken from a fast-food chain specializing in grilled food. The situation is described in the report as connected with problems of police manning levels and competence, and with a shortage of staff in the state legal sector.

Other forms of vigilante action, including much of that reported from the tense and violent 1980s, are more complicated. Here, my comments on the need to look quite carefully at the communities in which vigilantism develops are particularly appropriate. It is hard to imagine a country whose people and communities have been more divided from each other and among themselves. Potential problems of divisions along racial and ethnic lines have been sharply exacerbated by the systematic development by the state of political, economic and spatial cleavages between different sections of the population. The corrosive influence of apartheid and the grossly uneven distribution of power and wealth in the society have penetrated right down to relations between neighbours and between the generations even in a single family.

The South African black urban settlements of the 1980s, in which vigilante activity was particularly rampant, could not be understood without reference to several background factors of this sort. Among these are the history of many such 'communities' as at least partly squatter settlements, their location within the apartheid system, and the diverse origins of many of their members. Also, important divisions within them of power and wealth, when the South African economy was moving into recession, must be borne in mind when trying to understand the forms of vigilantism which arose there. In many cases, vigilante harassment of the opposition has been used to back the quest for and the maintenance of power of local political bosses, and often the state appears to have been involved on the sidelines or more actively behind the scenes. Vigilantism has also been a feature of the activities of political groups and parties, including both Inkatha and the supporters of the African National Congress.

The history of vigilantism in such areas has been documented in several publications. It is not easy to gain a clear view of the situation precisely because it was so heavily politicized. One problem here was the restriction of the term 'vigilante' to the activities of one side in the political struggle. As I have indicated, the term was generally used negatively by the opponents of apartheid and white domination to refer to violence and intimidation by those they saw as its supporters. Behaviour to which a disinterested or naive observer might be equally tempted to apply the term – the enforcement of boycotts, intimidation, arson and 'necklacing' by the so-called comrades – was not normally so designated.

A second difficulty concerned the role of the state. Much of the township violence in question took place between sections of the 'black community', and it was common for it to be labelled 'black on black' by officials and some other commentators. While this was literally true, it was also used misleadingly to dissociate the state from the events concerned (cf. Harris, 1989: 1). There has been ample evidence, including ultimately admissions by governmental officials themselves, to show that the state was seriously involved both indirectly and directly in black township 'vigilantism'.

It is clear that it was advantageous for the state and its security forces to let township leaders and their followers attempt to keep control of dissidents. The direct intervention of police and militia in township affairs was politically and economically less cost-effective and ultimately counter-productive. 'Black on black' violence had a lower profile, and at the same time it conveniently divided the communities that direct state action might easily serve to unite.

The situation provided an extremely useful façade behind which the involvement of the agents of the state could be concealed. The police often clearly sided with the 'vigilantes', refusing to intervene – even when on the scene – to protect their victims from attack, and refusing to respond to calls for help unless substantial legal pressure was brought to bear on them. Beyond this there are well-documented cases of police actually intervening to support 'vigilantes' who came under counter-attack, and of police collaboration with them in other ways.

Crossroads, 1975–1986

The area around the black settlement of Crossroads on the outskirts of Cape Town is a relatively well documented case in point.[12] Squatter settlement in this location began in 1975 and the population there had reached roughly 20,000 by 1978. From its inception, the history of the settlement was marked by a variety of strongly resisted governmental efforts to remove or at least control its growing population.

An attempt in 1976 to obtain a court order to demolish the settlement as a 'health hazard' was mishandled, and the area received the legal status of an 'emergency camp' for which basic services had to be provided. This was followed by a series of 'crime prevention' raids and pass-book arrests, culminating in a massive raid in 1978 in which almost 1,000 people were arrested and one was killed by a riot policeman.

Resistance to these efforts was organized internally by a small number of local men's and women's committees which, despite rivalries and conflicts, joined together in 1979 to form an all-male Executive Committee under the leadership of a controversial figure, J. Ngxobongwana. External support was organized by a 'Save Crossroads' campaign.

In 1978 the government initiated a new policy on black urbanization. This aimed at establishing a sharp distinction between 'permanent' residents, with rights to move within the towns and join trade unions, and others who were to be defined as rural homelanders. This policy provided the framework for negotiations between government and the Executive Committee, which at first demanded improvements for all residents, but which finally agreed to a compromise. A new township to be called New Crossroads was to be established nearby, but only a proportion of the residents could move there. Large numbers of other residents and their families, including those with 'no visible means of support' would have to be removed to live and work in rural homeland areas. The agreement caused dismay and anxiety for many of the residents, whose numbers now reached almost 50,000.

The Executive Committee collaborated with the Bantu Affairs Administration Board in a survey of the settlement and in the issuing of permits to those deemed to qualify for 'permanent residence'. Allegations of corruption in the conduct of this allocation were common.

More generally, the agreement marked the beginnings of authoritarian 'rule' in the settlement. Opposition to Ngxobongwana from within the Executive Committee was violently suppressed, and violence also began to characterize relations between the committee and other opponents to it in the settlement.

During 1981 and 1982, the state unsuccessfully attempted to evict the growing numbers of squatters in 'satellite camps' adjacent to the Crossroads area. This failure led to state proposal of a new solution – a new township was to be created at Khayelitsha on the coast about 35 kilometres from Cape Town, and officials spoke of this as a new 'home' for all blacks in the Western Cape. After a further comment by the deputy Minister for Co-operation and Development that Crossroads could not be tolerated and had to be destroyed, Ngxobongwana and the United Democratic Front (UDF) – which represented radical interests at the time – began to work together. Meanwhile raids on the squatter areas had continued, and more violent conflict between Ngxobongwana and some of his opponents erupted. His more violent henchmen, who were known as Witdoek, from the white cloths which they wore around their heads, burned down several houses and a school in the opponents' area, and some people were killed. Unity among all sections of the population was temporarily enhanced, however, when in spite of Cabinet announcements of more concessions to those granted legal residence, the new Minister for Co-operation and Development asserted that the movement of all residents, legal and illegal, to Khayelitsha remained a priority.

In February 1985, a violent confrontation between UDF-supporting comrades and the police left eighteen people dead and 230 seriously hurt. The minister then offered further concessions, including an expansion of the Crossroads area allocated for legal settlement.

Also around this time, Ngxobongwana himself was arrested after an affray arising from a meeting to protest against rent rises by the Administration Board. In June 1985, within a month of his return from prison, he announced that he was breaking with the UDF because they were creating divisions among his followers and had given him inadequate support during his trial. Rumours were rife that he had been 'bought off' during his detention.

However this may be, Phillips notes that differences of interests and of style were clearly present at this juncture. Ngxobongwana and many of his supporters stood to benefit politically and materially from the displacement of 'illegal' squatters, whereas these last constituted many of the UDF supporters. At the same time, his authoritarian style of leadership and the male domination of the Executive Committee appear to have appealed to patriarchal leanings among some of his supporters, whereas UDF was apparently less centralized and personalized, and women and youth had more say in its activities.

These activities and the radical stance against the state which informed them threatened the establishment of Crossroads on a stable legal basis and Ngxobongwana's position within it.

Some of the activities of younger UDF supporters also alienated many ordinary Crossroads residents. Although local usage and the literature restricts the term 'vigilante' to violent supporters of men like Ngxobongwana, to an outside eye behaviour of the UDF-supporting *maqabane* or 'comrades' also often seems to fit this label. Political campaigns including a consumer boycott were organized, and those who failed to participate or subscribe to them were harshly treated by the 'comrades'. Shoppers were stopped and forced to drink the fish oil or eat the detergent they had bought. Unofficial courts were set up and 'offenders' were 'punished' with extremely heavy beatings. Such behaviour was seized upon by Ngxobongwana and his supporters, one of whom is quoted as saying that 'unless the *maqabane* cool down, the people of Old Crossroads will hunt them down and beat them again ... The *maqabane* have to stop making petrol bombs and holding kangaroo courts. We will not allow them to beat and punish their own people.'[13]

Relations between the two sides deteriorated further during 1986, as police and Witdoek raids on squatter camps intensified. In May and June matters came to a head with what Phillips has described as 'probably the largest, most rapid and most violent forced removal in South African history'. Between 50,000 and 70,000 squatters had their homes burned down in a series of Witdoek attacks. The police are said simply to have stood by during these incursions, intervening only to help repel counter-attacks from 'comrade groups'. By 12 June, almost the whole of the main squatter camps had been destroyed and about 100 people had died violently. A national State of Emergency was declared.

This material reveals the acute difficulty involved in trying to attach firm labels to the aims and activities of conflicting individuals and groups in socially and politically unstable communities. The parties involved are variously contrasted locally and in the literature as 'vigilantes' or 'Witdoeke' and 'comrades' (*maqabane*), 'elders' or 'fathers' (*otata*) and 'youth', authoritarian and democratic, conservative and radical, legal residents and squatters, and supporters and opponents of apartheid. A further linked distinction is between relatively well-off businessmen and job-holders and the poor and unemployed. It is clear, however, that the above labels did not fit everyone to whom they were applied. Not all UDF supporters were young, for instance, and not all *otata* are elderly and conservative.

It is also clear that divisions in the population sharpened over time, as the unity in part inspired by the initial threat to the community gave way to cleavages between potential 'haves and have-nots' and between those willing to accommodate themselves to the wider system and its radical opponents. In addition, it seems clear that some people were much more active than others in the struggles which ensued. It is tempting to think that some of the labels adopted were more divisive than others – 'fathers' and 'youth', for example, seems to be a more complementary pairing than 'legal residents' and 'illegal squatters' – and that their use reflected at least the assertion of different attitudes to unity and division for different people at different times. Data to support or contradict this are, however, largely lacking, though the earlier quoted statement about the *maqabane* punishing 'their own people' suggests that ideas on this issue were at times incorporated into local rhetoric.

Sederberg and Rosenbaum's distinctions between 'crime', 'group' and 'regime' may help to throw some light on the situation, if only by indicating some of the questions one would like to answer if one could. There is evidence that elements of all three were present, but the problem is to disentangle them. Issues of group control emerge once 'the enemy' is defined openly or covertly as an undesirable group, and local questions of regime-control are clearly present when the aim becomes the preservation of a power system because of vested political and economic interests in it. Apart from problems which arise from mixed, disguised and even possibly confused agendas, the situation is further complicated by the escalation of the conflict along hardening factional lines. The issue of who was to control Crossroads became violently contested between opposing groups, and this led to the emergence of what might usefully be called vigilante factionalism as each side tried to arrogate legitimate authority and the moral high ground for themselves within the area. At the same time, conflict in this case appears to have degenerated ultimately into wholesale opposition, in which, at least for some, the aim became to eradicate the very presence of the enemy group from the community. The violence then became akin to local warfare.

The point at which one kind of vigilantism becomes another, or 'vigilantism' becomes 'war' or vice versa, is very difficult if not impossible to determine in such cases, given the capacity of humans to attribute political authority and good or evil motives to themselves and others, and to contest such attributions. As I argued earlier, one can do little more in such circumstances than try to establish ideal types against which reality might be measured. At the same time, the parties to a conflict will often agree more readily about the definition of such ideal types than about their applicability to their own and their opponents' actions.

Finally, the place of the state must be considered in this case. Vigilantism archetypically displays a grass-roots quality, which exists in the absence of or despite state machinery of law and order. The evidence of state complicity in the vigilante activity that supported local bosses like Ngxobongwana is very strong, and it was clearly convenient for the state to allow such men and their supporters to do some of its work and to define the kind of violence that ensued as 'black on black'. As in the case of death squads, which I discuss in chapter 6, one sees here that the 'frontier' between vigilantes and the state, like so much else in the political domain, may be more fictional than one is invited to assume.

Vigilantism and the politics of race: the first Ku Klux Klan

In discussing Sungusungu's efforts to hunt witches, I referred to our capacity as linguistic animals to dehumanize and demonize each other. The substantive and adjectival labels that we attach to others can be very damaging and even have, at times, a lethal quality. They permit and even encourage us to question or deny the common humanity between us and those we see as enemies, and they may appear to absolve us from the guilt that we would normally expect to feel if we harm other people.

The power of labelling in such situations also extends to what people call themselves. Sometimes there is simply emphasis on normality – on being simply ordinary, decent people. Sometimes, however, more pretentious words and phrases can be used in an attempt to endow even quite sordid aims and actions with a special aura of nobility and mystery.

Cultural, religious and linguistic differences all lend themselves to some degree to assessments of the otherness of others, but physical and so-called racial differences are especially prone to such use as indelible markers of quality and character. Nowhere is this clearer than in the history of black slavery and in the ideology of fundamental black inferiority that was claimed to justify it. Thus Francis Grund, a German commentator on America in 1837, writes deploring slavery in general. However, he goes on to say that if 'the negroes are naturally inferior to the whites . . . then [this] . . . would, at least, contain an apology for retaining [them] . . . in bondage'. After further exploration of the concept of slavery itself, he asserts that it is 'my honest conviction that the negroes *are* an inferior human race, and not capable . . . of enjoying the same degree of freedom as Americans'. In support of this he claims that they 'have very marked distinctions from any other race of men: and where nature points out a physical disproportion, we may in all cases safely conclude that a moral one corresponds to it'.

The violent 'punishment' of black slaves who were deemed to have offended their masters was commonplace in the American South. Like enslavement itself, it was partly justified in terms of black inferiority, but it also reflected a persistent fear of insurrection. Here other enemies were also involved – the at best misguided and at worst thoroughly evil traitors within white society who opposed slavery and gave its victims ideas and ambitions above their proper station. Such men too – the enemies within – were common targets of violent and self-righteous retribution. As Allen Trelease comments in his study of the first Ku Klux Klan, eternal vigilance was the price of white supremacy as well as of liberty.[14]

The Civil War saw the abolition of slavery, but this was, of course, but a first step in a campaign that is not yet over. Certainly in 1865, the vast majority of southern whites, and many others in the North, including many northern Democrats, were keen to see as little change as possible emerging from emancipation. Lincoln's successor in the Presidency, Andrew Johnson, appears to have largely shared this wish. The prime Congressional supporters of such change were northern Republicans and especially the Radicals, who advocated full legal and political equality for blacks.

In some respects emancipation left the former slaves in a more vulnerable position than before. They had their freedom, but little else. So-called Black Codes of 1865 and 1866 relegated them to lower status. They had no rights to vote and they found it more or less impossible to obtain their own land. As employees of whites they were subject to intimidation and harassment, and white violence was no longer tempered by the paternalistic feelings, or even the wish to preserve 'their property' in good condition, which had softened the behaviour of some slave-owners. Southern white fear and anger were also sharpened by federal efforts to consolidate control over the South. Some southern Democrats were disenfranchised and black freedmen were recruited and armed alongside white Unionists in new militias. Federal agents of a new Bureau of Refugees, Freedmen and Abandoned Lands were an additional thorn in their sides. In 1866, despite Presidential opposition, Congress also passed a Civil Rights Act, whose provisions were then enshrined in the Fourteenth Amendment to the Constitution, which came into force in 1868. United States citizenship was now extended to include blacks, who were at the same time granted equal rights to whites before the law, and rights to hold and transfer property.

Recalcitrant whites resisted such developments with whatever means they could muster. These included a variety of forms of vigilantism whose origins lay in the 'regulators' and old 'slave patrols' of pre-war days. During the late 1860s, however, these activities became identified more and more closely with the Ku Klux Klan, which was founded by six young Confederate veterans some time in the early summer of 1866, in the small town of Pulaski in Giles County, Tennessee.

Over the next few years, local chapters of the Klan conducted a massive campaign of terror throughout the South. It seems clear that the original Pulaski founders had no such intention. They established the society in an attempt to add some spice to the dull life of a post-bellum small community, as an opportunity for a few pranks and for surprise appearances in fantastic masquerade at local functions. Their standard outfit was white masks with holes for eyes, tall cardboard conical hats and a flowing robe of any colour they decided, but some also decked themselves out in other ways. They held private meetings, created a panoply of mysterious titles – Grand Magi, Grand Turk and so forth – and initiated new recruits. The name Ku Klux Klan itself is said to be derived from the Greek *kuklos* (a circle), to which Klan was added for alliterative effect. It seems that the name was modelled on the Greek forms used for college fraternities, and that one of these, Kuklos Adelphon, provided the immediate inspiration.

The founding of the Klan provides good support for a theory of unintended consequences. Its dramatic spread throughout the South and the swift shift to vigilantism as its main concern surprised and worried its founders, as it spiralled out of their control. The name itself and the mystery and grandeur of the Klan's titles and other paraphernalia quickly and sinisterly filled what its enemies no doubt saw as 'a much needed gap'. As Trelease comments, a name such as the 'Pulaski Social Club' would not have had a similar growth potential.[15] This attraction has managed to persist through several phases to the present day. Griffith's 1915 film, *Birth of a Nation*, was a crucial element in the rebirth of the Klan out of the flames of its invented symbolism of the burning cross.[16] In the years between the two world wars it developed into a massive, widespread organization with local variants of a broad aim of maintaining American white Protestant society against a multitude of enemies. These were variously identified as recent immigrants, union 'agitators', blacks, Catholics, communists, Jews and moral degenerates. Then, having died away in the 1930s in the wake of sexual, financial and political scandals, the Klan re-emerged in the 1950s and 1960s in the South. Once again the threat of black integration was met by a campaign of white terror dressed in the trappings of self-arrogated honour, chivalry and mystery.

I concentrate here upon the first Klan and the decades following its suppression in the early 1870s. It will be clear already that the time and circumstances were ripe for a widespread violent development of this kind after the Civil War. Several different organizations, with comparable aims, already existed throughout the South. Some were simply bands of 'rangers', 'moderators', 'nigger killers' and 'regulators'. Others had more ritualized organization and more pretentious names, such as Alabama's 'Men of Justice' and the 'Knights of the White Camelia' in Louisiana. As the Klan spread, many of these groups were subsumed under its label, though new ones were also sometimes formed. The Klan itself, despite its supposed overarching structure of Grand Wizards, Dragons and the like, was also quite decentralized in practice.

The Klan had spread throughout most of the South by 1868. Its practice and its membership varied from one area to another. Members of the local elite were more involved in some places than in others, and discipline and organization may have co-varied with this. Sometimes there were public appearances in parades and demonstrations, but the main activity was 'night riding', in which Klan members variously raided, harassed, tarred and feathered, flogged and hanged their chosen victims. Official counter-measures were hindered by the unpopularity of the Federal regime, and by the accompanying shortage of reliable recruits into state militias. The recruitment of blacks into these and the alternative of calling in Federal troops tended to serve simply to fan the flames.

The general aim of Klan activities was to maintain white supremacy and keep blacks under control. To this end many blacks themselves were savagely attacked and murdered, but the Klan also counted many whites – the northern 'carpet-baggers' and the southern 'scalawags' – among its enemies, who included Federal government agents and officials, and open supporters of the Union. As the Radicals pushed Federal policy more and more towards true black emancipation through education, property holding, voting rights, and rights to hold public office, resistance itself became stronger and more violent. The entrenched racialism of slave-owning days was if anything intensified by such developments and threats. Fears of violent black domination with Federal support were fanned by rumour and press agitation, and there were also strong anxieties about the perceived threat of a gradual and more peaceful, but none the less relentless, road to ruin. Sitting with blacks in the performance of one's public duties would lead to eating with them. The next humiliation would be intermarriage, and with that the degeneration of the North American white race and exclusion from the 'family of white nations'.

According to Brown, the Klan lynched over 400 blacks between 1868 and 1871, and Trelease provides a full account of the Klan's spread and activities throughout the South during these years. He describes the situation in York County, South Carolina as marking the climax of Klan terror.[17] The total population of the county was around 25,000 and about half of these were blacks. By the spring of 1871, around 1,800 of the 2,300 adult white males there were 'sworn members' of the Klan. Some had been intimidated into joining, as had a few blacks, and it seems that only some, mainly younger members, were active raiders. The Klan had started there in 1868, and was active in deterring black voters and gaining a Democratic victory in the November 1868 elections. It then became less active until 1870, when several black militia groups were armed, and then in October the Republicans won the county in the state elections.

That month Klan raids and violence against blacks flared up again, and these were resisted both by armed black militias and by threats and acts of arson. The militias were then officially disarmed and the Klan stole many of the confiscated weapons. Black homes were also searched in raids and any weapons found were taken by the Klan. Then between November 1870 and September 1871, a systematic series of nightly raids was carried out. Trelease estimates that there were eleven murders, over 600 whippings and other serious assaults, and many other instances of threats and personal abuse. The very large majority of victims were black and included women and children. Schools and churches were burned down as part of this 'record of sustained brutality which few places in the country ever matched'. Many of the attacks were overtly political as well as racial. One black was killed when he refused, after being flogged, to promise to vote Democrat. In one especially vicious case, a black political activist who had been paralysed since childhood, and whose limbs and body were those of a child, was threatened, punched and whipped, and was left with a warning to change his ways, vote Democrat and cancel his subscription to a Republican newspaper. A few months later, in despair of ever finding peace at home or in the West, he led a group of 136 emigrants out of America to Liberia.[18]

By this time Federal reaction was becoming tougher, and some of the more conservative Klan members seem to have worried that matters were getting out of control. Military rule was established in the county, *habeas corpus* was suspended, and large numbers of Klan members were arrested and indicted in the Federal court at the state capital, while many others fled. However, very few of those arrested were actually convicted, largely owing to the time that each case took, and the lack of funds that would have been necessary to expedite proceedings. The York County campaign was an important blow against the Klan, since it provided a clear demonstration to those elsewhere of Federal determination to suppress it. Yet it was only after many further outrages and conflicts, and after Democratic victories in South Carolina and other states, that the Klan was pushed into quiescence.

Even then, the struggle was continued by other means. In the 1880s, after Radical Republicanism had lost much of its earlier enthusiasm, southern whites began the process of reversing the developments of the Reconstruction years with a systematic programme of segregation and disenfranchisement of blacks. This was completed in the early years of the twentieth century. Meanwhile, violence against blacks relentlessly continued. Between 1889 and 1918, 2,460 blacks were lynched in the old slave states. Two-thirds of these were lynched for alleged offences against white women, but the standards of evidence demanded in such cases were often low, and many of the remaining 800 or so cases involved no clearly alleged offence at all.

5

The British Scene

Two men who attempted to clean up East Anglian villages plagued with petty vandalism have been jailed for five years for kidnap. The sentences have provoked a strong response from residents who described [the men] as 'upright citizens'. Judge John Binns jailed the pair for kidnapping James Last, aged 17, on January 12. Mr Last was described in court as a 'troublemaker' who had become a nuisance to villagers. (*Guardian*, 11 June 1993)

The case of the Norfolk vigilantes provoked strong reaction even after the two men had had their sentences reduced to six months. Fifty-nine per cent said they did not believe the two should have been jailed. (*Daily Telegraph*, 30 August 1993, report on Gallup Poll, 18–23 August 1993)

We have seen that in his study of vigilantism in the United States, Brown connects its vigour and persistence with the frontier and the revolutionary origins of the nation and its constitution. He also contrasts the situation there with Britain, which, he claims, despite a history of riots, lacks a vigilante tradition. This, of course, should not be too surprising in a relatively small country that has a long history of relatively dense and stable settlement under the 'rule of law', and it is certainly the case that vigilantism in the United States presents a very different picture from anything that Britain has to offer.

At the same time, as Philips and others have suggested, and in line with my earlier discussion of the ultimately global spread of information on such matters, it is clear that there has long been a substantial two-way traffic of news and ideas in this as in other contexts between

America and Britain, and that there are even direct links between some institutions, such as anti-horsethief associations, in the two countries. Such connections at least suggest that it would be a mistake to treat them totally separately from each other rather than as more or less favourable environments for the same seeds.

Here I want to draw particular attention to the flow of information from America to Britain, rather than vice versa, in both books and newspapers during the early nineteenth century, and also to some interesting use of American vocabulary in press discussions of events in England at that time.

In Edinburgh in 1833, James Stuart published his *Three Years in North America*, and he provides his British readers with an insightful account (vol. II: 178–9) of 'Lynch's law' in Alabama and elsewhere. He writes:

> In an extensive district of the country, where the expense of a police establishment cannot be borne by a few inhabitants, scattered at considerable distances from each other, no better scheme perhaps can be devised than that the inhabitants themselves should, with view to their security, place themselves under the control of some one of their number, in whom they have confidence. Many instances of this have occurred in Southern and Western America, and, in various cases, the newly established state governments have winked at the infliction of public punishment on depredators and criminals by such authorities as those I have mentioned, where it was obviously impossible to have criminals, and the necessary witnesses, carried to the circuit town, owing to its great distance, and to the almost total absence of officers of police.

He then goes on to discuss the origin of the name 'Lynch's law' in the activities of 'an individual of the name of Lynch' in Carolina, and he continues 'There are yet, on the western bank of the Mississippi, occurrences which require that this law should be resorted to, and even capital punishment inflicted.' He concludes that sometimes such courts have done wrong and been punished, and he adds that they dissolve themselves once a regular police force is established.

Four years later, Francis Grund published his two-volume account of *The Americans in their Moral, Social and Political Relations* (1837). Himself a German – a German edition was also published in the same year in Stuttgart and Tübingen – he presents the work to the 'English public' in an effort to correct current prejudices about the people. As Brown has noted (1975: 171), Grund presents a relatively favourable account of 'Lynch Law' – he focuses on flogging and tarring and feathering under this head – which he says has been the subject of discussions in 'the English papers'. He ascribes its origins to the original Pilgrim Fathers and their use of biblical precedents for the 'cheap, easy and salutary correction of flogging'. The penalties, he says, grew more severe as Puritan morality relaxed. Gamblers, disorderly persons and, more recently, 'itinerant ministers' who are 'a little too anxious for the emancipation of the Negroes in the Southern States' are described as the main objects of attention. He sees such activity not as 'opposition to established law ... but as a supplement, – a species of *common law*', and although he describes it as an interim measure till 'the regular physician could be called in', he notes that this may not be necessary.

In the 1850s, the activities of the San Francisco vigilantes were reported almost immediately in some detail in the London *Times* and in Australia, as well as in the newspapers of the eastern United States. As Bancroft notes, much such comment was highly critical. 'At the East and in Europe the Committee was thought of and talked of very much as we would think and speak of the Cannibal Island King and his Cabinet' (1887, vol. II: 549). At the same time, however, a more balanced and even a more positive note was struck occasionally. One *Times* report notes the popularity of the 1851 committee 'among a large number ... of the better classes of the people' and adds that there is no danger of a 'reign of terror'.[1] 'The non-vigilance citizen' is said to be on 'as amicable terms with the Vigilance Committee man now as ever'. Bancroft also quotes an ironic comment of the period from Charles Dickens' weekly journal *Household Words*, which berates the naive assumptions of 'John Bull' about his duty always to stand back and leave law enforcement to 'the person of the policeman who is not there' (1887, vol. II: 556–7).

A search of *The Times* in the first half of the nineteenth century also reveals references to 'lynch law' in America. The most detailed of these (*The Times*, 5 November 1835, p. 7, c. 1) concerns the publication of 'Proceedings of the citizens of Madison County, Mississippi, at Livingston, in July, 1835, in relation to the trial and punishment of several individuals implicated in a contemplated insurrection in this state'. *The Times* reports that five black slaves and five white citizens were executed and notes with some irony that 'if precedents, or principles, or the mode of enforcing Lynch law be required, here is a textbook for the admirers of such cheap and speedy jurisprudence'. Several of the cases are briefly described with information on the somewhat flimsy charges laid against those hanged, including being lazy, pretending to make a living by constructing washing machines (*sic!*), and having the 'audacity "to intercede with owners of runaway slaves, to save them from a whipping"'. The disdainful tone of the report appears to be inspired mainly by the intolerance shown to any questioning of slavery and violence towards slaves.

A search of local British newspapers for such reports would be a monumental task, but it seems likely that it too would reveal comparable references to American material. The earliest local British record of American activities that I have encountered reached me by accident in 1988 when the *Cambridge Daily News* reissued a copy of its issue of 24 December 1888. This contained an article under the heading 'Lynch Law' about the activities of the American 'White Caps', who seem to have borrowed their ideas about headgear from early Ku Klux Klan-style vigilantes. The article reports on their activities as follows.

> For several weeks the State of Ohio, which has been regarded as a civilized and highly developed region, has been the scene of a succession of serious outrages which the officers of the law have thus far found themselves powerless to check. The northern part of the State is inhabited by the descendants of the old Puritan stock. They have kept up many of the traditions of their ancestors, have pushed their religion to the verge of fanaticism, and are now carrying into practical effects the antiquated Puritan ideas of regulating the morals of their neighbours. This scheme was started in Southern Indiana. There a secret organization, as described in previous despatches exists, the leading spirits of which in order to improve the morals of the neighbourhood, study carefully the habits and manners of all the inhabitants in their locality, their society being known as the 'White Caps'.

The article goes on to relate how people who are unkind to their wives, or given to drink, or who are 'indolent and vagabondish' are seized at night by men disguised with white caps, and are given a thorough beating. Those individuals who try to oppose the movement themselves are also threatened and sometimes beaten.

The amount of published information on American developments clearly increased greatly in subsequent decades and, as I have discussed, the cinema and other media have also been involved in such dissemination. The main point in the present context is that Britons have long since been aware of 'lynch law' and 'vigilantism'. They have existed for them as elements in a repertoire of possible reactions to local-level problems of law and order and morality. Hostility to them has been strong, though perhaps mainly at the level of officialdom, which has generally been able to discourage competition to its own machinery. Their strong adoption by Americans, many of whom were of immediate or earlier British extraction, partly mirrors the sentiment of James Stuart that desperate times require desperate measures, and perhaps also partly shows that their emergence reflects freedom from, rather than simply absence of recourse to, state control. At the same time, as I mentioned earlier, some members of British associations for the prosecution of felons did occasionally overstep the mark in dealing with their captives, and there is also further evidence suggesting that some forms of 'do it yourself' justice have a long history in British local communities.

'Lynch law' in Britain

A number of other *Times* reports from the first half of the nineteenth century surprisingly involve the use of the term 'lynch law' in respect of British cases. On 8 April 1842 it published a brief article headlined 'Female Lynch Law in Scotland', which described the 'summary and severe punishment' of a man named Cameron in Maryburgh, Rossshire. The 'culprit' had circulated a number of 'improper assertions' about some of 'the fair villagers', who took the law into their own hands. All the women and children of the village gathered and surrounded his house. His wife tried to conceal him in a clothes chest, but the crowd burst in and found him. He was taken out and paraded around on a board to the accompaniment of loud jeers and a pelting with 'clods and other soft missiles'. When he laid a complaint to the authorities about this, he was seized again and carried shoulder-high astride the sharp edge of a plank or 'wooden mare', on which he was painfully tossed and jerked up and down outside the house of each victim of his slanders. The crowd, having decided not to duck him in the mill pond, as had originally been planned, deposited him in considerable distress at his door. The matter was said to be under 'judicial investigation'.

In another case from 1847 (16 December 1847, p. 5), headed 'Lynch Law in Cheshire', a woman is said to have tried to get a grocer's errand boy to steal some of the shop's goods for her. The boy brought her 'some parcels of sawdust etc', and when she took these, 'three stout men', who had been stationed by the boy's master, rushed out and beat her with holly branches and stinging nettles, and then dragged her through the horsepond. Again, in 1850 (29 October 1850, p. 3), *The Times* reports that a man in Newcastle was imprisoned for starving his two children. His wife, the children's stepmother, was discharged but her neighbours 'taking the law into their own hands, chastised her most severely'. They then broke down her door and only the intervention of the police is said to have rescued her from the destruction of her property and the possible loss of her life. It is also interesting that during this period, the term 'lynch law' also starts – like 'vigilantism' today – to be used more loosely to describe self-help in general.

These reports were mainly taken by *The Times* from British local newspapers, such as the *Chester Courant* and the *Rossshire Advertiser*. They suggest that, while it was itself illegal, such 'lynch law' was applied chiefly in cases which were of a moral rather than a strictly legal nature. Some other studies support this view, and the cases appear to fit fairly clearly within the zone of popular sanctions against disreputable behaviour, which has been classically explored by E.P. Thompson and others.

Rough music

The connection between one of the cases quoted and traditional British, French and other continental European custom is in fact extremely close. The Rossshire case is fairly clearly an example of a 'riding', which is one of a number of old British forms of *charivari* and 'rough music'. The forms taken by this kind of behaviour are described in some detail by Martin Ingram (1984), and have also been discussed in a well-known paper by Thompson (1972, 1991). 'Ridings' or 'skimmingtons', in which the victim of popular attention was paraded around mounted on an animal, were found in various parts of Britain, and the alternative form of riding 'the stang' (or pole) was particularly common in the north of England and in Scotland. Victims were subjected to a wild cacophony of noise and abuse, and might be thrown into a pond or mire or ducked on the 'cucking stool'. Rough music and related customs date back several centuries. By 1700 they had been declared officially illegal and had largely declined in Britain, but they went on to enjoy something of a revival there in the eighteenth and nineteenth centuries. The traditional victims were commonly men who had been beaten by their wives or had, in local view not unconnectedly, been cuckolded, though action was also taken against others who had committed a variety of offences, including adultery and seduction. Thompson's list of offences also includes cruelty to children (compare the Newcastle case above) and disloyalty and dishonesty towards one's fellow workers. One of the *Times* cases, headed 'Novel Mode of Punishment' in fact involves the parading of a miner around Whitehaven for having defrauded one of his fellow workmen of the product of his labour. Some evidence suggests that in some cases there were established local 'courts' that secretly decided upon taking action against chosen miscreants. In the nineteenth century, there was according to Thompson a significant shift to include men who beat their wives, and one such case he quotes took place in Cambridgeshire in 1904.[2] The report of 'White Cap lynch law' that appeared in the *Cambridge Daily News* of 1888 seems likely to have had a quite familiar ring to many of its readers.[3]

In many cases, the young men of the community played an important part in the proceedings. In France, many of the 'offences' dealt with were said to be concerned with the remarriage of a widower or widow, and many others were concerned with sexual relations, including affairs of young women with married men, and the rejection of a young suitor in favour of an older man or an outsider to the community. Sex relations between married women and younger men were also punished. Because of such cases, Lévi-Strauss and others have attempted to relate *charivari* to an anxiety of young men about guaranteeing access to a local pool of younger spouses of their own generation in a well-ordered way. This is almost certainly too narrow a view, and Thompson (1991: 534–5 and *passim*) has persuasively queried the evidence for it, but it is none the less closely resonant with some relatively modern Welsh material described independently by Emrys Peters.

Although published in 1972, when Thompson's work on 'rough music' first appeared, Peters' paper on 'Aspects of the control of moral ambiguities' was originally written ten years earlier. In his discussion there of rural Wales, he mainly makes use of a study by Rees (1961) of *Life in a Welsh Countryside*, and he shows no sign of awareness of traditional forms of *charivari* and 'rough music'. He describes how the village 'boys' – unmarried men from their late teens to their mid-thirties

gather regularly by a village shop and often spend the evening playing quoits, drinking soft drinks, eating tinned fruit, chatting and casting pointed jibes at passers-by. Occasionally, however, they also take more discriminate, concerted action against individual members of the community. In one case this involved the harassment of a middle-aged widow and her young lover. Whenever the two were known to be together, the 'boys' would stuff the chimney with straw and throw dead vermin and other 'obnoxious things' through the doors and windows. In another case, they attacked a married man who was having an affair, plastered him with dung and dragged him through a river. Peters also notes that the 'boys' were very hostile to their counterparts from other villages who came courting local girls. They would trail after such an intruder, insult him, throw things at him, hide his bicycle, and possibly set upon him. In a case from a different community known to Peters, the 'boys' took a woman's baby and left it in bed with its father, who had refused to recognize it. In general, Peters argues, the material suggests that the 'boys' act in such contexts with the tacit approval of the community at large.

All this is highly reminiscent of more traditional forms of community reaction to locally unacceptable behaviour described by Thompson. None the less, it should be seen not simply as some archaic survival from the past, but rather as living custom in a living community. Thompson's argument that the eighteenth and nineteenth centuries saw an active regeneration and modification of such custom, despite suggestions from historians that it was dying everywhere, strongly makes a similar point.[4]

I want now to turn directly to the present and the very recent past. My main aim in the preceding sections of this chapter has been to draw attention to two points. Firstly, I have highlighted the fact that Britons and Americans were over a long period well aware of the respective styles of handling unacceptable behaviour in their two societies, and that a two-way traffic of ideas and customs probably accompanied this awareness. It is interesting in this regard that Thompson, in a throw-away remark which makes no reference to *Times* usage, suggests the possibility of links between 'traditional' European *charivari* and lynch law and the Ku Klux Klan.[5]

Secondly, despite the fact that 'the rule of law' was generally respected in Britain, it is clear that in 'the dark village', as Hobsbawm and Rudé put it, and in the inner recesses of cities, Britons had their own resources for dealing with behaviour which the courts for one reason or another failed to handle to their satisfaction. Brown is right that Britons rarely took the law into their own hands when dealing with criminal offences, but this is not simply a matter of cultural and psychological predisposition, however significant that might be.

There has, of course, been a great deal of argument whether British respect for the authority of the law is deeply internalized or the result of social control from outside and above. Neither view seems satisfactory in itself, and both revolutionaries and 'consensus theorists' are likely to be disappointed by actual behaviour. It is beyond the scope of my personal expertise to attempt to comment with authority upon this issue. None the less, it seems important in the present context to recognize that deference and respect for the law are not necessarily as deeply ingrained as more consensus-oriented thinkers would like to assume, and that for Britons also the state has to earn its keep if it wishes to do more than simply use force, or its threat, to restrain its members from taking independent action. This is, of course, particularly true as British society has become more divided culturally and economically over recent decades.

None the less, it is clear that the British patterns of extra-legal social control that I have so far discussed differed from classical American vigilantism in several ways. Clearly, they tended to deal with a variety of moral misdemeanours rather than with serious criminal offences.[6] Also, if they did deal with the latter – as in the case of the various associations for the apprehension of felons and horse thieves – they were usually satisfied with handing over those arrested into the control of the formal legal system. Thirdly, with the main exception of such associations, it appears to be the case that many activities of this broad kind in Britain have historically and typically had a 'plebeian' quality, to use Thompson's term, rather than a local 'elite' one, as Brown asserts for most American examples of vigilantism. It is arguable that this kind of 'elitist' pattern is more visible in the current British middle-class penchant for Neighbourhood Watch, and also private policing, as against more violent and extensive vigilante action. At the same time, however, it is probably sensible not to overdraw this contrast. Palmer (1978: 49–57) has shown that both 'white-capping' and *charivari* in North America have also had a strongly plebeian flavour, and Ingram (1984: 104–9) notes that support for 'ridings' and similar activities was by no means uncommon among the English gentry during the seventeenth century and occasionally into the eighteenth century.

Vigilantism in modern Britain

I have already noted how 'vigilante' and 'vigilantism' have become commonplace in British English, and how this has been accompanied by increasingly loose usage of the terms. Things have clearly moved on since the early 1950s, at least as described in W.D. Campbell's Country Diary (*Guardian*, 13 October 1993). He comments on his own reactions to recent references to the formation of groups of vigilantes in built-up areas where vandalism and crime were problems. The word, he writes,

instantly transported me back 40 years or so when, at a parish council
... a not very literate councillor proposed that we should organise some
of 'these 'ere village-antis' – not quite a typical spoonerism, which is
accidental, but a genuine attempt to make sense of a new word.

Others had in fact adopted the word rather earlier. During the First
World War, the British politician Noel Pemberton Billing organized a
British 'Vigilantes' society, whose headquarters, in St James's Place,
London, were interestingly named the 'Grand Lodge'.[7] He published a
newspaper, the *Vigilante* (initially the *Imperialist*), 'in the interest of
purity in public life'. Billing's most celebrated activity in this area was
his attack in 1918 on 'private' productions of Oscar Wilde's *Salome*.
With the collaboration of Harold Spencer, who was later certified
insane, he linked these 'perverse' productions with an alleged German
'black book' containing thousands of names of people in high places
who were said to be willing to betray Britain and the Empire in favour
of the German cause. Foreigners, traitors, homosexuals and sadists
appear to have constituted more or less a single category for him.[8]

The *Oxford English Dictionary* (new edition) lists early uses of the
term in the work of Frankeau and Joyce (*Finnegans Wake*). It also notes
an article in the *Daily Telegraph* for 22 May 1948 which reports that the
Advertising Association had asked twenty-four advertising clubs to
form a 'vigilantes' committee to monitor and report advertising of a
'doubtful nature'.

Today, metaphors like 'the vigilantes of the race relations lobby' or
'the impatient monetary vigilantes' of the bond market have become
common alongside the use of the term for anyone engaging in almost
any form of violent self-help in the face of crime. Such usage is revealing both of the degree to which the word and its cognates are now
established elements in British vocabulary and, more importantly, of
the heightened awareness of crime and dissatisfaction with the state
machinery of policing and the courts.

As far as I am aware, there has been no carefully researched published study of contemporary vigilantism in Britain. In the absence of
such work, I have largely had to rely for information on numerous
media reports, particularly in the newspapers but also on the radio
and television. This clearly has regrettable consequences. It is difficult
to vouch for the accuracy and representative nature of some such
reports, and the material is likely to be coloured by the fact that the
topic is 'in the air' and has become part of a highly politicized debate
about law and order. At the same time, this itself is of some interest.

The background to this debate is a rise in recent years both in the incidence of crime and in anxiety about it. These are, however, difficult to document exactly. Crime rates themselves are notoriously problematic. Much depends upon how keen the public are to report offences to the police, and on how keen the police are to record such reports and to discover offences for themselves. More than 90 per cent of recorded crimes in Britain are property related, with burglary and vehicle crime constituting the largest categories. Yet it seems that many such offences are not formally reported to the police, and Home Office survey data suggest that real crime rates are perhaps four times as high as those recorded. Such recording is said to be mainly 'insurance driven', and the statistics are thus likely to reflect the patterns of insurance in the country. It has been claimed that 70 per cent of thefts, including unrecorded ones, involve money or goods worth less than £50, and claims on these may not be possible or sensible. Victims may have excesses on their policies, or may be afraid that premiums will rise if they claim. Some have no insurance at all, sometimes because it is impossible to get in the areas they live in, or is too expensive. Relatively low rates of successful 'clear-up' by the police, and increasingly complicated formalities, may also deter people from reporting a minor offence.[9]

Factors such as these throw into doubt some recent claims that rates of crime have fallen slightly during the last three years. Even if this is true, however, it seems clear that this has happened only after a long period of steady increase. Levels of recorded crime have doubled since 1980, and official survey figures suggest that the actual increase is somewhat higher than this.[10]

Coupled with this, anxiety about crime has also risen during the last decade, although anxiety is, of course, not necessarily a true reflection of the real risk. Home Office figures for 1994, for instance, show considerably more anxiety about terrorist activities than about household accidents, which are far more numerous. Anxiety is, of course, significant in itself, however, and it is by no means wholly irrational. Fears of property-related crime are greatest in poor council housing estates and in comparable areas, where the risks are almost three times higher than the average.

Other survey evidence provides further background information about attitudes to crime. The Gallup Poll commissioned by the *Daily Telegraph* and reported there on 30 August 1993 showed worrying levels of popular disaffection and anxiety about crime and the ability of the official system to cope with it. At the same time, the number of respondents whose house had been broken into at least once had more than doubled since 1980. Although a majority felt that the police tried hard in most cases of property-related crime and muggings, only small minorities considered it likely that police action would be successful in such cases, with the exception of recovering stolen vehicles. A substantial majority sympathized with police complaints that too much paper-work interfered with their attempts to deal with crime. Twenty-four per cent of respondents (as against 7 per cent in 1987) believed that miscarriages of justice, in which people were sent to prison for crimes they had not committed, were now frequent, and a much larger proportion believed that the guilty walk free or are too leniently treated. Only 1 per cent of respondents expressed strong confidence in government policies to combat crime, as against 35 per cent who were not at all confident and a further 47 per cent who were not very confident.

The front-page headline to the report on the poll was 'Public loses confidence in rule of law', and the page-two headline announced '75pc support those taking law into their own hands'. It appears to have been important that the poll took place shortly after the so-called Norfolk vigilantes were imprisoned, and the young killer of a music-teacher, who had tried to stop him slashing tyres, was acquitted. Fifty-nine per cent thought the Norfolk jailing was wrong, while only 27 per cent supported the decision. In the tyre-slashing case, 82 per cent said that the jury had been wrong to acquit the killer.

Apart from the possible influence of such cases on the views expressed, one also needs to bear some other points in mind here. 'Taking the law into one's own hands' covers a variety of reactions to offences, and this seems likely to be reflected in differences between some of the figures which the poll elicited.

There has clearly been a great deal of sympathy in recent years for those who tackle and even shoot intruders on their property, even if things have not moved as far in this context as in some areas of America, where a movement called 'Dead Serious' reportedly offers $5,000 rewards to members who shoot burglars or other criminals.[11] Several cases have been brought to public attention by television and other media (cf. *Daily Telegraph*, 4 October and 9 November 1995). Fairly typical was that of a 61-year-old vineyard-owner who was acquitted in November 1995 after shooting and wounding two burglars who were raiding his property at night, while another involved the prosecution and fining of a pensioner who shot through his allotment shed door at 'intruders'. The Home Secretary appears to have caught the mood of much popular sentiment in such cases, when he told the Police Superintendents' Association on 3 October 1995 that the police should use more common sense and not be so eager to arrest and charge those who attacked intruders in defence of their home and family. In its report on the speech next day, the *Independent* used the headline 'Howard demands sympathy for "have-a-go heroes"', and this epithet is highlighted in reports of the speech in both the *Guardian* and the *Daily Telegraph*.

It is probably significant in this regard that, while 76 per cent of the Gallup Poll's respondents supported the idea of 'taking the law into one's own hands' in some circumstances, only 59 per cent condemned the gaoling of the Norfolk villagers, who were not responding to a direct and immediate attack on themselves and their property. Between these two figures, some two-thirds of respondents supported the idea of people in villages, small towns or housing estates organizing their own 'patrols' if the police failed to protect them. The definitional limits for respondents of this concept of 'patrols' are not, however, clear. Sometimes, 'private policing', as opposed to straightforward vigilante action by citizens themselves, is referred to by such usage in the press, and even citizens' patrols may restrict their activities to surveillance rather than arrest or punishment.

Although many references are made to vigilantes in the newspapers and on radio and television, the term, as I have said, is very loosely used. Often it refers to single individuals acting in self-defence, or to one or two people spontaneously seeking revenge for some wrong they have suffered. Even when a group of people is involved in attempting simply to deal with criminal elements in their locality, the action concerned appears commonly to be a spontaneous and 'once-off' gesture of angry frustration. Sometimes such a group is small, but on occasion large 'mobs' have assembled in response to a local outrage.

Several cases have been highlighted by newspaper and television coverage. A *This Week* programme, produced by Thames Television in 1992, reviewed a variety of incidents ranging from vengeance attacks to mob action.[12] In one case, a large crowd in South Wales gathered outside the home of a family whose teenage daughter had allegedly been involved in the murder of an aged spinster. The crowd are shown shouting wildly and hurling stones at windows. The family concerned were, it seems, driven from the area by this show of violent hostility. In another case, a man tells how he attacked a man who had assaulted his daughter. He beat him with a hammer, broke his leg and also (apparently unintentionally) fractured his skull. In a further case, the father of a ten-year-old boy who had been killed by a lorry went out and shot the lorry driver. The driver had been gaoled for eighteen months, is said to have had a long list of driving offences, and appears on screen to have behaved somewhat arrogantly in the face of jeering crowds. The father of the boy was subsequently acquitted. The Director of Public Prosecutions, Barbara Mills, is shown generally condemning such self-help, which she describes as dangerous and 'medieval'. A further case of local residents setting a trap for young and noisy motorcyclists is also shown. A wire was drawn at neck height across a path frequently used by the intended victims, but in fact a young pedal-cyclist was almost killed by it.

Professor M. McColville, in an interview in the above documentary, rightly draws attention to an important feature of such cases. He defines what he calls 'vigilanteism' as 'enforcing the law by informal and unofficial means' and he notes that such people see themselves as seeking justice and not simply revenge. They are people who feel let down or ill served by the law, rather than being simply lawless. Yet their attitudes and behaviour mainly constitute at most a sort of 'proto-vigilantism', at least when compared with the groups I have documented in North America, Peru and Tanzania.

As this implies, organized vigilantism in which an established group regularly pursues and punishes offenders still seems to be rare in Britain. Defence groups have been established by some minorities – gay men, orthodox Jews and Asians, for example – to combat often seriously violent harassment by skin-heads and others. Guardian Angels also operate in London and elsewhere, though they are not typically local residents protecting their own communities.[13] Some small residents' groups, operating against thieves, drug-peddlers and other undesirables, have also been reported in Bolton, Nottingham and other towns and cities.

A recent newspaper article by Andrew Malone and Ciaran Byrne (*Sunday Times*, 26 February 1995) is entitled 'Vigilante gangs take over the mean streets'. It reports that

> People throughout Britain are increasingly taking the law into their own hands and delivering summary justice to violent criminals by forming vigilante gangs ... Scores of cases have emerged, including massed assaults on thugs, kidnappings and one incident where a thief was tied to a lamppost and beaten.

The article goes on to discuss several such attacks, but evidence of organized groupings is less clear. It mentions that vigilantes have 'restored order to a red-light district' of Birmingham, and tells how a vigilante group has also organized in Nottingham. There 'the residents have set up their own hotline for "emergencies"'. If there is trouble, a group of residents is called to patrol the neighbourhood armed with whatever weapons are available, including pick-axe handles for protection. Evidence suggesting the existence of another group on a Mansfield housing estate is also presented. Residents were said to have been criticized by police after a number of incidents, mainly involving young offenders. A councillor who lives on the estate appears to have supported the action, as did the Secretary of the Tenants' Association who is said to have described it as a fightback by previously helpless victims of crime.

In a 'crime-ridden Derbyshire estate', one 39-year-old man is said to have 'placed an advertisement ... in a local newspaper looking for like-minded people' to patrol the area. He is said to have 'snapped after three years of trouble'. He is quoted as saying, 'My men are ready to go on my orders. If there is one more incident on this street, it will explode. If these thugs draw weapons, my men will do likewise. We are just protecting our property. We have had enough.' His men 'carry baseball bats and walkie-talkies' and he appears to have support from his neighbours.

The Birmingham 'red-light district' mentioned in the article was Balsall Heath, and the case received a great deal of press attention, being also reported in the *Guardian* (Maggie O'Kane, 6 May 1994, 23 July 1994), *The Economist* (12 November 1994) and the *Daily Mail* (John Torode, 20 March 1996). This may partly have been due to the fact that the vigilantes in question were Asian Muslims. Similar action was reported among Bradford Muslims in the course of 1995. There was a comparable campaign in another area of Birmingham in the mid-1980s, when the North Mosely Residents Association Direct Action Committee was formed and set up regular street patrols. Its members are described as 'middle class, consisting of barristers, housewives and local business people, both white and Asian' (Johnston, 1992: 165).

The vigilante action of Asian men in Balsall Heath appears to have persisted for two years. Their leader is a former policeman who is said to have long-term political ambitions. The area is described by John Torode in the *Daily Mail* as a 'dreary inner-city suburb comprising Victorian terraces and bleak local authority blocks'. Prostitution was well established there, with women operating both from houses and on the streets, and kerb crawling was commonplace. There was also drug abuse. Earlier attempts by 'middle-class women' to deal with the problem are said (Maggie O'Kane, *Guardian*, 23 July 1994) to have failed. According to Torode, all the vigilante men have jobs, but put in the necessary hours. The leader says that he is used to shift work and getting sleep when he needs it. Others are said to be minicab drivers, able to work at hours to suit themselves. Alleged threats by prostitutes to call in the National Front appear to have faded. Prostitutes' reactions in 1994 and 1995 were often very angry, and included charges of hypocrisy against the group, now known as 'Streetwatchers'. A letter to the *Guardian* (12 May 1995) from Niki Adams, of the English Collective of Prostitutes, complains about another O'Kane article (6 May 1995), and claims that 'the property values of some residents' have received priority 'over the civil rights of others'. She also complains about vigilante violence against the women concerned.

Given the apparent persistence of activity over a two-year period, it is not clear how successful the campaign has been. Many prostitutes are, however, said to have been forced to move to other areas. Kerb crawling has been a main focus of the campaign, and it is said to have decreased with subsequent loss of income to the prostitutes. Large placards told motorists that their car numbers were recorded for police records and that 'The Wife Will Find Out'.

The Streetwatchers now have police collaboration and support, as opposed to the neglect which they claim to have suffered earlier, and Balsall Heath has been allocated a £6 million grant from the European Urban Fund. A police officer is described as working on a doctoral study of the movement. Police are also reported (*Sunday Times*, 26 February 1995) to have asked the men to turn their attention to drug dealers and violent criminals, and to have offered training in an attempt to combat drug-related robberies.

It is not very clear how widespread such cases are. Some commentators point to the possibility of a serious increase in behaviour of this sort, and both government and opposition take this and related law and order problems very seriously. Yet, one also wonders to what extent such 'doomsday scenarios' are not so much substantive prophecies as political rhetoric on the part of citizens and of the police themselves, in the battle for more resources to provide more effective policing, and for law and order policies in which more attention is paid to the plight of victims. These include not only those who have been attacked or burgled, but also those who feel surrounded and harassed by threatening behaviour, often on the part of young people who, it is commonly felt, are likely to 'get away' with only a caution, if they are apprehended at all.

One further area of vigilante action, where the frontier approximates more to that of a 'no go' area than to a neglected zone, also deserves mention here. So-called punishment squads, organized by both Loyalist and Republican paramilitary groups, have been a feature of street justice in Ulster over many years.

Johnston (1992: 163–4) quotes a *Listener* article (3 March 1988) by A. Thomson on these groups, and there have been more recent reports in the *Guardian* (22 February 1995) and *Sunday Times* (26 March 1995) as well as some television coverage. The 'squads' engage in beatings and 'knee-capping' shootings, and are said to operate against burglars, muggers, drug dealers and others.

Thomson's article deals with 'both sides of the sectarian gulf' and points to the existence of well-established procedures in which verbal warnings precede actual beatings, and attacks on the parents of young offenders. The groups are said to have enjoyed a great deal of local community support, but there has also clearly been considerable opposition to them.

The *Guardian* article, by David Sharrock, arose out of a protest by the US ambassador to Ireland after she had met a number of punishment victims. The article reports that seventy-five people had been beaten by Republican and Loyalist 'punishment squads' since the IRA ceasefire the previous September. The ambassador was presented with a letter of protest for President Clinton by a pressure group, Families against Intimidation and Terror (FAIT). The letter detailed a variety of abuses, including banishments, physical violence and assault, and abductions. The association claimed that since the ceasefire, thirty families had been forced to sell their homes and flee.

In the *Sunday Times* report, Liam Clarke writes that Sinn Fein and the IRA have tried 'to distance themselves from punishment beatings by setting up vigilante groups made up of former IRA members to carry out attacks'. This is said, according to 'Security sources', to be an attempt 'to stem public outrage which follows each attack'. The report describes how two youths were beaten with iron bars by five masked men in Belfast for 'anti-social behaviour'. This is said to be 'a typical punishment beating', but more severe attacks are also becoming common. Before the ceasefire 'victims had to attend kangaroo meetings in Sinn Fein offices, where they were forced to confess to petty crimes before being shot in the legs by the IRA'. More recently, responsibility for a majority of the attacks has been placed on 'ex-members'. This is denied by FAIT, who claim that there is evidence of direct IRA involvement.

Such squads have a truly vigilante quality inasmuch as they involve attacks on offenders within rather than between sectarian communities, but it is also worth noting here that inter-sectarian violence has also been seen locally as having the same character. This has a long history. Andrew Boyd's depressing chronicle of centuries of Ulster violence, *Holy War in Belfast*, reports how 'violence against people

who were unfortunate to live in the "wrong districts" increased' during the 1873 riots in the city. Some such people were given formal
notice to quit, and he quotes an example presented to Protestants in
North Street (1969: 98): 'It has been ordered by the committee that you
leave this dwelling before 7.30 this evening. Fail at your peril. Signed
by order of the Committee.'

Boyd also quotes a Protestant advertisement, in the *Belfast News
Letter* for 11 May 1886, inviting tenders for the supply of 20,000 Snider
rifles complete with swords or bayonets. The address for responses is
given as 'Vigilance Committee, 8335, Office of this paper'. Such
notices are interestingly reminiscent of notices of banishment and various advertisements published by American vigilante groups in San
Francisco and elsewhere in the American West.

Neighbourhood Watch

The material I have presented in this chapter so far will, I hope, make
clear that vigilante action is neither quite as alien historically to Britain
nor as rampant there contemporarily as is sometimes assumed.
Helping the police and courts has been a more typical response to
crime in Britain than attempting to do without them by turning to
vigilante action. Group responses of the kind that Johnston calls
'responsible citizenship' – as opposed to the 'autonomy' of vigilantism
– have recently become very widespread, mainly in the form of local
Neighbourhood Watch groups.[14]

Despite some initial concern, Neighbourhood Watch has been
generally supported by both government and police since its importa-
tion from the United States in 1982. Since then the number of groups
has increased dramatically, and it is said to have reached 130,000 by
1994, covering more than 5 million homes.[15] Their establishment
reflects both police encouragement and awareness of the recent rise in
crime. Initial advice from the police and subsequent liaison with them
are an integral part of the system. A recent survey in the
Herefordshire area found that 83 per cent of sixty-nine schemes studied there were started after joint meetings between residents and
police, and that in over a third of these cases the original suggestion to
establish a group had come from the police.[16] In Cambridgeshire, the
first groups were set up in 1985 with encouragement from both the
police and the local press.[17] It is common for the police to maintain
contact through newsletters and through the allocation of one or more

officers to the task of advising and monitoring the groups. Although a main reason for establishing the scheme was to help the police with the burden of crime control, the continued need for such liaison, as increasing numbers of new groups are founded, has itself caused some concern among the police that the groups are an extra demand on their time and energy.

The groups typically operate under the leadership of one or more 'co-ordinators', some of whom cover a wide area and several local street or other neighbourhood schemes. The existence of a local scheme is usually publicized by signs on lamp-posts, marking the group's boundaries, and by window-stickers. The members are encouraged to make their homes secure and to mark their property. They are also encouraged to restrict their 'watch' activities to surveillance, and to report any problems to the police via their co-ordinator. There is a keen awareness of the risks of taking independent action against suspected criminals, and press reports of statements of both police and group members often stress the difference between watch activities and vigilantism. Thus Peter Loyd, the co-ordinator of a large number of groups in the Hampstead area, was described as 'opposed to any suggestions of vigilantism' and is quoted as saying that 'Neighbourhood watch is about being alert and dialling 999. We would discourage any attempt by people to take the law into their own hands. Arresting criminals is a matter for the police' (Terry Kirby, *Independent,* 31 August 1993).

The fact that Mr Loyd was operating in the Hampstead area is probably not without significance. A British Crime Survey in the early 1980s suggested that the average Neighbourhood Watch member was male, in a non-manual job, with average or above-average earnings, living with his wife and children, and the owner-occupier of his own modern house.[18] This seems to fit American experience, with the main exception of a high level of black participation in such groups there. Some local variation is, however, found. Bennett, for example, studied two schemes in London in 1985 and 1986, and found a majority of women members, and a larger proportion of local women than of local men, in both. There was also a majority of manual workers, and a larger proportion of such workers living in the area, in one of the schemes. Judging from the overall distribution of respondents in the sample, members of both groups were predominantly white, but there was also a higher level of participation among whites in the sample in one scheme and a higher level of non-white participation in the other. The proportion of participating owner-occupiers was higher than that of renting tenants in both schemes.[19] The more recent Herefordshire survey suggests that a wider range of households may be included within rural, as compared with urban, area schemes. There the respondents to the survey were co-ordinators rather than ordinary members, and – like Mr Loyd above – they tended to be male (81 per cent), over sixty (64 per cent), and retired (69 per cent). They also tended strongly to be middle-class (81 per cent of those in employment were in Socioeconomic Groups I and II) (Yarwood and Edwards, 1995: 455). The relatively high age of co-ordinators seems clearly to relate to the amount of time that ordinary working people are likely to be able and willing to devote to such a task.

Offences against property, and especially burglary, were the chief concern of respondents in both surveys. In Herefordshire, burglary, vandalism, graffiti and litter, and vehicle theft were listed in that order, ahead of noise and assault against the person. In London, burglary, robbery and vandalism were the three chief sources of anxiety.

The sheer number of groups formed suggests that Neighbourhood Watch has been a popular and successful experiment in citizen response to rising crime rates. Notwithstanding its American roots, it seems to be an 'ideal' British compromise, combining elements of self-help with a good dose of deference to authority, while promoting some semblance of community concern and action as a morally desirable and potentially cheap solution to local problems of law and order. It draws upon the rhetoric of 'community' – as something valuable that society has largely lost but might regain – and fits well with modern tendencies of central government to govern indirectly via strict fiscal control, while decentralizing as much responsibility for services and welfare as it can to local institutions and to citizens themselves.[20]

A reliable evaluation of the success of the scheme is difficult, partly owing to a shortage of data, and partly because so much hope has been invested in it by government, the police and members of the groups themselves. Johnston nicely highlights how in 1988 the then Home Secretary, John Patten, seized upon apparently falling crime figures to proclaim the groups' effectiveness over a wide area, while asserting two years later that the subsequent rise in property-related crime was explicable in terms of its coverage of 'only 4 million households' (1992: 153). Independent studies suggest that ordinary group members especially are less active than was hoped initially, and that a palpable effect on crime is not readily detectable. Some commentators also note that, despite good intentions, the schemes are most likely to help those least in need – though need itself is hard to define. They point to the popularity of schemes among 'those people with the time and assets to help themselves' (Yarwood and Edwards 1995: 457) and to the prevalence of schemes in areas where crime rates are in fact relatively low. It has also been suggested that, even if Neighbourhood Watch is locally successful in deterring crime, it is likely to displace it into other, already more crime-ridden areas in which such schemes are less popular. Yarwood and Edwards also note the risk that Neighbourhood Watch, like other forms of voluntary activity, can lead to the further erosion of services by the state. At the same time, they agree that the schemes do appear to provide a *sense* of greater security to members in the Herefordshire area. Although they comment that such security may well be 'illusory', it is arguable that learning to live with crime through such feelings may be the only realistic short-term approach to the problems that it poses.

6
Death Squads

I have argued that vigilantism presupposes both the presence of the state and deep dissatisfaction with its handling of law and order. In what is typically seen as a three-sided structure, criminals and other undesirables disturb and harass ordinary citizens, who expect the state to deal with them, but such help is not always forthcoming. Criminals appear too often to escape arrest, or they may be felt to receive an unsatisfactory level of punishment. In the 'ideal' type of vigilantism, ordinary law-abiding citizens then turn to their own resources to cope with these problems. They bypass the state and react directly against offenders. Vigilante activity thus tends to constitute a criticism of both the police and the judicial system for failure to play their expected role.

I have already noted several contexts in which reality falls short in one way or another of this ideal type, as alleged battles against crime and immorality are turned to sectional political advantage. In this chapter I want mainly to discuss some further 'imperfect' forms, which can be loosely subsumed under the heading of 'death squad' vigilantism. For several reasons, this constitutes both ethnographically and analytically one of the least penetrable areas of vigilantism and related forms of 'social control'. Hard data on the subject are not easily obtained by researchers, or even by conscientious elements in the police and the judiciary, owing to official discouragement and deception, and also fear of retaliation among victims' families and other possible informants. The killing of potential witnesses, sometimes metaphorically referred to as 'burning the records', is a serious possibility when cases may take many years to process, and suspects are released for long periods pending trial. In some cases, threats against those charged with the investigation of death squad activities have also led to requests for transfer and the slowing down or abandonment of an inquiry. In addition, official propaganda has often played down or denied the existence of such groups, whose activities are commonly concealed beneath the apparently less sinister programs of 'democratization' and 'national security' proclaimed by their umbrella organizations. At the same time, those who write about the subject in particular countries or regions are likely to have their own political agendas, which sometimes clearly colour their accounts. This is scarcely surprising, however, when one is dealing with various forms of state and establishment violence, which have been responsible for many thousands of violent deaths, often accompanied by mutilation and torture, in a wide range of Latin American and other countries.

In its strictest sense, the term 'death squad' refers to groups composed of police or other agents of the state who are assigned, with varying degrees of secrecy, to carry out the extra-judicial extermination of a variety of people, who have been defined as 'public enemies' and 'undesirables'. Conceptually and in reality, however, such narrowly defined cases tend to merge with a wide range of others in which the military and police authorities are less directly involved. Sometimes current or former police personnel are employed by private individuals and groups as hired killers, and sometimes they may act on their own initiative. Sometimes too, 'ordinary citizens' may be recruited into state-sponsored activities, often following propaganda or harassment. Usually, however, the majority of citizens remain on the sidelines as critics or supporters, or as victims, of the violence.

It is in their nature that the activities and even the existence of 'death squads' are often denied. Some of their victims simply 'disappear', while others are typically said to have been killed by fellow 'criminals' or grass-roots vigilantes, or to have died in spurious 'shoot-outs' with the police. Others are claimed to have killed themselves or died in traffic accidents.

As with other topics I have treated, I do not attempt a systematic coverage of the available material, which would demand at least a volume in itself. However, the cases I discuss will, I hope, reveal some of the special features of this kind of phenomenon, and the wide range of forms it can take. Death squads, and related forms of police or paramilitary control of crime and dissidence, are most commonly associated with Central and South America, where a series of repressive military and authoritarian civil regimes have provided an especially fertile breeding ground for the phenomenon. However, the incidence of death squads is by no means restricted to this area, as cases from the Philippines and parts of Europe show. Moreover, as the material on northern Peruvian *rondas campesinas* illustrates, other forms of Latin American vigilante activity have been documented, though not in abundance.

Death squad targets vary widely. In some cases, criminals of a conventional kind, such as drug-traffickers, are dealt with. Labels of criminality may, however, sometimes be attached to targets as a legitimization of their killing. Often, death squad victims are politically 'undesirable' – for example, 'communists' and their 'supporters', and other 'troublemakers'. As the quotation marks imply, such concepts may be applied very loosely. Also, as one might expect, official involvement and support, whether open or covert, have often been a powerful influence in such cases. Children, and especially young male teenagers on the streets of major cities, are frequent death squad victims.

The wide range of death squad forms and members and their victims highlights the problem of drawing rigid boundaries in this area. As Huggins (1991: 9) has remarked, material of this sort falls somewhere on a continuum from spontaneous informal acts of violence by individuals or groups to organized extra-legal activity by police and military forces. How overt this last may be has naturally been influenced by the extent to which the state has wished to stem it or at least keep it 'clandestine', and this has varied from time to time and from one regime to another. None the less it is extremely clear, in this as in other contexts, that there is a great deal of room for deception and disinformation in societies with military or other forms of repressive regime, where there are vast differences in wealth and access to political resources, and where insurgents or internal dissidents and other 'undesirables' are or can be portrayed as a serious threat to political and economic stability.

As one would expect, it is in the middle area of such continua that most ambiguity and uncertainty reside. Clandestine state support may be denied or asserted by those in whose political interest such statements lie. Nor is the state itself always an undifferentiated monolithic structure. In some cases, democratically elected leaders and sections of the police and the judiciary may genuinely oppose such violence, but may be unable to act effectively when opposed by a powerful military and other influential interest groups. Current legislation may also be unhelpful and quite difficult to change.

In the present context, it is important to note two general points. Death squad activity – if it is to be described at all as vigilantism, as I have tried to characterize that term – should exhibit two main features. It should reflect popular dissatisfaction with the state's attempts to provide law and order, and it should be a substitute for such attempts. To the extent, however, that such activity is simply a reflection of the state's or its official instruments' dissatisfaction with the legal weapons at their disposal for the exercise and development of political power, it is perhaps better characterized as state, police or military 'extra-legal', or more simply criminal, activity, which may masquerade as vigilantism in the more usual senses of that word.

Although such lines of demarcation may be hard to draw in practice, it is clear that direct state support for or involvement in such action gives it a distinctly political flavour. Here the distinction between the maintenance of 'order' and the preservation or promotion of a particular 'order' or regime and its support base becomes quite obscure and is, in fact, often enough deliberately made so by the propaganda smoke-screens of the state and its agents on the one hand, and their more revolutionary opponents on the other. In such cases, the state's campaigns to combat crime often form part of a proclaimed political crusade against 'evil' generally. Political dissenters and common criminals, and by association the poor and unemployed, are compounded into an undifferentiated demonic threat which must be dealt with by whatever means, however brutal and illegal, are to hand.

It would be naive to believe that any of those in power in such regimes are unaware of the nature of these processes, though it is likely that at least some started as idealists. Their awareness, like that of many of their enemies, derives from experience and knowledge of a long history of revolution and repression in their own and other countries, and they have also commonly participated in the self-conscious development of their own machinery of terror, often with sophisticated help from other countries. It is less clear, however, especially when 'grass-roots' elements are recruited into such activities, that their perpetrators are all equally aware of the hand and strategy that guide them.

This is an important issue in the present context. Those in power in such states often have readily understandable motives for attempting to legitimize their extra-legal activities, either through the concealment of official action under a death squad or other vigilante cloak, or through the encouragement of 'grass-roots' vigilantism itself.

Grupos Anti-terroristas de Liberación[1]

An example of a relatively small-scale political death squad operation is that of the Spanish 'GAL' attacks against Basque separatists. Despite various disclaimers, evidence in a recent trial alleged the direct involvement of highly placed Spanish government officials in the affair. The prosecution claimed that a group of police and other government officers carried out a series of assassinations and attacks, under the name of Grupos Anti-terroristas de Liberación (GAL, or Anti-terrorist Liberation Group), with covert government support in the early 1980s. Between 1983 and 1986 the group is said to have undertaken a series of killings and kidnappings in which twenty-seven people were killed, and another thirty wounded. Most of those killed were members of the Basque separatist movement ETA, but the court was also told that several people were killed or kidnapped by mistake. Two former Guardia Civil police chiefs received long prison sentences in 1991 following their confessions of responsibility for some of these attacks on separatists, and the Office of State Security is said to have paid the two defendants and their wives large sums of money to keep silent. In 1994, however, the two men decided to publicize their story, which implicated and led to the trial of fourteen police and government officials, including the Interior Minister. The Prime Minister, Felipe Gonzalez, denied knowledge of the plot and was eventually cleared of complicity, but the case forced him to bring parliamentary elections forward and contributed to his defeat in them. At the time of writing, the case has not been finally resolved.

The death squad in question is alleged to have arisen from a meeting of high government officials in 1983, in which the problems of dealing with the Basque separatist movement ETA were discussed. One former official testified that 'the Israeli' solution to this kind of problem, involving the kidnapping and killing of terrorists, was discussed. Many of the terrorists were in hiding over the French border, but the official claimed that, while the group discussed 'doing something in France', nothing illegal was planned.

One of the two prisoners, however, claimed that he was given a suitcase full of money to be delivered to a contact in France, and this money is reported to have come from a secret government fund set up to finance the new anti-terrorist unit and to hire assassins in France and Portugal. GAL claimed to be a terrorist organization in its own right, issuing communiqués and taking credit for killings and bombings. Operations are said to have ceased in 1986, when the question of

GAL's government support became controversial, and the group is said to have been finally disbanded in 1987 when France agreed to provide official collaboration against the separatists.

Guatemala and El Salvador

In an article about such groups in Central America, Cáceres (1989) usefully refers to 'a publication of the US-administered School of the Americas', a military training institution in the Panama Canal Zone. There a distinction is made between two kinds of armed force – 'regular' and 'special'. In addition to their standard active units (army, navy, police, etc.), regular forces typically contain intelligence services, whose prime acknowledged duty is to gather information useful for security. They also commonly maintain useful links with foreign governments and also with influential private citizens. Special units may be either 'irregular' (armed groups or individuals that do not formally belong to the various regular forces) or 'paramilitary', which are different from regular armed forces, but typically liaise with them and possess similar organization, training and equipment.

According to Cáceres, all these kinds of unit have been connected at one time or another with death squad activity in the region. Security forces have allegedly been active in a variety of Guatemalan death squads, known by such names as Mano Blanca (White Hand), Ejército Secreto Anticomunista (Secret Anti-Communist Army) and Ojo por Ojo (Eye for an Eye). Such groups, which operated in the late 1960s and 1970s, are said to have been financed by wealthier members of society, and to have enjoyed 'total impunity'. Though allegedly beyond official control, they had close connections with the army and the police (many of their members were off-duty or former security personnel), and government ministers are said to have helped to draw up their 'death lists'. Their many thousands of victims consisted mainly of workers and peasants, and their sympathizers of students, teachers and the professions, all of whom tended to be branded as 'guerrillas'.[2]

In El Salvador, the 'Treasury Police' and, later, military intelligence units were apparently main bases of this kind of action. As an example of a paramilitary organization, Cáceres (1989) cites the Salvadorean ORDEN (Organización Democrática Nacional), which was organized in the 1960s by the head of the National Guard. The proclaimed purpose of ORDEN was to 'disseminate democratic ideas within the peasantry', but its members were largely engaged in hunting out 'communists' in the rural areas and in death squad activities.

Irregular forces in the region have included a variety of partially clandestine organizations of extreme right-wing civilians devoted to the defeat of opponents of the prevailing social and economic order. The members of such groups have seen themselves as participants in a global anti-communist crusade justified by the activities of Marxist subversives in the region. Secret death squads are said to have been formed by such groups to look after 'the political side' of their struggle, and some of the groups have maintained a wide range of national and international connections with state military and security units.

Alsa Masa in the Philippines[3]

More widespread military and paramilitary activities, operating under a populist vigilante cloak, have been described for South America and for the Philippines. Despite official secrecy and propaganda, the Philippine case of the Alsa Masa (Masses Arise) movement is relatively well documented, partly owing to an easing of restrictions on investigations and reporting in the post-Marcos era. The material illustrates well the complex and at times impenetrable mixtures of state and citizen involvement which often characterize such cases.

Alsa Masa arose in and around Davao City in South Mindinao in the aftermath of the Marcos government. Marcos's regime had been a fertile breeding ground for communist and socialist resistance groups and parties, including the New People's Army (NPA), which were co-ordinated under the umbrella of the National Democratic Front. South Mindanao was a key area of violent action by the NPA and its 'liquidation squads', known as 'Sparrows', as well as by pro-government detachments of the paramilitary Civil Home Defence Force (CHDF), whose summary executions were locally described euphemistically as 'salvaging' operations. Davao City and its environs became known as 'Murder City' and the 'Mindanao killing fields'.

In her election campaign, Corazon Aquino had promised to disband the Civil Home Defence Force after her accession to the Presidency, and the subsequent constitution of February 1987 explicitly ordered its dissolution. None the less, it managed to survive. At the same time, partly with her support, new groups of 'spontaneous vigilantes' arose with the avowed aim of countering left-wing insurgency. Alsa Masa, which is said to have been founded in April 1986, was the best known of these. Others include various fanatically religious groups of so-called Tadtads (from the verb 'to chop'), whose main weapon against the insurgent 'enemies of God' has been the machete.

One of Marcos's key supporters in Davao City was Wilfredo 'Baby' Aquino (unrelated to the President), who was particularly powerful in the squatter district of Agdao. In April 1986, after Aquino's election victory, he and several of his bodyguards are said to have started Alsa Masa, allegedly with military intelligence encouragement, though this has been denied. They obtained arms and began their activities by killing an alleged NPA member, but they were disarmed shortly after by the local chief of staff.

This man was replaced in July 1986 by Major Calida, who called a number of the organizers to his office and told them they could count on his support in the struggle against the NPA. The group began to organize patrols and it was soon accused by local Agdao residents of harassment in the course of its campaign to recruit new members. Accusations that the group was being armed by Calida were somewhat unconvincingly denied. He admitted that they had firearms, however, and that some were unlicensed. He also claimed that 'The Alsa Masa is the entire people of Agdao. The entire population of 60,000 residents are all Alsa Masa.' This was patently untrue, and it is also clear that many people were terrorized into joining the movement, either through fear of violence or simply to make life easier for themselves more generally. It was explicitly stated by Calida, at a 1987 Alsa Masa meeting, that there was no room for neutrality in 'the war between communism and democracy'. The groups also received strong support from local radio stations, particularly through the violently anti-communist broadcasts of a self-proclaimed former NPA member, Juan Pala. 'Harassment for democracy' and 'extortion for democracy' were his key slogans in support of the movement. He warned that those who refused to join Alsa Masa would be attacked by them, and their homes would also be marked with an 'X' and attacked. Any group questioning or opposing such activities was dubbed 'communist', including a variety of church and other socially concerned organizations. In the wake of this campaigning, membership of the movement grew rapidly, and several groups of Tadtads and others also began to operate in the urban areas. These activities were highly valued by both military and civil officials, and there is strong evidence, despite denials, that top-level military and ultimately American CIA support for 'Reagan-inspired low-intensity conflict' was behind the movement and provided a great deal of disinformation to fuel its enthusiasm.

Youth murders in Brazil

I noted earlier that children have also figured as the targets of some death squad vigilantes. A number of reports have recently been published on the killing of young people in Brazilian cities. An article published in the *Guardian* (5 January 1993) draws on a report by Anthony Swift for Unicef. It notes that, although the assassination of children and adolescents is not a new phenomenon in Brazil, it has only relatively recently been investigated. It appears that over 1,000 children and adolescents were killed in São Paulo in 1991 and the first half of 1992. In Rio de Janeiro, 277 were killed from January to July 1992. The large majority of them were boys, and most were sixteen or seventeen years old. Thirty-two had appeared at some time before a court.

Further statistics, along with a detailed sociological analysis of the situation, are provided in an article by Huggins and Mesquita (1996). They note that more than 7,000 poor children and adolescents were murdered in Brazil between 1988 and 1991, and they stress that the rate of such killings has risen dramatically in recent years, as compared with adult murders and with population growth. In Brazil as a whole, the number of child and adolescent murder victims is estimated to have grown by 161 per cent between 1985 and 1992. In Rio de Janeiro, São Paulo and Recife, one youth was killed 'every 2 days' in 1988. By 1993 the number had risen to five per day in the four largest cities, and in Rio de Janeiro there was a 50 per cent increase between 1992 and 1993.

Huggins and Mesquita confirm that the very large majority of victims (almost 90 per cent) are teenage males. They also stress that they are typically extremely poor and black. At the same time they – and others, such as Penglase in his study *Final Justice*, published by Human Rights Watch (1994) – seriously question the common designation of such victims as 'street children', with its implications of living permanently as strays on the streets. Although a substantial minority clearly fit the stereotypes of young criminals living off theft and peddling drugs, or of drug addicts, most of them do not. While they often pass their daylight hours '*on* the street', a majority live with their families, often in make-shift homes, in the poorest areas of the city, and many of them work as best they can in extremely low-income occupations. Moreover, despite many claims that they are dangerous as well as criminal, even those involved in crime are relatively rarely violent – unlike the military and civil police, who often engage in common criminal activities themselves. As the authors note, however, such stereotypes are used to dehumanize *all* the children concerned and to classify them more or less as social vermin and 'feral discards', whose destruction is essential for the survival of respectable society. They also argue plausibly that such labelling, combined with their high degree of public visibility, renders poor black youths on the streets especially vulnerable to violence from more 'respectable' citizens who fear or resent their presence.

Unlike most other murder victims, who are killed by members of their families or some other close associate, these young males are typically killed by strangers. Homicide data on 15–17-year-olds in São Paulo for 1990 show that, in cases where the perpetrator was identified, public police accounted for almost half of the killings and 'extermination groups' for almost a third. Although the perpetrators remained unidentified in 64 per cent of cases, there are reasons to believe that 'police-related extermination groups' (*grupos de extermínio*) were most commonly responsible. The large majority of the victims were shot, and many of them were also badly mutilated and tortured. Many of the killings are said to be carried out for money by off-duty police or security guards working for local businesses and hotels, and some shop-owners and commercial associations keep 'assassination teams' on a retainer. Shopkeepers and others claim, not altogether convincingly, that 'street children' scare away desirable tourist and other business. The fact that some of them sell similar goods at cheaper prices on the street also probably causes some anxiety.

Although death squad members and other killers of such children are often known to the police, few have been prosecuted. An exception has been the recently reported trial (*Independent*, 1 May 1996) of a policeman who was sentenced to several life sentences for his part in the killing of eight street children in Rio de Janeiro in 1993, and this trial is said to have been the first of a number scheduled against several men accused of these killings. The sheer scale of this incident – usually only one or two children at a time are found dead in suspicious circumstances – along with a massacre of twenty-one civilians in a police raid some days later, seems to have roused public opinion and heightened official sensitivity to the wave of adverse national and international publicity that followed the killings.

The policeman was found guilty on six counts of murder, five of attempted murder, two of grievous bodily harm followed by murder, and one of causing grievous bodily harm. Most of the victims had been part of a large group of about seventy children who were sleeping not far from the Candelária church in the city when a group of men drove up in two cars and indiscriminately opened fire on them.

Four were killed instantly, and two died later of their wounds. Three more, of whom one survived, were shot some blocks away. Human rights groups were reported to have described the case as a 'small breakthrough' in the 'wall of impunity', though the convicted man was hoping for a retrial on appeal. Meanwhile, both the number of street children and the number of killings are said still to be growing.

There appear to be several reasons for general police inability and reluctance to pursue the guilty parties in such cases. Investigations are often hindered by, and advantage sometimes taken of, the cumbersome nature of the judicial process, and both witnesses and police themselves have been deterred by threats. Moreover, except under extreme pressure, many members of the police are not enthusiastic to hunt out the killers when it is known or suspected that these are police themselves or their associates. At the same time, as Huggins and Mesquita comment, such reluctance and, indeed, the killings themselves are understandable only in the context of a society whose more 'respectable' members are in general little concerned with the fate of the young people in question. In fact, many citizens are critical of the apparent inability of police and courts to keep such undesirable elements off the streets, and their attitudes often range between acquiescence in and positive support for the killings, which are seen as necessary if decent society is to be protected. Such citizens are also willing to connive in and help foster the claims that the young people in question are often victims of each other's violence or of individual 'lone wolves' rather than organized groups of police and others.

Huggins and Mesquita interestingly contrast such blinkered attitudes in a 'democratizing' Brazil with the more widespread hostility towards the violence directed against 'enemies' of the previous military regime (1964–85). They describe such earlier Brazilian violence as more 'visible', partly because much of it was perpetrated by armed and uniformed police and military personnel, and partly because of the social standing of the victims. They comment that at that time

> the primary victims of murder were middle- and upper-middle-class political dissidents whose alleged transgressions were challenging the military regime; the visibility of victims was increased by the fact that they were young adults with indisputable civic status as university students, or priests, nuns, or professional people, children or adolescents being much less likely to be direct victims of this political repression.

They also note that the social class of many of the victims of violence at that time was higher than that of its perpetrators.

Some further light is also indirectly thrown on the acquiescent attitudes in question here by what is in some respects contrasting material from another part of Latin America. Although the case does not fall within the category of 'death squad vigilantism', I have thought it worth discussion here both for the way in which it was marked by violent public reaction to police inefficiency and for the further variant of triangular relations between police, criminals and public that it illustrates.

The case of Tres Arroyos, Argentina[4]

In this case, which I outline briefly, members of an Argentinian community interestingly turned their anger and frustration on the police themselves rather than condoning their failure to arrest the murderer of a child. Here, a combination of police inefficiency and criminality – as opposed to the activities of 'ordinary' criminals – became the direct focus of violent popular attention.

Although police criminal activities that lead to failure to combat crime are always liable to criticism from the general public, violent attacks on police for reasons of this sort seem relatively rare, and – with the partial exception of the threatening confrontation between Peruvian *campesinos* and the Public Prosecutor mentioned in chapter 2 – the Argentinian case in question is the only one I have encountered in the literature. Like grass-roots vigilantes, those who criticize or physically attack the police in such circumstances tend to prefer peace and security to revolution, and this in itself seems likely to inhibit violence of this sort. In addition, a high level of police inefficiency and criminality suggests a high level of police power to do harm to those who venture to oppose them. This is also, of course, likely to be true when police engage in 'over-performance' of their duties in death squad and other criminal activities, in their self-styled 'war' against alleged enemies of society. On the other hand, as earlier material in this chapter suggests, and as one might expect when idioms of war are used, police crimes in such contexts are often subject to less widespread criticism than some of the relatively minor offences of other criminals that they fail to deal with effectively by legal means.

The incidents in question took place in the small town of Tres Arroyos, 350 miles south of Buenos Aires. At 8.30 p.m. on 31 December 1989, a woman asked the police for help to find her nine-year-old daughter, who had failed to return home after an afternoon swim. The police declined to help. At 10 p.m. she returned – apparently for a fourth time – to ask for help again. She was told that the police were celebrating New Year's Eve and she should come back later. At this point the woman asked the local radio service to ask listeners to help her. Many people who heard this appeal went out to search for the missing girl, and her body was discovered seven blocks away from her home after only a few minutes. She had been raped and strangled. It was estimated that she had been killed at 10.30 p.m. – two hours after the woman made her first attempt to get the police to help.

The discovery sparked off a serious disturbance. The Subchief of Police got into an argument with the Director of the radio station at the scene of the crime, accusing him of starting a disturbance. Then, sensing that his life might be in danger, he and his two companions fled, leaving without their car, which was then burned. The crowd then moved on to the Municipal Building, where they demanded that the senior police officers and the local *intendente* (governor) should be removed from office. Over a thousand people then gathered at the police station, where they threw stones and denounced the police as 'bribe-takers, thieves and killers'. The police, who were the worse for wear after their celebrations, retaliated with tear gas and plastic bullets. By 6 a.m. when peace had temporarily been restored, fourteen police cars had been overturned and burned. Violence then broke out again during the day, and police reinforcements were called in from neighbouring cities. All told, twenty-seven people were wounded in the disturbances and further cars were subsequently burned. The entire police force at the station was eventually replaced. Two weeks later the Director of the radio station died in a reportedly suspicious car accident.

The author of the source material draws attention to two aspects of the situation. One is that willingness to engage in the disturbances appears to have been encouraged by the end of military rule and its replacement by a democratic system. This element of transition seems important for an understanding of the relative rarity of such disturbances, which are likely to be impracticable under a harsh regime and unnecessary under a more benign one. At the same time it must be said that there is a great deal of evidence to suggest that the iron hand of the military and of the powerful civil forces that supported them is only lightly concealed beneath the glove of new 'democratizing' governments in many parts of this region.

The second point is that many of those who were involved in the violence were drawn from more 'respectable' sections of the community. They were normally firm believers in the need for law and order, and many of them had previously acquiesced in substantial levels of state violence. The Director of the radio station was no radical 'trouble-maker' – indeed, during twenty years of military rule no reference was ever broadcast from his station about any of the twenty-five local people who 'disappeared' in this period.

Beyond the immediate horror of the rape and murder of a young girl left unprotected while police celebrated New Year's Eve, the more general rapacity of the police and their failure to provide responsible and honest policing for the benefit of the respectable members of society appear to have been a major factor influencing such citizens' assessment of the situation. Following the disturbance, several hundred accusations were levelled against the police concerning thefts of cars and cattle, clandestine banking, prostitution and drugs. It was said that they charged people for investigating crimes, and that they aided and abetted criminals.

In this respect, the angry citizens have much in common with spontaneous 'respectable' vigilante groups elsewhere, with the added complication that the common criminals, whose behaviour threatened their well-being, were the police themselves.

Conclusion: death squad vigilantism?

Much of the material discussed in this chapter pushes the concept of vigilantism to its limits. The typical triangulation that I noted earlier is short-circuited by the complex merging in different contexts of the categories of 'police' and 'criminal' and 'police' and 'vigilante'. At the same time, it appears that influential sections of civil society – usually the rich and powerful – have often given active support to such extra-legal 'vigilance' by the state security and police personnel, and that many other members of 'respectable' society are willing to applaud or at least acquiesce in such activities 'beyond the call of duty', providing that they remain within limits and do not approach too close for their comfort. The conceptual waters become even more muddied when 'ordinary citizens' are recruited into such state- and establishment-sponsored activities, as in the Philippines. A part of the problem is that we are clearly dealing here with various extreme forms of social cleavage, where it is often almost meaningless to attempt a genuine definition of the 'public interest'. However, although some of the material seems to fall within what one might better label 'pseudo-vigilantism' (state violence masquerading as grass-roots reaction to crime), conceptual connections with more clear-cut vigilante action seem worth retaining. It is not so much the presence of sectional interests in such cases, as the extreme form that they take, which helps to make them special. The fact that many death squad activities have been at least tolerated and sometimes even praised by substantial sections of the population is important here, especially when they are portrayed as valuably suppressing threats to 'decent' society. The suspicion which such cases automatically arouse about assertions of the need to protect 'society' from its enemies seems worth remembering, even when one is considering more obvious cases of popular reaction to unacceptable levels of crime and disorder.

7
Vigilantism and Gender

Vigilante action discussed in this book has typically been male action and, with significant exceptions, most of it has been directed at other males. While it is arguable that this at least to some extent reflects my choice of source material, such an argument cannot take us very far. On the basis of my study of much more material than is included here, I am confident that the large majority of those who are currently and historically identifiable as vigilantes are and have been men, and few women have apparently been keen to stake their claim to an active share in the proceedings. It is less clear, however, that this pattern will continue in the future.

At the same time, women have not been wholly absent from the vigilante scene in one role or another, as I have from time to time described. They probably appear most often as the targets of male vigilantism, but they also sometimes serve as its auxiliaries and accomplices, and occasionally they even emerge as prime movers in their own right. In at least one case, they are said to have intervened to mitigate male vigilante violence. They have also appeared, most notably in the southern states around the time of the American Civil War and the first Ku Klux Klan, as a complex symbol – largely fashioned by their menfolk – of values that male vigilantes seek to preserve.[1] All this is not surprising when politics and law more generally – and also violent crime, which often attracts vigilante action – are commonly male-dominated areas, and inasmuch as sex and gender are rarely likely to be far away when questions of morality are under scrutiny.

The American West

Perhaps the archetypical example of male-on-male vigilante violence is that of Montana in the 1860s. Partly this is a demographic issue, since the mining camps and the towns that sprang up in their vicinity had predominantly male populations. There appear to have been relatively few women in such settlements, and many of them seem to have worked in the brothels and in the 'hurdy-gurdy houses', where men paid to drink and have a dance.[2] A few of the more 'respectable' men, like Wilbur Sanders, came to Montana with their wives. Others, like Dimsdale and Granville Stuart, married after they arrived. Little is known about Dimsdale's wife, Annette Hotchkiss, beyond the statement that she was 'the first white woman who settled in Virginia City' and before that one of the 'pioneers of Colorado Territory'. She arrived in 1863 or 1864. She and Dimsdale were married in 1866, a few months before he died, and she subsequently remarried.[3] Stuart, like several other white males in the area, married a girl from one of the local Indian groups. A Snake Indian, known as Aubony and as Ellen, she and Stuart were married in 1862 and had nine children. She died in 1887. The marriage is mentioned in his brother's diary, which notes that she was 'a sister of Fred Burr's wife. She had been living with Burr's family, is a fairly good cook, of an amiable disposition, and with few relatives'.[4]

A case reported by Langford (1890: 42) from nearby Florence, Idaho, in the early 1860s suggests that respectable pioneer wives were keen to make sure that less reputable women were kept out of more genteel social events. A saloon keeper, known as Cherokee Bob, had a mistress, Cynthia, whom Langford describes as 'the fallen wife of a very worthy man' and as 'the cause of more personal collisions and estrangements than any other woman in the Rocky Mountains'. She was anxious to attend the New Year supper and ball, and Bob agreed that she should be accompanied there by his friend Willoughby. When the couple arrived, they were met by 'scowls and sneers' from other women, who threatened to leave if Cynthia remained, and the men in charge of the ball told Willoughby to take her home. Next day Cherokee Bob, accompanied by Willoughby, vowed to take revenge on those involved, but their attempts resulted in a gun fight in which both were killed. Cynthia herself survived the loss, as she did the violent death of her next lover in the following year.

Beyond this case, and that of Alice Sterling discussed below, I have not seen other evidence of women's 'policing' the community in the old West. Moreover, Montana vigilantism, at least, seems to have been quite self-consciously male. This is said to have crystallized after the intervention of some local women prior to a first attempt to hang some members of the Plummer gang. The women interceded tearfully on the men's behalf, and persuaded the assembled men to commute their sentence. Dimsdale wrote:

> We cannot blame the gentle-hearted creatures; but we deprecate the practice of admitting the ladies to such places. They are out of their path. Such sights are unfit for them to behold, and in rough and masculine business of every kind women should play no part ... A woman is a queen in her own home; but we neither want her as a blacksmith, a plough-woman, a soldier, a lawyer, a doctor ... As sisters, mothers, nurses, friends, sweethearts and wives, they are the salt of the earth ... and the humanizing and purifying element in humanity. As such, they cannot be too much respected, loved, and protected. From Blue-Stockings, Bloomers and strong-minded she-males generally, 'Good Lord, deliver us'. (1866: 80–1)

After this case, women seem to have been kept away from hangings. Clearly for Dimsdale, and his friends, their 'humanizing and purifying' role was a quite unwelcome distraction in the harsh world of road-agents and vigilante executions. Yet, it is also likely that some women posed a tougher threat to vigilante justice. Joseph Slade's wife, whom he was not allowed to see before his former colleagues hanged him, was a woman of notoriously strong character. On her eventual arrival at the hotel where his body was laid out, her cries of grief were 'mingled with deep and bitter curses upon those who had deprived her of her husband', and it seems likely that his executioners' haste was fired more by fear of her anger than by her fragile femininity.[5]

Women as victims

Women are, as I have said, also sometimes vigilante targets. I described in chapter 2 how Tanzanian Sungusungu vigilantes have partly directed their energies to keeping women 'in their proper place' as faithful and obedient wives. In France, in the immediate aftermath of World War II, women who had collaborated with the German occupying forces were common victims of popular vigilante action. Women have also been victims of Sungusungu witch-hunts, and of *samosud* activities in this and other contexts, in nineteenth-century Russian villages.

As I have described, much *samosud* activity in late nineteenth-century Russian *mir* communities was highly reminiscent of western European 'rough music'. Mainly prior to the nineteenth century, in Britain, France and other countries, 'deviant' women seem to have been common victims of this form of folk retribution and ridicule. Those who beat or cuckolded their husbands, and those who other-wise were deemed to have disturbed the proper forms of sexual and marital arrangements, were likely *charivari* targets. The husband of an overbearing wife was also liable to comparable treatment for putting up with her behaviour, but the 'ridings' or other humiliations to which such men were subjected were also a shameful public indict-ment of their wives. A new pattern became visible in the nineteenth century, however, when men were more commonly subjected to rough music for beating and otherwise maltreating their wives, and similar developments connected with 'white-capping' – and echoed later in the second Ku Klux Klan – also took place in America.[6] Starn (1992: 106) also reports some punishment of wife-beaters in northern Peru. He comments, however, that despite some female participation, the groups are mainly male-dominated and 'perpetuate the oppres-sion of women', if only through discouraging their participation in assemblies and excluding them from patrols and holding major office.

Despite some exceptions, typically in murder or in witchcraft cases, women seem to be less liable than men to extreme vigilante violence. Although they have, of course, suffered deeply through the killing of their menfolk, they themselves are more likely to have been beaten and humiliated than actually killed. While women in California and other parts of the old West were sometimes the focus of a quarrel and a fight that ended with a lynching, there as elsewhere they seem rela-tively rarely to have engaged directly in the kinds of crime that pro-voked vigilante hangings. More generally, Bancroft remarks that it was extremely rare for 'rough men to lay their hands upon a woman'. He goes on to comment in one of his more florid passages that 'A woman to a mining-camp brought the odor of Araby, brought the sunshine of Eden. The atmosphere was mellowed by her influence; the birds sang sweeter for her coming, the ground was softer to sleep on, the pick was lighter, and whiskey less magnetic' (1887, vol. I: 578).

The hyperbole of this optimistic passage prefaces Bancroft's account of what he calls the Downieville Tragedy of July 1851, when a group of miners hanged a woman, known as Juanita, who had killed one of their number (pp. 577–86). For Bancroft this was not strictly speaking 'vigilantism'. He is keen to note that a Downieville Vigilance Committee was only formally established after this event, and he sees her killing, albeit after her conviction in a trial that he describes as far-cical and one-sided, as mob vengeance.

Juanita was hanged for the killing of a man called Joe Cannon. Bancroft describes him as a large, strong and honourable miner, very popular with his fellows. He was originally an Englishman who had come to California from Australia, but he was 'not a man of Sydney in the sense then current'. He had got drunk in the 4 July celebrations, and kicked at the door of a Mexican gambler. The door collapsed and next morning he is said to have gone round, still drunk, to apologize. The man's wife, Juanita, who is said to have been quite tiny by comparison, leapt at him with a knife and killed him as he spoke with her husband in his broken Spanish. The Sacramento *Times and Transcript* described her hanging as a 'blot upon the history of the state'. Bancroft retorts that 'the people were right to hang her, but they were wrong to do it madly and in the heat of passion' (p. 587). It seems clear from other comments in the text that the fact that she and her husband were Mexicans outweighed any sentiments of gallantry to womenfolk that the miners felt.

Partly similar male vigilante attitudes to women are displayed in the Brazilian material discussed in chapter 6. As I discussed there, the 'street children' murdered by death squad and other vigilantes are predominantly poor young males, who are often petty criminals and drug-takers. In contrast, poor young women, who may work as maids, child-minders or prostitutes, are rarely victims of such killings by men who are 'strangers' to them. In their discussion of this issue, Huggins and Mesquita draw attention to the fact that murdered young women are typically the victims of men who are close to them – brothers or lovers, for example – rather than men who are unknown to them, unless they happen to be closely attached to a male death squad victim (1996: 82–3).

The subordinate status of women *vis-à-vis* men seems to be involved here in complex ways. It seems likely that the men who kill them feel that they 'own' them or arc, in some way, personally responsible for keeping them in line. At the same time, it is arguable that the death squads and the forces behind them are inhibited from killing them for various reasons. Huggins and Mesquita suggest in this context that women may be protected by paternalistic 'Brazilian male stereotypical attitudes concerning female vulnerability'. They also note that gender stereotyping may make poor young women seem less criminally dangerous than men, and that this may be reinforced by the fact that many of them work indoors and are less visible than their male counterparts. Finally, they comment with particular reference to prostitutes that male perceptions of the 'services' they render may 'save' them from murder by 'extermination groups', while leaving them extremely vulnerable to other lethal hazards, such as botched abortions and AIDS.

Women and the Ku Klux Klan

Women figure relatively prominently in the history of the Ku Klux Klan. In the first Klan of the later 1860s, they constituted important symbols of white male supremacy. The idea of rape was central here. The South itself was seen as a defenceless woman ravaged and ravished by the 'nigger-loving' North.[7]

More directly, white women were themselves constantly portrayed as potential victims of black lust through rape or seduction. This partly reflects their image as weak and in need of protection, but Blee (1991: 15–16) has argued convincingly that much more is involved than this, and than expressed fears about the dangers of miscegenation for American whites within the international brotherhood of white societies. She sees the long history of enforced white male access to black women, which continued with the Klan, as an integral part of the picture. Sex in general, and rape in particular, were central symbols in an ideology of white male power over blacks. The seduction or rape of a white woman would constitute a vital threat to white male masculinity and power. Similarly, sex with black women, whether through violent rape or other forms of duress, was a blow to black *men* whatever other pain or pleasure it provided. The long-standing custom of violently castrating blacks, sometimes as a prelude to their lynching, also clearly fits within this pattern.

In the reborn Ku Klux Klan of the 1920s, comparable ideas form a small part of a much more complex picture. This second Klan was far more widespread than the first, and it was especially strong in Indiana and elsewhere in the Midwest. There it had been preceded by a range of earlier vigilante institutions, including the White Cap movement of the 1880s and also an old Horse Thief Detective Association, which now widened its remit to include sexual morality and the use of alcohol.[8]

The new Klan's enemies were similarly more numerous and varied than those of its southern predecessor. Apart from blacks, the list included Jews, Catholics, immigrants, communists and socialists, trade union 'agitators', drinkers and other local reprobates – in short, anyone who could be locally identified as an enemy of '100 per cent' American white Protestant society. At the same time, many wily politicians sought to exploit the alleged threat from such enemies for the achievement of their own political ambitions.

The Klan's spread and development also coincided with changes in the legal status of women – most importantly, they were enfranchised – and with contested perceptions of their place in society. As Blee's (1991) study *Women of the Klan* describes, women began to demand and achieve a place within the second Klan. The first major expansion of the Klan around 1920 had been spearheaded by a woman, Elizabeth Tyler, who had formidable organizing skills and experience in fund-raising and publicity campaigns. The reborn Klan had, however, been sold to the nation – almost literally, in a well-organized 'pyramid-selling' operation – as an epitome of American manhood, and neither it nor America more generally was ready for a woman like Tyler. Internal quarrels and adverse publicity led to her removal.

Tyler died in 1924. However, pressure had already begun to develop for broad-based female participation in the Klan. Letters from, or purporting to be from, the wives of Klansmen complained that the Klan was ruining their marriages. The absence of husbands on Klan business was aggravated by the fact that they were sworn not to divulge its content to anybody, including their non-member wives. Such demands, which were used to fuel competition and conflict between rival factions in the Klan, led to the establishment of several women's groups, including the Queens of the Golden Mask and the Ladies of the Invisible Empire. In June 1923 the WKKK (Women of the Ku Klux Klan) was formed. This was open to white 'Gentile' women owing no allegiance to any foreign government or sect – Jews, Catholics and communists were thus excluded – and they defined themselves as an organization 'by women, for women, and of women'. By November of that year there were WKKK chapters in thirty-six states, and by 1925 one estimate put membership at three million or more. Blee notes that this was probably exaggerated, but agrees that the real figure must have been very high (1991: 30).

The second Klan is said to have been less intensively violent than the first, at least in some of its main centres such as Indiana. Much of its members' energy was given over to fund raising, expanding membership, mass gatherings and parades, and political power seeking. What violence there was – beatings and some lynchings – was done by males, and the Women of the Klan concentrated upon other methods of social control. These included gossip and the ostracism of other women, but they appear to have done most damage to Klan 'enemies' through trading boycotts. Many Catholic and Jewish businessmen and shopkeepers in Indiana suffered badly through such boycotts, and many Jews left the state as a result.[9]

In addition, the WKKK provided highly valued opportunities for comradeship among its members. It also served as a platform for the pursuit of white Protestant women's rights, which members claimed could be protected and developed only by the Klan's attacks on Catholicism – the entrapment of girls into sexual slavery as nuns was a common propaganda theme – and on Jewish businessmen, drunken males in general, and other enemies of decent society. Many male members found it convenient to pay little more than lip-service to these particular ambitions, and as has happened more than once in such cases, the Klan's attempts to take the high ground on sexual and other moral issues ultimately contributed strongly to its downfall.

Disaster struck at the very heart of the Klan empire in Indiana, and its repercussions were felt nationally by Klan members and were put to good use by their opponents. In 1925 the Indiana political boss, and a leading local Klansman, D.C. Stephenson, was charged and convicted for the second-degree murder of a young woman called Madge Oberholzer. He already had a reputation as a drinker and a womanizer, but this only brought him into open conflict with the national leaders of the Klan when he quarrelled with them and openly declared his independence and that of his followers. The Klan leadership, and those loyal to them, began to spread stories around about his sexual and alcoholic excesses, but matters ultimately came to a head with the death of Oberholzer.

At Stephenson's trial, it was revealed that he had first attempted to seduce her, and had eventually abducted her by train. There he had raped her and savagely and grotesquely bitten her in several places. She poisoned herself and eventually died from a combination of the poison and the bite wounds. Stephenson hoped that the jury had been 'fixed' and would acquit him, but a dying declaration made by the young woman sealed his fate. He was given a life sentence and was not released until the 1950s.

The trial and its revelations had a very powerful effect. By 1928 overall membership of the Klan had fallen from several million to several hundred thousand, and by 1930 there were said to be fewer than 50,000 men and women members nationally. The fall in Indiana was especially steep, from almost half a million at its peak to a few thousand by 1928.[10]

Vigilante women

Women as prime movers, separate from and even against men, appear to be rather rare. Modern television and cinema has its fair share of individual rape victims or other wronged and angry women who are, like their male 'counterparts', seeking what is commonly called 'vigilante vengeance'. Bancroft (1887, vol. I: 545–6) tells one such story of a woman, Alice Sterling, in California in 1851. Her fiancé had been killed in a fight arising from a card game, and the killer fled. Attempts to trace him ended with the further deaths of two of his pursuers. Sterling herself disappeared at this time and was thought to have killed herself. Three years later, when the killer was playing cards in a saloon in Pioche, she secretly came in and shot first him and then herself.

More organized patterns of crime control by groups of women appear to be relatively rare, though this may well change as women's roles and status in contemporary society take new forms. At the same time it is true that, even in some so-called traditional societies, groups of women have customarily been able to bring more pressure to bear on rule-breakers of both sexes than one might expect, given the common high levels of male control over judicial processes in most such societies.

In a classic study, Margaret Green reported that, among the Ibo of Nigeria, village women levied fines from any of their number who stole things.[11] They also treated some offenders – those who did not join in their activities or tried to refuse to pay the fines – to their own variations of enforcement through 'rough music', typically in the form of scurrilous songs performed outside the victim's home (1964: 198ff). These Ibo women were also said, in the manner of Aristophanes, to have forced their menfolk to agree to raise their behavioural standards by decamping to the market place and refusing to sleep with or cook for them (pp. 212–14).

Barabaig women in Tanzania are also said to make and enforce judgements against men who violate their rights. Klima (1970: 88ff) describes how women of a neighbourhood belong to a 'council' which can punish men for a variety of offences, mostly involving violence against one of their number. The guilty man is typically fined a bull, which will be killed and eaten by the women. Men are said to resent these women's councils and the punishments they impose. Most men accept the penalties, however. Klima describes a case from the 1950s when a man refused to pay the fine. Women simply took a beast in his absence, and placed him under a death curse when he tried to stop them skinning it. They sent his wives away, threw ashes over their beds and the floor, and made traditional mourning cries as if he were already dead. The situation was resolved after a year when a further fine was paid.

However, such behaviour only hovers on the edge of vigilantism. The societies in question, though incorporated within colonial states, lacked their own chiefs or other centralized authorities, and the behaviour of the women in such cases, while unpopular with men, does not appear to compete with or substitute for the exercise of judgement on such issues by a normally recognized higher authority. The unmarried women's wing of Sungusungu, which I encountered in some Nyamwezi villages in the mid-1980s, is a more straightforward example which was set up to deal with offences committed by women. It also appears to have been short-lived, however. By 1992 Bukurura encountered no such units in the villages he studied, and he found few women actively involved in the main local committees, despite official pressures to encourage their participation.

Other female initiatives occurred in some of the cases of nineteenth-century British 'lynch law', such as that of the Rossshire women described in *The Times* of 8 April 1842, and such cases seem to have arisen both in Scotland and in England in the eighteenth century as well.[12]

A more modern case is discussed by Camilla Guy in a recent paper on 'Feminism and sexual abuse' (1996). Subtitled 'Troubled thoughts on some New Zealand issues', Guy's paper begins with an account of a vigilante assault in 1984 on Mervyn Thompson, an Auckland University lecturer and playwright. The vigilantes were six unidentified young women, who dragged him out of his car and chained him to a tree. They also sprayed the word 'rapist' on his car. Posters were later placed on the walls around the university, asserting that he was a rapist who forced students to have sex with him. The facts of the case were clearly complex – the definition of rape remained unclarified and the truth of allegations of sexual exploitation of his power as a teacher remained unproved. The main point in the present context, however, is the fact that the women concerned took 'the law into their hands'.

Camilla Guy expresses serious disquiet about this case, and about what she sees as related attitudes – expressed through formal medical and social service channels – which seem to underlie some recent identifications of male sexual abuse against children. She relates it to the radical feminism of the 1970s and 1980s, and she draws attention to her own and some other feminists' more recent questioning of the assumptions behind such strongly accusatory behaviour.

Violently Aggressive Women?

The Mervyn Thompson case tempts speculation on the possibility that forms of women's vigilantism, involving some degree of hands-on violence, may begin to emerge more frequently in contemporary western society as women play a more assertive role within it. At the same time, recent reported increases in physical assaults committed by young women may seem to point to a growing female proclivity for violence more generally. For several reasons, this is an extremely difficult question to pursue with any rigour. Reliable comparative data are difficult to obtain, and their interpretation is in any case by no means easy.[13] Theories abound – increased 'masculinization', increased involvement in the workforce and increased 'marginalization' are among those noted in a recent American study – but testing them is quite another matter.[14] Also, recent feminist and other studies make it clear how hard it is to generalize about sex and gender both between and within societies.[15] This is especially difficult in modern, complex social systems; and even allowing for age, class and ethnic differences, one is still left with a problem of a link between different forms and contexts of criminal and other violence. None the less, a brief and tentative discussion, at least of the British situation, may be useful here if only to highlight some of the difficulties involved.

A case that seemed to many to mark a shift towards more female violence in Britain occurred in April 1996, when a young teenage girl was violently killed by other girls after trying to stop a fight between two of them. Reporting the case in the *Guardian*, Yvonne Roberts (2 May 1996) comments that such incidents have 'traditionally ... been the business of a certain type of lad' and she notes that the previous day's *Sun* headline read 'Kicked to death by 30 schoolgirl yobs'. She also reports that there has been an alleged 250 per cent increase in female violent crime in Britain since 1973, though more recent figures that she cites are less dramatic. Over the last five years, female violent crime is said to have increased by 12 per cent, as against around 3 per cent for similar male crime. This suggests a slowing down, and in any case the actual number of offences remains relatively low.[16]

As I have already noted, the relation between 'crime statistics' and reports and the reality that they set out to represent is problematical, not least when 'law and order' has become so heavily politicized. A wide range of interest groups – party political, police, the media and, in the present context, feminist and anti-feminist lobbies – are all keen to make what they can of such 'information'.

Beyond this, violent crime itself is a complex category, and it has not always been classified in the same way from year to year. Official British figures for offences of violence against the person recorded by the police, or for those for which offenders were cautioned or found guilty, are of little or no help here.[17] Apart from difficulties of interpreting changing gaps between recording and conviction, for example, the figures tell us too little about the actual form and circumstances of violence.

The 1996 British Crime Survey for England and Wales, published by the Home Office and based on respondents' reported experience of crime in 1995, is potentially more helpful, though it is mainly concerned with victims over sixteen years old. It distinguishes between different categories of violent crime – domestic, mugging, 'stranger' violence and 'acquaintance' violence. In 1995 women offenders were mainly found to be involved in domestic violence against males and in stranger and acquaintance violence against females, while their involvement in mugging was extremely low.[18]

Comparison between such figures and those reported for 1981 show some increase, with the special exception of muggings. In 1981, 14.2 per cent of muggings were reported to have been committed by women as compared to only 2 per cent in 1995. The proportion of muggings committed by mixed-sex groups also decreased, from 16.3 to 5 per cent. Female (as opposed to mixed-group) involvement in other forms of common assault and woundings rose from 9.5 to 13 per cent, and from 9.9 to 11.9 per cent for all violent incidents (including muggings).[19] At the same time, the actual number of female violent offences reported to the survey rose from about 214,000 to about 483,000, an increase of around 269,000 or 126 per cent, as against an overall increase in such incidents of 87 per cent (from 2,161,000 to 4,055,000). More detailed figures comparing different types of violent offence over this period suggest that the main area of increase in the proportion of offences committed by women is in violence against female strangers. There was a 100 per cent increase (from 16 to 32 per cent) in such reported cases between 1981 and 1991, though the increase fell to just under 40 per cent (22 per cent of all such crime) by 1995. Such incidents rose overall (i.e. ignoring sex of the offender) by approximately 70 per cent. On the other hand, the main areas of increase in violent crime more generally (ignoring sex of both the victim and the offender) were domestic (3.4 times more frequent) and acquaintance violence (2.2 times greater). At the same time, however, there is also reason to believe that a larger proportion of such offences may be being reported – certainly to the police and perhaps also to the survey – than previously.[20]

Such figures partly run against and partly reinforce western and many other cultural stereotypes, and also some research data, which portray women's violence as out of character except under severe domestic or personal emotional pressure.[21] It is true that women's involvement in terrorist and other revolutionary violence has been fairly common in recent decades at least, and in some cases rather earlier, though this – like such behaviour generally – tends to be seen as either pathological or a reaction to exceptionally strong political pressure. Also, as with women's presence in mixed violent gangs, one cannot simply assume that they are always playing 'masculine' as opposed to more traditionally feminine roles in such contexts.[22]

Western culture distinguishes between the aggressive and pacific in both attitudes and behaviour, and within the aggressive we also distinguish between physical and verbal or other non-physical modes. Within this framework, women are often stereotyped as normally and normatively pacific or, at worst, non-physically aggressive, and this is often claimed to be due to their psychobiological constitution.[23] More than is the case with men, and in spite of some apparent evidence to the contrary, such as that noted above and their participation and even leadership in eighteenth-century English 'food riots', violent women are commonly seen as unnaturally deviant.[24] Aggression in women may be recognized, but it is usually expected to find typical expression in verbal form or in covert violence, rather than in open physical assault.[25]

Although witchcraft beliefs are no longer widely held in our own society, stereotypical ideas of women as witches are extremely common in many cultures, and they cast a further interesting light on such views of female aggression. From one perspective, alleged witchcraft can be seen, like any violently aggressive action, as the opposite of what Fortes (1969: 251) called the 'axiom of amity', which should ideally mark relations between close kin. On the other hand, it is also often seen as different from simple violence. A reported ironic comment from one area of East Africa that 'We don't need witchcraft here, we just stab each other' makes this point. Witchcraft is secret, underhand and sinister, and the common tendency to accuse women of its practice is often held indigenously to reflect their character.

In an early treatment of such accusations against women, the psychologist and anthropologist Nadel (1954) argued that perceptions of female witchcraft among the Nupe of Nigeria were expressions of male–female conflict. He suggested that an important element in the situation was the lack of fit between women's 'ideally' subordinate position and the realities of their powers in the economic sphere, and he also suggested that deep-seated psychosexual anxieties might be involved. Esther Goody (1970) rightly points to the specificity of Nadel's economic argument, which focuses on trading, and suggests a more general theory on the basis of her Ghanaian research among the Gonja. She notes that Gonja women, unlike men, have no legitimate channels for the expression of aggression, and she sees the attribution to them of evil mystical power as a corollary of this. As I have argued elsewhere (1994: 20), this approach also helps to make some sense of the commonly asserted Nyamwezi belief that witches are mostly women, though the situation there, and in some other cases, is further complicated by the fact that stereotypes of the typical witch are not borne out by the actual incidence of accusations.

Such ideas and beliefs occupy an intriguing middle ground between our own more polarized conceptions outlined earlier. Witchcraft beliefs and accusations against 'women witches' partly fit our view that open female violence is abnormal, but at the same time they seem to acknowledge that women might engage in much more open forms of aggression if given the chance.

It is arguable that recent developments in modern western society and culture are beginning to provide just such a chance. Along with the struggle for and moves towards an enlarged and more active role in economic, legal and political life, many women are also becoming increasingly aware of the possibility – explored in sport, the arts and media and in their own minds and actions – of thinking and behaving beyond the boundaries of stereotyped pacificity in their relations both with men and with each other. Films and novels about violent female 'avengers' and 'spree killers' appear to be part – it would be facile to see them as 'a' or 'the' cause – of this development.[26] The latent is becoming patent, and men may perhaps have to cede a greater share of more generally increasing violence and crime to women along with their increased hold on basic rights and their penetration into more legitimate zones of activity.

I am well aware how difficult it is to gain a clear picture of such processes of cultural and social change, and of the danger of turning one or two ephemeral snapshots into a grand but highly simplified scenario.[27] It is clear from vigilantism itself and from recent legislation, however ill-conceived some of it might be, that 'society' does not simply sit back unreactively in the face of increased violent crime and other undesired social change. Such issues create anxiety and provoke responses from a wide variety of formal institutional and other quarters, and the outcome of these is not easily predictable. Moreover, negative reactions to increasing female violence are likely to emanate from a wide variety of women, including many feminists, as well as from men.

The idea of 'a wide variety of women' is important here. It has arguably always been mistaken to generalize without due caution about 'women in society', as about many other topics. As I have noted, this is recognized in much recent feminist writing, where differences of ethnicity, class and generation receive much attention, and it is also reflected in the many different points of view that have developed within feminism itself. Certainly, the high level of diversity among different sections of contemporary western society makes such generalization extremely hazardous.[28]

The violent teenagers of Rotherham are very different from the radical feminists on a university campus, and both may have very little culturally or socially in common with the many women – such as the widow Frances Lawrence, the young mothers of Dunblane and the Women for Peace in Belfast – who devote much of their energy to trying to diminish violence in society. The teenagers in question also seem, at least superficially, quite different from the mothers and aunts trying to keep young Geordie tearaways out of trouble, as recently described by B. Campbell, and also from the grandmothers and mothers of Stirling's Raploch estate, who in January 1997 drove a convicted paedophile out of the area.[29]

Yet here two caveats arise. Such women may perhaps be the more responsible adults into which the vast majority of working-class and other teenage women grow. Also, the behaviour of the Raploch women, hammering on their victim's door and shouting through the letterbox – or the previous year allegedly driving out another who had attacked his wife – is not so far away from that of the nineteenth-century Rossshire 'rough musicians' described in chapter 5. Lastly, if one wants to talk of a decreasing 'gender gap', the question arises here as elsewhere of what constitutes the male side of the supposed emerging equation. Are women becoming, or trying to become, more like 'macho man' or 'new man' or both?

This said, however, it appears to be another and fairly widespread feature of the same high levels of diversity that relatively little can be taken for granted without contestation in today's society. Like other stereotypes, the view of what it means to be male or female, and the perception of men as culturally and genetically programmed to be the more violent sex are, for better or worse, under critical review and challenge in a variety of forms and contexts. If this is indeed the case, violent female vigilantes, either in their own groups or in collaboration with men, and variously aimed at common or more sectionally defined enemies, may become a more frequent 'informal sector' component of changing patterns of social order now under construction.[30] Some may be opposed to simple criminality, while others may target those men or women who oppose the moral or political direction in which they wish themselves or society more generally to move. And like the 'Regulators' of the old American frontier, they may well inspire the formation of new female 'Moderators' to keep their excesses within bounds.

8
Limits of the Law

The many ambiguities and complications of relations between vigilantism and the state have been a recurrent focus of attention in this book. In this final chapter, I give further consideration to some of the special qualities of these relations, particularly with regard to the state's claims to provide law and order for its citizens. One approach to this is through a direct discussion of the concept of law and the paradox that vigilantes often see themselves as breaking the law in order to respect it. A second approach is through comparison and contrast between vigilantes and some of those whom I describe as 'other dwellers in the twilight zone' of state law and authority, such as mafias, bandits and guerrillas.

Vigilantism and the law

The nature of law is a contentious issue that has taxed the minds of lawyers, social anthropologists and many other scholars. One key question has been how the 'rules of law' relate to actual behaviour in the handling of crimes and disputes, and arguments about this between 'realists' and 'idealists' have at times been heated. Idealists see the judicial process as the clear-headed application of an authoritative and well-structured set of rules and concepts, which should permit a wise judge to arrive at a true assessment of events in the 'real world'. Realists are not convinced, and see the process as contingently dependent on a wide variety of personal and other factors that lead to one of several possible decisions in a particular case.[1] There are, of course, also political, as well as intellectual, versions of such arguments, in which judges and their decisions may be portrayed as a fundamental element in the maintenance of elite domination and unequal access to society's resources. Even a relatively mild version of this kind of 'realism', such as Griffith's *The Politics of the Judiciary*, quickly roused the protests of more 'idealistic' figures in the legal establishment.[2]

Further problems have arisen with attempts to apply western definitions to societies elsewhere, as Howell nicely brought out with his comment (1954: 22) that, although the Nuer of the Sudan lacked law in a strict sense of the term, they were not lawless. The diversity of social forms that social anthropologists have encountered, together with the intensive fieldwork base of their research, has in fact led many of them to veer away from 'law' itself, defined in abstract or in narrow institutional terms, towards a more empirical stance akin to that of legal realists.[3] They have not ignored the rules of a society, but they have insisted upon studying them in action, and they have not restricted their attention to those strictly definable as legal. Their concern has been with such broader questions as the nature of 'social control', 'social sanctions' and 'dispute settlement'. This appeared to beg fewer questions than a focus upon 'law' itself, and their attempts to document and generalize about such processes have proved relatively fruitful.[4]

This kind of approach also leaves the question of relations between vigilantism and 'the law' more open. For a doctrinaire lawyer, vigilantism is likely to appear as simply illegal. For someone interested in 'social control', and in the functions of 'the law' as part of a set of sanctions, it commands more receptive attention. Vigilantes themselves, all over the world, complain that the official legal system has failed to satisfy their thirst for order, and a narrow focus on the law itself – whether 'realist' or 'idealist' – does not seem ultimately to have much to offer them. At least for 'classic vigilantism', the big question is not 'what is law?', but 'what is the relation between law (as an official system) and "decent" standards of order and justice?' Moreover, 'justice' in this context is not so much a deep philosophical issue as a gut-level feeling of satisfaction that perceived wrongs are righted through the identification and punishment of those who perpetrate them. Whatever the reasons legal and other academics might adduce – human error, wickedness, particular concatenations of events, or any combination of these – the relation between law and justice often remains painfully unclear to those whom the official legal machinery claims to serve.

None the less, some distinctions stemming from more narrow, academic definitions and analysis of law remain useful at least for the student, if not the practitioners, of vigilantism. The idea that law is essentially a dual system of first-order rules about human behaviour and second-order rules about these rules is particularly relevant here.[5] The rules about behaviour can be variously classified. Some are prescriptive, stating what we must do, and others are proscriptive, simply defining what we must not do. In either case, some – typically defined as 'legal' – are officially sanctioned by the state or other wider authority, while others have a narrower constituency within local communities or other sub-groups of society. Often there is overlap between the two, but this cannot be taken automatically for granted.

The second-order rules about the rules also take several forms. Some are 'legislative' inasmuch as they define how and by whom first-order rules can be made. Others are 'jurisdictional', defining who is allowed to apply and enforce the rules. Others again are rules of 'due process', defining the proper circumstances and procedures for such application and enforcement. It will immediately be clear that, when a group of vigilantes seize and punish a suspected cattle rustler, they are enforcing a first-order legal rule against theft, while clearly breaking rules of jurisdiction and due process. If such a group seizes and punishes someone for being a witch, or for organizing a strike, or for being sympathetic to the social equality of blacks and whites, they are also likely to be in conflict with the state's legislative rules, since they are dealing with 'offences' that most states do not recognize. At the same time, it is clear that there is overlap between the first-order and second-order zones to the extent that the former typically includes assertions of the rights of citizens to be dealt with in accordance with the latter.

Many people have stressed the fundamental illegality, and therefore the unacceptability for them, of vigilantism. Such criticisms were quite common in America, despite the generally high levels of support for vigilantes there, and they have been often voiced in Britain when the threat of vigilante action has been raised. As I have shown, such views were also frequently expressed in Tanzania when Sungusungu first emerged. From this perspective, there appears to be no room for argument. The activities in question are illegal and there is nothing more to be said. Nor can one usually deny the charge of illegality itself, though some implausible attempts to do so were made in Tanzania on the basis of the Sungusungu groups' 'traditional' character and also on other grounds. A Parliamentary question asked under what authority these groups fell. The official reply stated, not altogether accurately, that although no law provided for their establishment, they were organized under the guidance of regional party leaders and were as such comparable to the People's Militia (cf. Tanzanian *Daily News*, 19 July 1986).

Yet, despite its fundamental illegality, arguments in defence of vigilantism also abound, and the assumption of a necessary link between strict illegality and unacceptabilty has often been denied. Many have claimed that the mere existence of a law or laws is not enough, and that other questions must be asked. Nyerere's reported comment that the law under which Sungusungu members were being charged was 'a bad law', since it worked against the people's interests and created conflict between people and the state, is one of many versions of this line of argument.

The American historian Hubert Bancroft similarly asserts in his monumental *Popular Tribunals* (1887, vol. I: 9) that 'Law is the voice of the people' and (I: 43) that 'Law is the servant and not the master of men'. He also claims (I: 36) that 'Law we must have ... But to talk of the sacredness of law ... is to clothe rules and prescriptions with the superstitious veneration which enshrouded them of old'. He goes on to discuss the influence upon people's minds of 'the words and symbols of authority, such as legal verbiage, red tapes and seals, and all that claptrap of justice of which wigs, gowns, and divers hollow ceremonies are a part'. He stresses the uselessness of law if effective courts are unavailable to people, and he also questions the integrity of many of those whom he calls the 'law and order party' (vol. II: 141ff and *passim*). 'Crime fattens on the fruits of industry, and lawyers fatten on crime', he tells us, and he describes those concerned as 'office-holders, judges, lawyers, sheriffs, policemen, jail-keepers, politicians, law-makers, and such nondescript subalterns, contractors, demagogues, manipulators of elections and hangers-on as found food or profit in the law' (II: 142). Others, including many vigilantes themselves, have emphasized the absence of effective policing and the unreliability of those courts that exist as reasons why resort to vigilantism may be 'a regrettable necessity'.

As Bancroft's term 'popular tribunal' suggests, this position in its simplest expression emphasizes that law, society and the state exist for 'the people', and that the people must and will fend for themselves when necessary. This idea is, of course, enshrined in the United States constitutional doctrine of 'popular sovereignty', but its attraction is much wider. In many different parts of the world, vigilantes and their sympathizers – and indeed some of their critics – argue that, if the state and other institutions worked as they were meant to, no one would look elsewhere for security of life and property. But when police and courts are non-existent, weak or corrupt, the people will naturally fall back on their own resources. They will form posses and committees, and criminals and other public enemies will be hunted down and punished.

This kind of 'democratic' argument has considerable attraction for critics of the 'dead hand' of bureaucracy and other pathological conditions of the state. However, as usual with such rhetoric, the problem is what lies behind it. When one enquires who 'the people' are, the answer varies from one case and context to another, and there may well be different answers from within the same 'community'. In the Tanzanian case, as I have shown, one comes comparatively close to a genuinely popular movement. Differences of wealth and differences of interest between villagers were relatively small, and local support for Sungusungu was widespread and, on the whole, enthusiastic. Yet even there, what I have called a 'proto-elite' of middle-aged and older men were largely speaking for the people, and their interests were not always concordant with those of at least some women and younger men. In the townships of South Africa, we saw local factions, with distinct political and economic interests, competing with each other to assert their claims to satisfy the true needs and identify the enemies of 'the community'.

In the United States, as Brown has argued, vigilantism has typically had a more obvious elitist character. Indeed, long before Brown, this character was proudly boasted of by Dimsdale, Langford, Stuart and Bancroft in their celebrations of the vigilantes of Montana and of San Francisco. In both cases, the vigilantes were 'the best and most intelligent men' in their pioneer communities. Bancroft is especially explicit on this feature of the San Francisco vigilantes, and emphasizes the difference between the disciplined activities of the leading members of the Vigilance Committees and the undisciplined tendencies to 'mobocracy' of the populace at large. He devotes several pages to this question (1887, vol. I: 8–15).

> The terms vigilance committee, mob-law, lynch-law, are not, as many suppose, synonymous...The vigilance committee is not a mob ... Indeed prominent among its other functions is that of holding brute force and vulgar sentiment in wholesome fear. The vigilance committee will itself break the law, but it does not allow others to do so. It has the highest respect for law ... yet it has a higher respect for itself than for ill-administered law. (p. 8)

He admits to superficial similarities with mob-violence – they emerge in similar conditions and 'become a law unto themselves'. However:

> One is an organization officered by its most efficient members, aiming
> at public well-being, and acting under fixed rules of its own making; the
> other is an unorganized rabble, acting under momentary delirium, the
> tool, it may be, of political demagogues, the victim of its own intemper-
> ance. Underlying the actions of the one is justice; of the other revenge.

One need scarcely say that such distinctions are more easily sustained
on paper than in hangings. Nor are one's anxieties about them
necessarily allayed by learning that many of the elite in question were
businessmen or Freemasons, however proud of this they were themselves, or that the 1858 committee in San Francisco was largely concerned with the destruction of its political opponents, however
corrupt their political machine.

The issue of reality and rhetoric looms much larger when one shifts
attention from such cases to the covert operations of the state's own
personnel in the asserted vigilantism of death squads and 'counter-
insurgency' groups in Central and South America and the Philippines,
and in the 'black-on-black' conflicts of South Africa. In such cases, we
have seen how regime-support and control, and elite economic interests, may be disguised by specious claims that such activities essentially constitute a popular reaction to problems of personal and
national security.

The material I have considered makes it clear that vigilantism is
rarely simply a popular response to the failure of due legal process to
deal with breaches of the law. 'The people' and 'the community' are,
on inspection, complex concepts, and the populism of much vigilante
rhetoric conceals, or in Bancroft's case goes hand in hand with, a self-
satisfied elitism.

As Smurr has argued for Montana, this may go with a contempt for
more populist forms of 'trial by jury' and 'miners' courts', which the
vigilantes choose to neglect rather than support and protect.[6] It is also
clear that many vigilantes are concerned in other ways with much
more than the legal system's failure to uphold the law. Anti-witchcraft
vigilantism in Tanzania and South Africa, and racist and anti-labour
vigilantism in the Deep South and elsewhere in America, show that
the problem is commonly the definition of the primary rules of law
themselves, rather than a failure of police and judiciary to uphold
existing legislation. Similarly, the activities of 'White Caps' in the
American Midwest and of exponents of 'rough music' in Britain were
largely directed against legally non-indictable offences. And the hanging of the 'bummer' Rawley in Montana seems to have been a more
serious example of this kind.

Yet, if it is mistaken to take vigilante claims about the failure of the formal legal process at face value, it would equally be wrong simply to dismiss it as a sham. One does not need to be a Marxist or an anarchist or a vigilante to perceive that state machinery is often flawed. Corrupt police and lawyers, and 'nobbled' or intimidated witnesses and jurors, are not figments of the radical imagination, and due process no doubt does make it more difficult to convict the guilty, especially if they are clever and well connected. Legal sentencing is often at loggerheads with public sentiment, as in recent anger about the perceived 'light sentences' in vehicle offences causing death.[7] Anxiety about crime levels and the apparent inability of state machinery to cope is also real enough in Tanzania, Britain and elsewhere.

Nor are Bancroft's hyperbolic comments simply to be dismissed as florid bunkum. Large numbers of societies have managed satisfactorily without the state. Indeed, the French anthropologist Clastres tells us that it is insulting to such societies to describe them in this way, as if they lacked the state.[8] For him, at least, they are societies successfully against it rather than without it. Bancroft would doubtless not approve this anarchistic point, but he would heartily agree that authority must earn its keep. Pomp and ceremony – or theatre, as E.P. Thompson puts it – are not, or at least should not be, enough.[9]

Max Weber too is interesting on this point. He is naturally well aware that political stability is a variable, and he notes that, although expediency and habit may form a basis for political solidarity, they are incapable in themselves of maintaining a stable regime and need more lasting bases of support. As is well known, he identifies these in three 'ideal' bases of legitimacy – charisma, tradition and a 'legal-rational' constitution.[10] For some, of course, this is simply a function of a fundamental political deceit, concealed by ideology and underlying state claims to public service. For others, less sinister issues of 'political elasticity' and predictable phases of short-term unpopularity for almost any regime are at least partly involved. Problems are bound to arise, and errors of judgement to be made. Some continuity of personnel and of state institutions is arguably desirable, as an alternative to the constant replacement and reshuffling of staff and attempts at instant structural readjustment at the institutional level. Often, of course, governments are able to survive minor crises of unpopularity by the 'sacrifice' and replacement of particular personnel. Such personnel may indeed be to blame for some problems, but it is a commonplace that they are also often short- or long-term scapegoats for the ineffective or unrealistically demanding machinery that they operate.

The typical conservatism of vigilantes, and their accompanying claim to want the state to operate effectively, seem to constitute an alternative, grass-roots solution to this kind of problem. They present themselves as a stop-gap rather than a permanent replacement for malfunctioning state institutions, but they none the less let it be clearly known that the state must work for its living if it is to receive their respect.

At the same time they, and their apologists, play down the more problematic elements in their own activities. As I have shown, the arrogant elitism of many groups is – like state authority itself – clothed in the finery of public service. The cruelty of hanging men like Rawley is excused in terms of the dire threat he posed to public order, and the hanging of Joseph Slade is dismissed as 'the protest of society on behalf of social order and the rights of man'.[11]

Similarly, the opportunities for error that summary justice amply provides, and which Walter van Tilburg Clark's classic 'western' novel, *The Ox-bow Incident* (1940), vividly portrays, are often denied or represented as exaggerated.[12] The Vigilance Committees are said to be cool-headed and immensely careful in their investigations, or such charges are dismissed in more cavalier fashion by claims such as that of Charles Bonaparte, that 'very few innocent men are lynched, and, of those who have not committed the past offense for which they suffer, a still smaller proportion are decent members of society'.[13]

Bonaparte, who was to go on to be Attorney General of the United States under President Theodore Roosevelt, himself a firm friend of vigilantism, also noted that many a miscarriage of justice took place in the formal courts. In addition, vigilante justice is often argued to be not only just as good or better than its inefficient official counterparts, but also far less demanding on the taxpayer and the public purse.

It is useful to return to Brown's analysis of the special situation in North America here. He argues that the vigilante tradition is a firmly established feature of American society and culture. It arose, he argues, from the peculiar combination of a revolutionary tradition, the post-revolutionary inheritance and persistence of an outdated legal framework, the emphasis on 'popular sovereignty' and the state's obligations to its citizens, and the special nature of the frontier and accompanying ideas of 'do-it-yourself' localism. He sees vigilantism as an intrinsic, if informal, feature of the total social system, coexistent with the formal legal and judicial apparatus. Commenting on the view that vigilantes would have done better to provide direct support to this apparatus, Brown notes (1975: 148) that the criticism, while laudable, 'misses the point'.

The reality is that during the nineteenth century and on into the twentieth Americans supported a dual system of legal and extralegal justice by adherence to the primary role of repression of crime with little regard for procedural safeguards. Thus Americans did not feel themselves any less public spirited when they participated in lynch law. Instead they saw the vigilante participation as an act of public spirit as important . . . as the election of upright officials.

It is arguable that this 'special character' of the American tradition serves not so much to mark it off as radically different from others as to highlight in particularly trenchant form a problem fundamental to relations between people and the state wherever they occur. Unless the state achieves a truly 'totalitarian' domination of all aspects of their practical, emotional and intellectual lives, its citizens will think, and at least be tempted to act, for themselves in a varying range of contexts.

This seems to apply as much to questions of the administration of justice as to anything else. States, of course, vary in the degree to which they arrogate to themselves more or less exclusive power and authority in this particular field, and with this in the space that they allow their citizens to pursue matters for themselves. Yet there seems good reason to suspect that the more control the state demands, the less successful its attempts to satisfy its citizens will be. The typical bureaucratic structures and processes that such increased control requires are intrinsically flawed. They are bound to oversimplify and, of course, depersonalize the situations they attempt to deal with, and, as Rappaport has argued, it is very likely that the information on the base of which a highly centralized officialdom attempts to act is subject to considerable distortion as it travels from periphery to centre.[14] Beyond this, there is the further point that a large proportion of the lives of citizens is taken up with personal and local issues which are, as parts of chaos theory remind us, likely to be none the less complex for being localized.[15]

When one adds the difficulties noted earlier of human error, the time-consuming and expensive nature of the formal judicial process, and the opportunities for its manipulation by both legal and illegal means, it begins to seem surprising that the legal system provides any satisfaction at all to any but the well-paid professionals who operate it. The various problems to which vigilantism responds seem likely to be givens anywhere, and there seems little hope of eradicating them at source. The dissatisfactions they engender have then to be kept under control in other ways, typically through ideology and the threat of force. Yet these too are imperfect instruments, and at least some people usually have the inclination and the space for some self-help on the shadowy edges of state discipline.

At the same time, it would clearly be mistaken to assert that vigilantism's relation to the law is, in all significant respects, everywhere the same. An important issue is the role played by officials in this context. Brown highlights how many high-ranking lawyers in the United States, such as Bonaparte quoted earlier, have been apologists of vigilante action. His analysis goes well beyond this, however, and indeed beyond his emphasis on the idea that American vigilantism and the formal legal system have been in shifting but persistent equilibrium with each other. For he also points to a history of collusion with and even active participation in vigilante projects by official personnel, especially but not only in the nineteenth century.[16]

We have already seen something of this in the material documented by Ingall for Tampa, Florida, where police officers were active members of the Ku Klux Klan, and there are 'many instances', Brown tells us, 'of sheriffs and officials who have collaborated with vigilantes and lynch mobs' (1975: 147). Judging from the cases that Brown refers to, the most commonly reported form of such collaboration was inaction, typically a failure to make any effort to prevent a lynching taking place, but he notes that 'the open cooperation or collusion of officials with lynchers had become such a scandal that after 1892 a number of states adopted legislative or constitutional procedures designed to end the evil' (1975: 161). He adds that although 'these measures were largely ineffective, they were an index of a growing public opinion that, in the 1920's, began to turn decisively ... against lynching'.

The situation that Brown documents sits somewhere between that found in Britain on the one hand and that found in parts of Latin America and the Philippines. Despite isolated allegations of police collusion, as in the Norfolk vigilantes case, police, courts and politicians have more regularly expressed hostility and alarm when vigilantism has raised its head in Britain, and it is not at all clear that the current level of popular acquiescence in such activities would continue if their scale increased. In Latin America and the Philippines, on the other hand, the extent of collusion and merging between vigilante and official forces has at times been so great as to render the two indistinguishable, and this pattern has enjoyed a high degree of acquiescence and support at least among the middle and higher echelons of society.

Other dwellers in the twilight zone

This discussion of the links and contrasts between vigilantes and the law may also help to throw some light on similarities and differences between vigilantism and other patterns of relatively autonomous 'informal sector' grouping and activities. Heald (1986b) interestingly explored some aspects of this question in her paper 'Mafias in Africa: the rise of drinking companies and vigilante groups in Bugisu, Uganda' and also in her later book (1989). Her discussion draws on Hobsbawm's work on early mafias as filling sociopolitical space left empty by a weak state structure. Partly following her lead, I include here forms that are commonly labelled 'social bandits', 'mafias', 'guerrillas' and 'resistance movements'.[17]

At a general level, all of these – like vigilantes – typically involve groups that operate within or on the edge of society and constitute an (often enough violent) alternative to the institutions of the formal political and economic sectors. All are also commonly engaged, either among themselves or more widely, in one or other form of social control, and they all lay claim to some constituency of support. Moreover, the differences between them are not always clear in practice, because they all share the 'labile' tendencies that I outlined earlier for vigilantism. The activities of all of them, whatever their starting point, may fairly easily degenerate into a lowest common denominator of less discriminating criminality. Because of this, it is valuable in each case to bear in mind the possibility of sharp distinctions between definition and reality that ideal-type analysis anticipates.

The concept of 'social bandit' was developed by Eric Hobsbawm in his study of 'primitive rebels' (1959). Like classical vigilantes, bandits – 'social' or otherwise – are violent and operate on the spatial and social edges of normal mainstream society. Their activities are illegal, but in the case of social bandits, there are popularly acknowledged extenuating circumstances that mitigate their criminality.

Bandits are criminals in a relatively straightforward way, inasmuch as they break the law by attacking people and depriving them of property that is legally theirs. They therefore clearly differ from vigilantes in their breaking of first- rather than second-order legal rules, and it is not surprising that they have often been prime targets of vigilante activity.

None the less, the criminality of bandits also has its complications. Property itself is seen by some as highly problematic. Proudhon, the first self-styled anarchist, responded to the question 'What is property?' with the well-known answer 'Property is theft', and such radical views still persist in one form or another, with pick-pocketing, burglary and other forms of robbery sometimes described as the poor's own way of redistributing wealth in society. Only a minority, of course, take such a position, but a substantial number of people would perhaps be willing at least to entertain the less extreme idea that persistent extreme differences in wealth are often symptoms of a shortfall in social justice.

Hobsbawm's idea of the 'social bandit' contributed importantly to an understanding of such matters. As Hobsbawm sees him, the social bandit is a kind of rebel against the unjust inequalities within society. He is a Robin Hood figure, who robs the rich to feed the poor, and consonant with this, the social bandit is often loved and protected by the poor whom he helps to feed. Typically, he himself is a victim of injustice, which then drives him to crime. A major problem with this characterization, however, is that very few real bandits seem to fit the bill. Robin Hood did not even clearly exist, let alone fit the specification in question, and many others often turn out on closer inspection to have been more bandit than social.

None the less, Hobsbawm does seem to have been on to something interesting. As Maxwell Brown notes, some of the bandits of the American West, like Billy the Kid, and men like Pretty Boy Floyd in the depression era, do seem to have been loved and protected by some of the less fortunate elements in society, and many bandits have enjoyed at least the admiration of those who are too poor for them to rob.[18] Taken as an ideal type, rather than as an adequate description in itself of real people, the concept of the social bandit is a useful one because it points so clearly to the absence of complete consensus and support for the structural status quo in a society. Like vigilantism, social banditry highlights the idea of justice. Also like vigilantism, bandits, social or otherwise, are tinkerers with the social system rather than true revolutionaries. Yet it is also clear that, unlike social bandits, vigilantes typically tend to represent established interests and try to maintain the socioeconomic status quo in their communities. Their protection rather than subversion of property rights places them in direct opposition to the aims of banditry, and the justice they seek is that of retribution rather than redistribution.

Hobsbawm's comments upon mafias, on which Heald draws, are also problematic. He mainly refers to what he claims were embryonic forms of mafia, which arose in the early history of the Italian state and provided elements of local law and 'government' where political change had left a rural power vacuum.[19] The relation of this model of early mafia to the development of mafia in rural Sicily has been strongly contested by Blok (1974), and its relation to more modern, often urban, forms is even less clearly apparent. Blok has, in turn, been taken to task by Gambetta (1993) for vagueness and inconsistency in his use of the term.

If, as with vigilantism, we leave aside more figurative uses of the term – the 'Oxbridge mafia' in high places, for example – there is still room for argument about its meaning. For many people, whose main sources of information are novels, films and newspapers, the word 'mafia' refers to an underworld of large-scale and often violent organized crime, conducted by secret associations with a strong internal code of honour, reinforced by rituals of entry. The criminal activity in question is focused upon drugs, prostitution and extortion, in places such as Sicily and on the Italian mainland, in North America in major cities such as New York, Chicago and Miami, and in the former Soviet Union.

Despite uncertainty about the levels of organization involved nationally, the extent of international collaboration and how much similarity there is between the groups concerned over both space and time, it is clear enough that such organized crime exists and that its practitioners are often extremely powerful. It is also reasonably clear that their operations sometimes involve the collusion of major figures in both state and local government. Evidence supporting such assertions has been built up over many years, partly through the 'state's evidence' of *pentiti* (repentants), who have come to the conclusion that they are better off collaborating with official investigators, and partly through phone tapping and other undercover police work.[20]

If we assume for the moment that this popular stereotype of organized criminality usefully delineates the main features of contemporary and much historical mafia, direct comparison in terms of similarities with vigilantism seems misplaced. As with banditry, the clear central focus on the breaking of first-order legal rules appears to preclude this, though one may still note a partial overlap of functions in some cases, along with vigilantism's capacity to conceal sectional and sometimes criminal interests under the mask of public service and community well-being.

The stereotype has, however, recently been questioned by Gambetta (1993) in a persuasive book on the Sicilian Mafia. For Gambetta, the essential characteristic of mafia, whatever else it might do, is its trade in a commodity – protection. It provides this commodity to businesspeople and others who wish to carry out their activities prosperously and without undue interference, and to avoid being cheated by those

with whom they deal. The fact that much of the business activity concerned is illegal is significant, since it pre-empts the possibility of protection by the formal state machinery, and it also partly predicates the
violence that mafiosi commonly resort to as a demonstration of their
power to punish those who create difficulties for or default on their
clients.[21] The threat and execution of such violence is also an important instrument for warning off competitors within the protection and
security 'market', and for maintaining discipline among group members. Although mafiosi often engage in organized crime themselves
along the lines of the popular stereotype outlined above, this is not
their quintessential quality. Nor are they simply to be understood as
offering extortionate protection mainly against themselves.

Gambetta thus sees the mafia as engaged in the maintenance of
order in 'the market', and he also notes that it may sometimes be
involved more generally in order maintenance in other contexts. Most
of the examples he gives, however, concern the behaviour of the
mafia's own members, or slights and insults to those members or their
wives and relatives. He clearly acknowledges this and dismisses
claims, which have sometimes been made, that mafia genuinely constitutes a broad-based alternative judiciary.

If we accept Gambetta's well-documented position as providing the
basis for an informed ideal type of mafia, we approach closer to
Heald's original assertion of comparability. Johnston, for example, as I
noted in chapter 1, describes vigilantes as offering assurances or guarantees of security to participants and other members of a given established social order. None the less important differences remain.

Most important is the twofold economic focus of mafia activity.
Mafias protect those in business and the provision of such protection
is their own economic business activity. It is true that the promoters of
vigilantism, such as those in the San Francisco movement of 1851,
have often been businessmen anxious to create and maintain a stable
environment for their business activities. Yet this is secondary in the
context of vigilantism itself. Vigilantism is contingently rather than
intrinsically connected with business in such cases, whereas it is central for the mafia in Gambetta's model. Nor are vigilantes, as an ideal
type, operating an economic profit-making business for themselves.
Accusations that the Montana vigilantes of the early 1860s were looking for a direct economic pay-off from their activities would, if sub-
stantiated, seriously damage their vigilante status.[22] Such accusations
would, in contrast, be quite meaningless if levelled at the mafia, since
such activities *are* their business.

Conversely, the 'good works' of the mafiosi are secondary to their business activities. This becomes clear in Gambetta's statement about mafia contributions to law and order that 'Unless they have a direct interest at stake, mafiosi do not protect a nameless, faceless "public", which would be difficult to "tax". Only in small towns, where everybody can be controlled, do mafiosi occasionally appoint themselves caretakers of anything that could be called law and order' (1993: 167–8). Thus if mafia activities possess a 'law and order' flavour at all, it is that of a particularistic and informal *civil* law, involving supportive participation in the disputes of private individuals and organizations unable to avail themselves of more open and formal procedures. Vigilantism, in contrast, essentially provides an ideally universalistic, informal substitute for the *criminal* justice system.

The concepts of guerrillas and resistance movements merge into each other, and examples are relatively well documented from several areas including Europe, though – as with other secret organizations – it is not always easy to assess their character in particular cases. Guerrillas are technically members of small fighting units which typically engage in armed raids upon the forces and supporting institutions, including transport and buildings, of an established government whose legitimacy they contest. As its name suggests, 'resistance movement' is a broader concept in which the key element is covert organized resistance, typically against an 'occupying power'. Such movements commonly include guerrilla units which they use to harass the enemy, but they may also engage in a wide range of other and more individual forms of sabotage, disruption and intelligence work. Both are more clearly revolutionary in their relations to the political and economic status quo than other forms under consideration here.

As Lan's work on guerrillas in Zimbabwe shows, however, such groups may well establish themselves within local populations, and they may then actively engage in the punishment of what they and villagers assert to be offences, in addition to conducting more direct attacks against the 'occupying' regime.[23] In other cases, such as that of the Forest Brethren in Estonia and elsewhere in the Baltic region during the Soviet occupation, the groups were forced to hide away from village settlements, though some contact was maintained with individuals within these. Raids were carried out against Soviet military and KGB units, and also in some cases against villagers who were deemed to have collaborated with the occupying power. Predictably, personal revenge killings also sometimes seem to have been carried out under the resistance banner, and some members of the bands are said, even by strong anti-communists, to have been more criminal

than political activists.[24] Ranger has also noted how some
Zimbabwean guerrilla groups moved into banditry, and this appears
to be true also of groups like Quantrill's Guerrillas, whose members
included the celebrated Jesse and Frank James, after the American
Civil War.[25]

The most obvious case in which vigilantism and political resistance
seem to merge is that of the first Ku Klux Klan, discussed in chapter 4.
There we find a movement whose prime aim is resistance to the political aftermath of the North's victory in the Civil War, and whose prime
mechanism of resistance is the harassment and 'punishment' of blacks
who were attempting to realize the benefits that this victory appeared
to proffer them.

But this does not mean that ideal-type starting points cannot be usefully distinguished, and the main terms of such distinctions are, it
seems, relatively simple. Firstly, the distinction that I noted earlier
between breaches of first- and second-order rules is relevant. Bandits
and mafiosi, to the extent that their main purpose is the pursuit of
gain through activities like robbery, drug dealing and corruption, tend
to be more openly in breach of first-order rules than vigilantes. These,
as I have suggested, are archetypically interested in the control of
first-order crime, rather than its commission – though they may also
disagree with the state about some first-order rules – and this focus
leads them mainly into breaches of the second-order rules of jurisdiction and due process. Secondly, some insight into differences between
the ideal types involved here can be gained through almost everyday
distinctions between law, politics and economics, though once again
the slipperiness of actual activities can blur this in practice. In these
terms, vigilantes are, at least ideally, mainly interested in legal issues
of crime control, while bandits' activities are more clearly focused
upon economic gain. This is also true of mafias, but these additionally
appear to have characteristically strong interests in the development
of political power, either directly at a local level or through the infilt-
ration and corruption of the formal political system at the centre.
Again, guerrillas and resistance movements aim primarily at mount-
ing a subversive political offensive against the regime currently in
power in the state. However blurred these distinctions may be in reality, they appear to be worth maintaining analytically as points of reference against which shifts and extensions of actual behaviour can be
measured.

As this last point makes clear, I consider that the comparison of
vigilantism with such other forms of challenge to 'mainstream' society
and the state is at least as enlightening for the differences between

them as for broad similarities that may emerge. In focusing upon such similarities, Heald rightly sought to emphasize that Gisu vigilantism was not simply a piece of African 'exotica', but a fundamentally 'human' response to particular kinds of social and political problem, and especially a perceived shortfall in the maintenance of order in society. While deeply sympathetic with this aim, my own premise in this volume has been that a more direct exploration of vigilantism itself offers the best road for its pursuit.

Vigilante days and ways

The title of Nathaniel Langford's reminiscences of old Montana provides the heading for this final section. He tempts one to believe that North American vigilantism made sense only as part of the taming of the West, but subsequent events, such as the re-emergence of the Ku Klux Klan in the Midwest and the South, belie this wishful thinking. Nor can this be simply explained in terms of the persistence of populist revolutionary and frontier traditions. Although it is clear that these are a force to be reckoned with in the United States – for instance, in the rise of urban 'self-defence patrols' and various 'militia' groups – vigilantism has appeared in too many different times and places in the world for any culturally specific explanation to be wholly satisfactory.[26]

We have also seen, in the United States and elsewhere, that the 'frontier' character of vigilantism must be understood in relatively broad terms. It is true that many of its recent manifestations outside North America, such as in eastern and southern Africa, or in Peru, are understandable only in terms of the state's inability to penetrate to physically remote areas of its domain, though even in such cases 'remoteness' is not simply a matter of distance, but depends partly on available communications and resources. Yet it is also apparent that a variety of other frontiers may be present even where spatial distance in itself is not a serious problem. In such situations, the frontier is an inner one of state or 'ruling class' legitimacy, and the problem is one of reaching hearts and minds rather than actual places.

As I have argued, these and other problems of authority and power seem likely to be endemic to most modern, complex state systems. Also, we have seen that there are many examples where government itself or other powerful forces within the state may instigate and provide material, or at least moral, support to vigilante activities as a means to the destruction of political enemies under a banner of order maintenance.

All this suggests that vigilantism in its various forms responds to a range of persistent imperfections in state systems. I mentioned earlier my own ambivalence to the phenomenon, and I must confess that the more I have explored its nature, the more I tend to agree with much on both sides of the arguments it generates. Although vigilantism and the official apparatus are often praised or criticized in contrast to each other, both seem to serve some of their avowed purposes and at the same time to be full of dangerous potential. Each seems capable in its own way of fostering both the common good and sectional interests, and of confusing them in the process. Each similarly seems capable of both the protection and repression of those whom it claims to represent. Both can produce serious miscarriages of justice, and both can employ claims to the provision of 'public service' to camouflage less noble aims. It is true that the state typically operates at a much more massive scale, but the scale of movements like the Ku Klux Klan has also been terrifyingly large.

Perhaps the best that can be said of both of them is that, sometimes at least, they may positively combine their virtues and counteract each other's faults rather than simply compound them. This last too unfortunately happens, as we have seen, when the state's own personnel engage in covert vigilante action, and the distinction between police and criminal begins to become purely academic.

Of course, not all cases are the same. Both vigilantism and the law, like community and state themselves, vary from time to time and from place to place in accordance with such factors as political ideology, social and cultural homogeneity, internal sanctions and controls, and commitment to duty. In the case of vigilantes, locally developed political skills and local knowledge of the character and background history of actual and potential participants are also clearly important.

At first glance, such differences might suggest that vigilantism is a category with little content, though the same would also have to be said of the state. It seems more sensible, however, to view this kind of variation as evidence of fundamental dualities and ambiguities in the realm of law and order and politics. Moreover, we have seen that 'vigilant citizens' in many different places organize themselves in recognizably comparable ways to pursue demands for justice and security in the absence, or the locally asserted inefficient presence, of the state's machinery.

Their propensity to do so is, I have suggested, partly a natural 'given' of their experience of state organization itself. One might suppose that, as states become more complex and developed, the need for vigilantism might wither. Yet it is especially in such states that the idea of legitimate authority itself has been increasingly questioned in many different contexts. These have varyingly included differences and conflicts of class, ethnicity, regionalism and, more recently, gender, in which people are tempted to bypass the state as old norms are contested and the challenge to them is resisted. Similarly, the tendency towards contemporary state tolerance of such 'traditional sins' as homosexuality and abortion, or of perceived cruelty to animals for scientific or commercial purposes, has sometimes led to violent 'popular' reaction against those concerned. Again, contemporary anxiety and argument about the safety of children and the proper limits of state and local reaction to known sex offenders – including the publication for some areas of their identity through varieties of 'Megan's Law' – also suggest that the list of potential focuses for vigilante action is unlikely to get shorter.[27]

Lastly, even if particular groups and communities should fail to think up vigilante action for themselves, plenty of exemplars are regularly brought to their attention. I have argued that this 'global' quality of knowledge about vigilantism has a long history – witness *Times* reports of the 1830s – which may well be as old as travel and the state themselves. But it is, of course, especially relevant in the contemporary world, in which the notion of culturally bounded communities immune to the spread of information and ideas from elsewhere has become increasingly fanciful.

It is theoretically conceivable that this process might lead to an anarchic melting pot in which the very notion of authority becomes discredited, and cultural and social relativity prevails. It seems more probable, however, that struggles for political hegemony and the demand for order will, if anything, intensify. Both despite and because of challenges to boundaries and regimes, the state itself and its claims to legitimacy seem well set to persist as the predominant form of polity and focus for political ambitions. Similarly, one may assume that, within it and to varying degrees apart from it, 'community' values old and new will still be authoritatively asserted and contested with the same and possibly increased vigour. In such a world, vigilante days and ways, with their detractors and supporters, seem likely to be with us for some time to come.

Notes

Chapter 1 Vigilantes

1 For a brief survey of many such developments in the United States since the 1960s, see Johnston's excellent discussion and list of sources (1992: 166–73).

2 Early Chinese material is suggestive rather than conclusive. Cf. Kuhn (1970: 24ff) and Schurmann (1968, chapter 7).

3 Thompson (1991: 530–1) makes a similar point about 'rough music' in historical communities in Britain. Arguing, he says, partly with himself because he finds much attractive in 'rough music', he notes that 'Because law belongs to people, and is not ... delegated, it is not thereby made necessarily more "nice" and tolerant, more cosy and folksy. It is only as nice and as tolerant as the prejudices and norms of the folk allow.'

4 Caughey (1957: 228 and *passim*). As I describe in chapter 8, the suitability of the term 'mob' for 'true' vigilante groups is strongly contested by Bancroft (1887, vol. I: 8–15). A comparable point is also made by Thompson (1991: 260 fn. 1 and 289) in defence of his preference for the term 'crowd' over 'mob' in his discussion of 'food riots'. Caughey's choice of the term is, of course, consonant with his strongly critical stance on vigilante violence.

5 The 1960 book contains a version of his 1957 paper as an introduction, followed by an interesting collection of excerpts from a large number of reports, both contemporary and historical, of various forms of American vigilantism – in a broad sense of the term – ranging from classical western patterns to McCarthyism and the activities of local 'American Minute Women' in modern Houston, Texas. The title is taken from the letters of 'Dame Shirley' (Louise Clappe), a doctor's wife at one of the early mining camps, to her sister. The letters were published in the San Francisco *Pioneer* in 1854–5.

6 See Nicolosi (1968). Little and Sheffield (1983: 805) comment on the 'remarkable similarity' between American anti-horsethief associations and English prosecution societies, and suggest the need for further research on such links.

7 Philips (1989), Little and Sheffield (1983) and Brown (1963, 1975).

8 See also Burrows (1976) for an interesting general discussion of American vigilantism.

Chapter 2 On the Frontiers of the State

1 Cf. Kuhn (1970) and Schurmann (1968).

2 For detailed discussions of the first Ku Klux Klan, see Wade (1987: 31–118) and Trelease (1972).

3 In addition to Melbin discussed here, Little and Sheffield (1983: 797) suggest the concept of a frontier of transition between major social forms, as in the shift to industrial capitalism in Britain. They see the rise of private prosecution associations as a response to problems of this transition.

4 See Abrahams (1967, 1981) for an account of life in the area in the late colonial period and after independence.

5 The main sources on Sungusungu are Abrahams (1987, 1989), Abrahams and Bukurura (1993), Bukurura (1994a and b, 1995) and Masanja (1992). Sabasaba and Rweyemamu (1986) and Campbell (1989) are also of some interest, though the former concentrates heavily on the question of the movement's illegality and the latter sees it, mistakenly in my view, as resistance to capitalist developments in the area.

6 Richards (1935) gives a classical account of Mchapi in the 1930s in neighbouring Zambia. The movement also reached Tanganyika, and was revived there in some areas in the early 1960s (Iliffe 1979: 367; Willis 1968).

7 See Tanner (1970) and Mesaki (1994).

8 Cf. Slapper (1993).

9 Bukurura (1994a: 195–8) found a similar situation in the Kahama village of Mwalugulu in the period January–September 1992. There were 27 cases during that period: 7 were concerned with (mostly petty) theft, 1 with adultery, 1 with neglect of children, 1 with threatening behaviour, 4 with disorderly behaviour, 3 with breaches of ostracism, 1 with witchcraft, 3 with procedural rules and the rest with minor (mainly interpersonal) offences.

10 For a more detailed account, see Abrahams and Bukurura (1993).

11 Cf. Abrahams (1967, chapter 8).

12 Gitlitz and Rojas (1983) and Starn (1992).

13 For further discussion of *charivari*, see chapter 5. According to Professor Juhan Kahk (personal communication), such behaviour was not a feature of the historical Estonian peasant scene, even though Estonia was part of the Russian empire. The country population was more closely adminis-

tered than many sections of its Russian counterpart within the framework of government, church and the baronial estates.

Chapter 3 Early San Francisco and Montana

1 See Bancroft (1887, vol. I, *passim* and vol. II). For a discussion of Bancroft's research methods and output, see the entry in the *American Dictionary of National Biography*.
2 Quoted in Senkewicz (1985: 17).
3 Reported in Lotchin (1974: 192).
4 Quoted in Senkewicz (1985: 85).
5 Bancroft (1887, vol. I: 215); see also Stewart (1964: 304).
6 Callaway (1982: 46).
7 Bancroft (1887, vol. I: 698) and Langford (1890 [1966]: 296–7).
8 See Writer's Program (1941: 274–5).
9 Cf. Howard (1943: 127) and Dimsdale (1866 [1953]: 226).
10 Langford (1890 [1996]: 10).
11 Langford (1890 [1996]: 112–90), Brown (1975: 106) and Smurr (1958: 20).
12 Mather and Boswell (1987: ix, 97–8, 226).
13 Callaway (1982: 104, 106).
14 Smurr (1958: 19–20).

Chapter 4 Vigilante Politics

1 Cf. Marx (1904) (in Feuer 1959: 84). The complications of the situation include the influence of the inner logic of the professionalized legal system (cf. Engels 1890: 442–3). Marx was, of course, also sharply aware of the way in which apparent 'formal' equalities, guaranteed by law, worked to the sectional advantage of the economically powerful. Cf. Popper (1957, vol. II: 123).
2 Brown (1975: 134).
3 Bancroft (1887, vol. II: 666).
4 Bancroft (1887, II: 114).
5 Bancroft (1887, II: 666) and Senkewicz (1985: 62–90).
6 Bancroft (1887, II: 707).
7 Ingalls (1988: 11).
8 See Wade (1987: 119–248).
9 Brown (1975: 28).
10 Dumenil (1984: 122–3, 129–30, 147). She notes that 50–60 per cent of the first 4,000 Klan members in Oregon were Masons according to one estimate. The link was also present in the women's wing of the Klan. See Blee (1991: 111, 116, 121).

11 Ingalls (1988: 184).
12 Cf. Phillips (1989) and Haysom (1986).
13 Quoted in Phillips (1989: 22).
14 Trelease (1972: xx).
15 Trelease (1972: 4).
16 Wade (1987: 119–39).
17 Brown (1975: 214) and Trelease (1972: 362–80).
18 Trelease (1972: 371–2).

Chapter 5 The British Scene

1 Quoted by Bancroft (1887, vol. I: 404).
2 Thompson (1991: 505). He also reports some eighteenth-century cases of this sort, including some organized by women (1991: 511). See also the discussion in chapter 7 on vigilantism and gender.
3 Palmer (1978: 40) discusses 'whitecapping' and 'charivari' in the United States and Canada. He sees the former overtaking the latter as a preferred way of dealing with wife-beaters and the like during the late decades of the nineteenth century. At the same time, despite their similar functions, he asserts their completely separate origins. I feel less sure about this than he is. Cf. Thompson's 'throwaway' suggestion, noted below, of a contribution from 'shivaree' in the southern States to the development of the Ku Klux Klan and similar organizations, which Palmer sees as lying at the historical roots of the 'White Cap' movement. In any case, it is difficult to imagine that the historical conjunction of the two forms of activity would not have led to some convergence in the minds and actions of the members of Midwestern and other North American communities.
4 Thompson (1971: 53–4; 1981: 279). See also Ingram (1984: 110).
5 Thompson (1972: 308; 1991: 523). As Thompson (1991: 470) notes, forms of *charivari* (commonly called 'shivaree') were very widespread in the United States and Canada. As mentioned in note 3, Palmer (1978) also provides a detailed discussion and comparison with 'whitecapping'.
6 Macfarlane's (1981) discussion of 'law and disorder' in seventeenth-century England is interesting in this respect. Some of the account of lawlessness in the Kirkby Lonsdale area and elsewhere is reminiscent of the 'Wild West' of the nineteenth century, described by Dimsdale, Langford and others. But he notes that there was 'no sign that the neighbours went outside the law and set up vigilante groups' in response to threats and violent nuisance caused by criminals who lived in their midst. There is no discussion of 'rough music' as a response to other kinds of offence in the area.
7 Cf. my discussion of Freemasonry and vigilantism in North America in chapter 3.
8 For an interesting discussion of these events, see Barker (1993: 151–60 and *passim*).

9 I am very grateful for help from Dr G. Slapper on this issue (personal communication and also cf. Slapper (1996: 570). See also the discussion in Mirrlees-Black, Mayhew and Percy (1996). Home Office crime statistics for England and Wales show an increase in notifiable offences recorded by the police from 3,611,900 in 1985 to 5,100,200 in 1995, an average annual increase of 3.5 per cent (Home Office, 1996). Violent crimes rose by 6.2 per cent per annum over the same period. In contrast, convictions in the courts fell from 443,900 to 314,100 during this period.

10 Slapper (1996: 570).

11 Cf. D. Jeffreys, *Independent*, 5 July 1995.

12 *Vigilantes*, Thames TV, 10 September 1992.

13 Cf. C. Maclean, 'Whose Guardians?', *Independent Magazine*, 14 January 1989; Rees (1994). Johnston (1992: 168–73) usefully surveys material on Guardian Angels in the United States.

14 Johnston (1992: 136–58) provides a very useful overview of these schemes and also a discussion of Neighbourhood Watch and other forms of 'responsible' citizen action in the United States. For a discussion of Australian schemes, see Darian-Smith (1993).

15 A. Travis, 'Alarm over "patrolling by citizens" plan', *Guardian*, 20 September 1994.

16 Yarwood and Edwards (1995: 454).

17 Cf. *Cambridge News*, 18 and 23 July 1986, and 6 November 1986. I am very grateful to Pauline Hunt for helping me to obtain relevant cuttings.

18 Yarwood and Edwards (1995: 450), quoting Hough and Mayhew (1985: 49).

19 Bennett (1989: 211) and Bennett (1990: 84 and 195–201). A simple numerical account of Bennett's material is difficult, since he is comparing participation rates of different categories of respondents in his samples. Thus around 80 per cent of those in the samples were white, and it is not clear how representative this is of the local populations in question.

20 For an interesting discussion of the ideological rhetoric of 'the community' in such contexts, see Lacey and Zedner (1995: 301 and *passim*).

Chapter 6 Death Squads

1 My main sources for this part of my discussion are newspaper reports. Cf. articles by Elizabeth Nash in the *Independent* (16 January 1995, 20 January 1995, 7 February 1995, 11 January 1996, 25 January 1996, 22 February 1996) and also other articles in *The Times* (19 August 1995), *Sunday Times* (10 September 1995), and *Independent* (10 March 1995, 9 May 1996).

2 See also Jonas (1991: 62–3).

3 My account here is drawn mainly from Arguillas (1989). For other work on vigilantism and related phenomena in the Philippines, see Diokno (1989) and Kowalewski (1991).

4 My data source for this section is Kalmanowiecki (1991).

Chapter 7 Vigilantism and Gender

1 Cf. Wade (1987: 20–1) and Trelease (1972: xx–xxi).
2 On hurdy-gurdy houses, see Dimsdale (1866, chapter 1).
3 Towle (1966: 153–62). Towle provides accounts of several of the women concerned, including Mrs Dimsdale, Mrs Sanders and Mrs Slade. As she notes, Dimsdale's wife is not mentioned in the main sources.
4 Stuart (1925, vol. I: 206). One may speculate that the fact that she had 'few relatives' was seen as an advantage, since it would limit the demands upon her husband from his in-laws.
5 Langford (1890 [1996]: 289).
6 Thompson (1991: 505–6). Dobash and Dobash (1979: 56–9) discuss this feature of 'rough music', but do not consider it very significant as a weapon against male violence against wives.
7 Cf. Blee (1991: 14).
8 Recent media reports suggest that such moralistic attitudes are alive and well today in many American western and Midwest communities.
9 Blee (1991: 147–51).
10 Re Stephenson, see Blee (1991: 94–8) and Wade (1987: 215–47).
11 Green (1964). The study was originally published in 1947.
12 Thompson (1991: 511) mentions cases from London, Sussex and the Scottish Lowlands.
13 Lloyd (1995: 58–9).
14 White and Kowalski (1995: 495–503).
15 Cf. MacCormack and Strathern (1980) and Moore (1988, chapter 1).
16 White and Kowalski (1994: 487) note that only 13 per cent of those arrested for aggravated assault in the United States in 1990 were women, though they question the accuracy of such figures and suggest (pp. 490–1) that they may be lower than they should be.
17 The figures show an increase from around 121,700 in 1985 to around 212,600 in 1995, an average rise of 5.7 per cent per year. These figures, however, even if taken at face value, do not distinguish between offences committed by males and females. Figures making this distinction are available from the same source about both cautions and convictions, but then other difficulties emerge. The number of males convicted of violence against the person actually fell during the same period from about 43,900 to 26,400, and the number of convicted females also fell from about 3,600 to 2,800. At the same time, cautions in such cases rose, from about 7,100 to 15,500 for men and from about 1,900 to 4,900 for women. It is impossible to read any trends for changing rates of female crime from such data.
18 Domestic violence constituted about one-quarter of all violent incidents reported to the survey, and may well be more frequent than this figure suggests. Most domestic offenders were males – female offenders constituted 21 per cent of the total with a further 1 per cent of offences committed by a 'mixed sex group'. Most women's domestic violence was directed against men.

Mugging constituted about 10 per cent of all offences, and was almost wholly committed by men irrespective of the sex of the victim. Stranger violence (about 23 per cent of the total) was also a predominantly male offence, but 12 per cent of offences were carried out by mixed-sex groups. The sex of victim was also significant in this context – only 1 per cent of attacks on males were carried out by females (10 per cent were committed by mixed groups) whereas 22 per cent of attacks on females were carried out by other females (with a further 16 per cent by mixed-sex groups). Acquaintance violence (43 per cent of all cases) shows a roughly similar pattern. Only 1 per cent of attacks on males as against 39 per cent of attacks on females were carried out by women (7 per cent of attacks on both males and females were by mixed-sex groups).

19 Female and mixed-group violence combined rose from 16.2 to 17.9 per cent over the same period.

20 A number of sources note that men may have become more willing to report female violence against them. This seems particularly likely to be important in domestic violence – the only major area of female violence against men. I am extremely grateful to Catriona Mirrlees-Black of the Home Office Research and Statistics Directorate for her help in obtaining the British Crime Survey data used here. I am also grateful for her advice on the reliability and significance of some of these data, though I must assume full responsibility for any shortcomings in my use of it.

21 White and Kowalski (1994) review a wide range of research findings which support such a picture. As their title 'Deconstructing the myth of the nonaggressive woman' suggests, they are suspicious of its validity, at least as a source of evidence for female pacificity. For a valuable exploration of theory, fact and public fantasy concerning violent women, see Lloyd (1995). I am grateful to Loraine Gelsthorpe for drawing this and other texts to my attention.

22 For a discussion of some of the complexities involved in such political participation, see Moore (1988: 171–8). Quoting Molyneux (1985), Moore notes that, although women constituted about 30 per cent of the armed revolutionary force in Nicaragua, their special interests faded in the aftermath. Interestingly, she also notes that women's active participation in the Iranian revolution partly accounts for the largely non-violent nature of the struggle. The best study of women in gangs is Anne Campbell on New York (1991). See also Campbell (1995: 113ff).

23 White and Kowalski (1994: 500–1).

24 On women in English food riots, see Thompson (1991: 233ff and 305–36). Thompson drew attention to their role in such activities in his 1971 paper on 'The moral economy of the English crowd in the eighteenth century' (1991: 185–258) and in 'The moral economy reviewed' (1991: 259–351). Such material, of course, raises the question of the historical particularity of contemporary ideas on the subject. He notes ironically (p. 234) that these 'women appear to have belonged to some pre-history of their sex before its

Fall, and to have been unaware that they should have waited some two hundred years for their Liberation'.

25 White and Kowalski (1994: 487) themselves note that 'men are more likely than women to express their aggression publicly and physically' and that 'women's aggression is restricted primarily to the home and to more indirect modes of aggression'.

26 For a discussion of such literature and its feminist political implications, see Harris and Baker (1995).

27 For a critique of simplistic models of role convergence and increased female crime, see Morris and Gelsthorpe (1981). The thesis was classically proposed by Freda Adler (1975), and has been subjected to both attack and defence. See references in Austin (1993) and A. Campbell (1991: 278, 290). Campbell (pp. 278–80) provides a well-argued assessment of the problems that the thesis raises for feminists and others interested in male and female violence.

28 For a useful general discussion of such issues see Moore (1988: 1–11 and *passim*).

29 Campbell (1993: 204–10), *The Times*, 11 January 1997, p. 7.

30 Evidence from Neighbourhood Watch groups, discussed in chapter 5, is hard to interpret in this context. Most group members are male, but there are exceptions that may be significant. At the same time, patterns of membership in such 'responsible' groups (in Johnson's terms) may be a poor guide to participation in more 'autonomous' and violent activity.

Chapter 8 Limits of the Law

1 The argument appears to have been particularly sharp in the United States, where Kurt Llewellyn was a leading promoter of the realist case. His work with Hoebel (1941) on the Cheyenne Indians, with its emphasis upon detailed case study, was very influential in anthropology.

2 Cf. Drewry's (1978) positive review, which draws attention to such protest. For a detailed and moderately critical review that none the less ends on a positive note, see Devlin (1978).

3 Apart from their natural investigation of detailed case material in such circumstances, several anthropologists have encountered a 'realist' awareness of the special nature of each case in the societies they have studied. Cf. Epstein (1967: 210) for central Africa. Llewellyn and Hoebel (1941: 22) make a similar point for the Comanche Indians.

4 Cf. Gulliver (1963: 1). The very title of this work, *Social Control in an African Society*, points in this direction. See also Radcliffe-Brown (1952) for a classical statement on sanctions, partly based on Durkheim, and Epstein (1967: 206). For a 'realist' lawyer's frustration with the concept of law, see Frank (1949: vi). Gluckman (1972) makes it extremely clear that neither rules nor cases can be studied in isolation from each other.

5 Cf. Hart (1961: 77–96) and Fallers (1969: 11).

6 Smurr (1958: 15).

7 Devlin (1991: 404) serves as a reminder that public opinion on such issues is changeable, when he notes that juries at one time refused to convict in such cases because of the perceived severity of the penalties then in force.

8 Clastres (1977: 159–60).

9 Thompson (1991: 46).

10 Weber (1947: 114ff, 297ff). Weber notes (p. 114) that transitions from expedience and habituation to full-blown legitimacy are 'empirically gradual'. He also comments (p. 121) that 'submission to an order is almost always determined by . . . a wide variety of interests and by a mixture of adherence and belief in legality'. He has less to say about the kind of mixture involved in the case of vigilantism, where a belief in the legitimacy of the state is tested by the failure of its institutions to satisfy its citizens' expectations. He does, however, note (p. 123) that 'changes of natural and social conditions have some sort of effect on the differential probabilities of survival' of different forms of social action.

11 Dimsdale (1866: 205).

12 Brown (1975: 367) describes Clark's book, which was the basis of a classic film, as 'the best novel ever written about American vigilantism', and he notes that it 'marked an important shift in public attitudes, from favoring to condemning vigilantism'. For an earlier and more sympathetic treatment of vigilantism in a popular American novel, see Wister's *The Virginian* (1902). Wister was a friend of Theodore Roosevelt. The novel's widespread success was once ascribed to its being written by an easterner about a southerner in the far west (Cf. Webb, 1936: 456).

13 Quoted and discussed in Brown (1975: 173–5).

14 Rappaport (1977).

15 For an interesting discussion of this in a social science context see Strathern (1991: xx and *passim*).

16 Brown (1975: 159–62).

17 There is also a useful discussion of mafia and banditry, as particular forms of 'peasant violence', in Macfarlane's study of 'law and disorder' in eighteenth-century Westmorland (1981: 181–99).

18 Brown (1975: 16).

19 Hobsbawm (1959, chapter 3).

20 Gambetta (1993: 9, 116–17, 296).

21 As an anthropologist, I am reminded here of Barton's classic ethnographic study of the Kalingas of the Philippines (1949). There a variety of powerful individuals known as *pangats*, along with others to whom Barton refers as 'pact holders', keep the peace and enforce agreements through their reputation for being violently dangerous if crossed.

22 Mather and Boswell (1987: 97–8). See the discussion of the background to this point in chapter 3.

23 Lan (1985: 149, 167–70).

24 For a general, if somewhat idealized history of Forest Brethren resistance, see Laar (1992). I collected a few less flattering accounts in the course of rural fieldwork in Estonia in 1991–2.

25 Ranger (1986: 379, 383–4) and Brown (1975: 8–9).

26 On the relation of such self-defence patrols to vigilantism, and the possible significance of the 'frontier tradition' in their development, see Marx and Archer (1976).

27 For 'Megan's Law', see Martone (1995), and for reaction to proposals for a paedophile register in Britain, see the *Guardian* (16 August 1997, p. 7). The *Guardian* (19 August 1997, p. 14) reports the publication of identities on the Internet in California. For a recent British case involving the expulsion of a convicted paedophile from a local community, see that of Raploch women mentioned in chapter 7.

References

Abrahams, R. 1967: *The Political Organization of Unyamwezi.* Cambridge: Cambridge University Press.

    1981: *The Nyamwezi Today.* Cambridge: Cambridge University Press.

    1987: Sungusungu: village vigilante groups in Tanzania. *African Affairs.* 86, 179–96.

    1989: 'Law and order and the state in the Nyamwezi and Sukuma area of Tanzania'. *Africa,* 59, 3, 354–68.

    (ed.) 1994: *Witchcraft in Contemporary Tanzania,* Cambridge: African Studies Centre.

Abrahams, R. and Bukurura, S. 1993: Party, bureaucracy and grass-roots initiatives in a socialist state: the case of Sungusungu vigilantes in Tanzania. In C. Hann (ed.), *Socialism: ideals, ideologies and local practices,* London: Routledge, 92–101.

Adler, F. 1975: *Sisters in Crime: the rise of the new female criminal.* New York: McGraw-Hill.

Arguillas, C. 1989: 'Masses Arise': the making of a vigilante group. In M. Kirkwood (ed.), *States of Terror,* London: Catholic Institute for International Relations, 69–90.

Austin, R. 1993: Recent trends in official male and female crime rates – the convergence controversy. *Journal of Criminal Justice,* 21, 5, 447–66.

Bancroft, H. 1887: *Popular Tribunals* (2 vols). San Francisco, CA: History Company.

Barker, P. 1993: *The Eye in the Door.* Harmondsworth: Penguin.

Barton, R. 1949: *The Kalingas.* Chicago, IL: University of Chicago Press.

Bennett, T. 1989: Factors relating to participation in neighbourhood watch schemes. *British Journal of Criminology,* 29, 3, 207–18.

    1990: *Evaluating Neighbourhood Watch.* Aldershot: Gower.

Blee, K. 1991: *Women of the Klan: racism and gender in the 1920s.* Oxford: University of California Press.

Blok, A. 1974: *The Mafia of a Sicilian Village.* Oxford: Blackwell.

Bohannan, P. 1957: *Justice and Judgment among the Tiv*. Oxford: Oxford University Press.

Boyd, A. 1969: *Holy War in Belfast*, Tralee, Republic of Ireland: Anvil.

Brown, R. 1963: *The South Carolina Regulators*. Cambridge, MA: Harvard University Press.

1975: *Strain of Violence*. Oxford: Oxford University Press.

Bukurura, S. 1994a: Sungusungu: vigilantes in west-central Tanzania. Unpublished PhD dissertation, University of Cambridge.

1994b: Sungusungu and the banishment of witches in Kahama Tanzania. In R. Abrahams (ed.), *Witchcraft in Contemporary Tanzania*, Cambridge: African Studies Centre, 61–9.

1995: Combating crime among the Nyamwezi and Sukuma. *Crime, Law and Social Change*, 24, 3, 257–66.

Burrows, W. 1976: *Vigilante*. New York: Harcourt, Brace, Jovanovich.

Cáceres, J. 1989: Violence, national security and democratisation in Central America. In M. Kirkwood (ed.), *States of Terror*, London: Catholic Institute for International Relations, 95–114.

Callaway, L. 1982: *Montana's Righteous Hangmen*. Norman, OK: Oklahoma University Press.

Campbell, A. 1991: *The Girls in the Gang*, 2nd edition, Oxford: Blackwell.

1995: A few good men: evolutionary psychology and female adolescent aggression. *Ethology and Sociobiology*, 16, 99–123.

Campbell, B. 1993: *Goliath: Britain's dangerous places*. London: Methuen.

Campbell, H. 1989: Popular resistance in Tanzania: lessons from the Sungusungu. *Africa Development*. 14, 4, 5–43.

Caughey, J. 1957: Their majesties the mob. *Pacific Historical Review*. XXVI, 3, 217–34.

1960: *Their Majesties the Mob*. Chicago, IL: University of Chicago Press.

Chinnery, E. and Haddon, A. 1917: Five new religious cults in British New Guinea. *The Hibbert Journal*. XV, 3, 448–63.

Clark, W. 1940: *The Ox-Bow Incident*. New York: Random House.

Clastres, P. 1977: *Society against the State*. Oxford: Blackwell.

Colson, E. 1975: *Tradition and Contract: the problem of order*. London: Heinemann.

Darian-Smith, E. 1993: Neighbourhood Watch – who watches whom? *Human Organization*, 52, 1, 83–8.

Devlin, P. 1978: Review of Griffith 1977. *Modern Law Review*, 41, 5, 501–11.

1991: The conscience of the jury. *Law Quarterly Review*, 107, 398–404.

Dimsdale, T. 1866, new edition 1953: *The Vigilantes of Montana*. Norman, OK, and London: Oklahoma University Press.

Diokno, M. 1989: 'Guardians of democracy': vigilantes in the Philippines. In M. Kirkwood (ed.), *States of Terror*, London: Catholic Institute for International Relations, 37–68.

Dobash, R. and Dobash, R. E. 1979: *Violence Against Wives*. London: Open Books.

Drewry, G. 1978: Review of Griffith 1977. *New Law Journal*, 128, 8–9.

Dumenil, L. 1984: *Freemasonry and American Culture, 1880–1930*. Princeton, NJ: Princeton University Press.

Engels, F. 1890: Letter to Conrad Schmidt. In L. Feuer (ed.), *Marx and Engels: basic writings on philosophy and politics*, London: Fontana, 1969, 439–45.

—— 1894: On the history of early Christianity. In L. Feuer (ed.), *Marx and Engels: basic writings on philosophy and politics*, London: Fontana, 1969, 209–35.

Epstein, A. 1967: The case method in the study of law. In A. Epstein (ed.), *The Craft of Social Anthropology*, London: Tavistock, 205–30.

Fallers, L. 1969: *Law without Precedent*. Chicago, IL: University of Chicago Press.

Favret-Saada, J. 1980: *Deadly Words: witchcraft in the Bocage*. Cambridge: Cambridge University Press.

Fortes, M. 1969: *Kinship and the Social Order*. Chicago, IL: Aldine.

Frank, J. 1949: *Law and the Modern Mind*, 6th edition. London: Stevens.

Frank, S. 1990: Popular justice, community and culture among the Russian peasantry, 1870–1900. In B. Eklof and S. Frank (eds), *The World of the Russian Peasant*, London: Unwin Hyman, 133–53.

Gambetta, D. 1993: *The Sicilian Mafia: the business of private protection*. Cambridge, MA, and London: Harvard University Press.

Ghai, Y. 1976: Notes towards a theory of law and ideology: Tanzanian perspectives. *African Law Studies*, 13, 31–105.

Giddens, A. 1984: *The Constitution of Society*. Cambridge: Polity Press.

Gitlitz, J. and Rojas, T. 1983: Peasant vigilante committees in northern Peru. *Journal of Latin American Studies*, 15, 1, 153–97.

Gluckman, M. 1972: Limitations of the case method in the study of tribal law. *Law and Society Review*, 7, 1, 611–41.

Goody, E. 1970: Legitimate and illegitimate aggression in a West African state. In M. Douglas (ed.), *Witchcraft Confessions and Accusations*, London: Tavistock, 207–44.

Green, M. 1964: *Igbo Village Affairs*. London: Frank Cass.

Griffith, J. 1977: *The Politics of the Judiciary*. London: Fontana.

Grund, F. 1837: *The Americans*. London: Longman, Rees, Orme, Brown, Green and Longman.

Gulliver, P. 1963: *Social Control in an African Society*. London: Routledge and Kegan Paul.

Guy, C. 1996: Feminism and sexual abuse: troubled thoughts on some New Zealand issues. *Feminist Review*, 52, 154–68.

Harris, A. and Baker, D. 1995: If I had a hammer: violence as a feminist strategy in Helen Zahavi's *Dirty Weekend*. *Women's Studies International Forum*, 18, 5/6, 595–601.

Harris, P. 1989: The role of right-wing vigilantes in South Africa. In M. Kirkwood (ed.), *States of Terror*, London: Catholic Institute for International Relations.

Hart, H. 1961: *The Concept of Law*. London: Oxford University Press.

Haysom, N. 1986: *Apartheid's Private Army: the rise of right-wing vigilantes in South Africa*. London: Catholic Institute for International Relations.

Heald, S. 1982: Chiefs and administrators in Bugisu. In F. Robertson (ed.), *Uganda's First Republic: chiefs, administrators and politicians 1967–1971*, Cambridge: African Studies Centre, 76–98.

1986a: Witches and thieves: deviant motivations in Gisu society. *Man*, NS, 21, 1, 65–78.

1986b: Mafias in Africa: the rise of drinking companies and vigilante groups in Bugisu, Uganda. *Africa*, 56, 446–67.

1989: *Controlling Anger*. Manchester: Manchester University Press.

Herzfeld, M. 1992: *The Social Production of Indifference: exploring the symbolic roots of western bureaucracy*. New York: Berg.

Hobsbawm, E. 1959: *Primitive Rebels*, Manchester: Manchester University Press.

Hobsbawm, E. and Rudé, G. 1969: *Captain Swing*. London: Lawrence and Wishart.

Home Office 1996: *Criminal Statistics: England and Wales 1995*, London: HMSO.

Hough, M. and Mayhew, P. 1985: *Taking Account of Crime: key findings of the second British Crime Survey*. London: HMSO.

Howard, J. 1943: *Montana High Wide and Handsome*. New Haven, CT: Yale University Press.

Howell, P. 1954: *A Manual of Nuer Law*. London: Oxford University Press.

Huggins, M. (ed.) 1991: *Vigilantism and the State in Modern Latin-America*. New York and London: Praeger.

Huggins, M. and Mesquita, M. 1996: Exclusion, civil invisibility and impunity as explanations for youth murders in Brazil. *Childhood*, 3, 77–98.

Hyden, G. 1980: *Beyond Ujamaa in Tanzania: underdevelopment and an uncaptured peasantry*. London: Heinemann.

Iliffe, J. 1979: *A Modern History of Tanganyika*. Cambridge: Cambridge University Press.

Ingalls, R. 1988: *Urban Vigilantes in the New South: Tampa 1882–1936*. Knoxville, TN: University of Tennessee Press.

Ingram, M. 1984: Ridings, rough music and the 'reform of popular culture' in early modern England. *Past and Present*, 105, 79–113.

Johnston, L. 1992: *The Rebirth of Private Policing*. London: Routledge.

1996: What is vigilantism? *British Journal of Criminology*, 36, 2, 220–36.

Jonas, S. 1991: *The Battle for Guatemala: rebels, death squads and US power*. Boulder, CO and Oxford: Westview.

Kalmanowiecki, L. 1991: Police, people and preemption in Argentina. In M. Huggins (ed.), *Vigilantism and the State in Modern Latin-America*, New York and London: Praeger, 47–59.

Klima, G. 1970: *The Barabaig: East African cattle herders*. New York: Holt, Reinhart and Winston.

Kopytoff, I. (ed.) 1987: *The African Frontier*. Bloomington and Indianapolis, IN: Indiana University Press.

Kowalewski, D. 1991: Cultism, insurgency and vigilantism in the Philippines. *Sociological Analysis*, 52, 3, 241–53.

Kuhn, P. 1970: *Rebellion and its Enemies in Late Imperial China*. Cambridge, MA: Harvard University Press.

Laar, M. 1992: *War in the Woods: Estonia's struggle for survival 1944–1956*. Washington, DC: Compass.

Lacey, N. and Zedner, L. 1995: Discourses of community in criminal justice. *Journal of Law and Society*, 22, 3, 301–25.

Lan, D. 1985: *Guns and Rain*. London: James Currey.

Langford, N. 1890, new edition 1996: *Vigilante Days and Ways*. Helena, MT: American and World Geographic Publishing.

Leach, E. 1977: *Custom, Law and Terrorist Violence*. Edinburgh: Edinburgh University Press.

Little, C. and Sheffield, C. 1983: Frontiers and criminal justice: English private prosecution societies and American vigilantism in the eighteenth and nineteenth centuries. *American Sociological Review*, 48, December, 796–808.

Llewellyn, K. and Hoebel, E. 1941: *The Cheyenne Way*. Norman, OK: Oklahoma University Press.

Lloyd, A. 1995: *Doubly Deviant, Doubly Damned: society's treatment of violent women*. Harmondsworth: Penguin.

Lotchin, R. 1974: *San Francisco 1846–1856: from hamlet to city*. New York: Oxford University Press.

Luhrmann, T. 1989: *Persuasions of the Witch's Craft: ritual magic in contemporary England*. Oxford: Blackwell.

MacCormack, C. and Strathern, M. (eds) 1980: *Nature, Culture and Gender*. Cambridge: Cambridge University Press.

Macfarlane, A. 1981: *The Justice and the Mare's Ale*. Oxford: Blackwell.

Martone, E. 1995: Megan's Law – response – mere illusion of safety creates climate of vigilante justice. *American Bar Association Journal*, 81, 39.

Marx, G. and Archer, D. 1976: Community police patrols and vigilantism. In H. Rosenbaum and P. Sederberg (eds), *Vigilante Politics*, Philadelphia, PA: University of Pennsylvania Press, 128–57.

Marx, K. 1904: Excerpt from *A Contribution to the Critique of Political Economy* translated by N. Stone. In L. Feuer (ed.), *Marx and Engels: basic writings on philosophy and politics*, London: Fontana, 1969, 83–7.

Masanja, P. 1992: Some notes on the Sungusungu movement. In P. Forster and S. Maghimbi (eds), *The Tanzanian Peasantry: economy in crisis*, Aldershot: Avebury, 203–15.

Mather, R. and Boswell, F. 1987: *Hanging the Sheriff*. Salt Lake City, UT: University of Utah Press.

Melbin, M. 1978: Night as frontier. *American Sociological Review*, 43, 1, 3–22.

Mesaki, S. 1994: Witch killing in Sukumaland. In R. Abrahams (ed.), *Witchcraft in Contemporary Tanzania*, Cambridge: African Studies Centre, 47–60.

Mirrlees-Black, C., Mayhew, P. and Percy, A. 1996: The 1996 British Crime Survey. *Home Office Statistical Bulletin*, 19, London: Government Statistical Service.

Molyneux, M. 1985: Mobilisation without emancipation? Women's interests, the state, and revolution in Nicaragua. *Feminist Studies*, 11, 2, 227–54.

Moore, H. 1988: *Feminism and Anthropology*. Cambridge: Polity Press.

Morris, A. and Gelsthorpe, L. 1981: False clues and female crime. In A. Morris and L. Gelsthorpe (eds), *Women and Crime, Cropwood Conference Series 13*, Cambridge: Institute of Criminology, 49–72.

Nadel, S. 1954: *Nupe Religion*. London: Routledge and Kegan Paul.

Nicolosi, A. 1968: The rise and fall of the New Jersey vigilant societies. *New Jersey History*, 86, 29–32.

Palmer, B. 1978: Discordant music: charivaris and whitecapping in nineteenth-century North America. *Labour/Le Travailleur*, 3, 5–62.

Penglase, B. 1994: *Final Justice: police and death squad homicides of adolescents in Brazil*. New York: Human Rights Watch/Americas.

Peters, E. 1972: Aspects of the control of moral ambiguities: a comparative analysis of two culturally disparate modes of social control. In M. Gluckman (ed.), *The Allocation of Responsibility*, Manchester: Manchester University Press, 109–62.

Philips, D. 1989: Good men to associate and bad men to conspire. In D. Hay and F. Snyder (eds), *Policing and Prosecution in Britain (1750–1850)*, Oxford: Clarendon Press, 113–51.

Phillips, M. 1989: Divide and repress: vigilantes and state objectives in Crossroads. In M. Kirkwood (ed.), *States of Terror*, London: Catholic Institute for International Relations, 15–36.

Pocock, D. 1985: Unruly evil. In D. Parkin (ed.), *The Anthropology of Evil*, Oxford: Blackwell, 42–56.

Popper, K. 1957: *The Open Society and its Enemies* (2 vols). London: Routledge and Kegan Paul.

Radcliffe-Brown, A. 1952: Social sanctions. In *Structure and Function in Primitive Society*, London: Cohen and West, 205–11. Originally published in *Encyclopedia of the Social Sciences* (1933, XIII, 531–4), New York: Macmillan.

Ranger, T. 1986: Bandits and guerrillas: the case of Zimbabwe. In D. Crummey (ed.), *Banditry, Rebellion and Social Protest in Africa*, London: James Currey, 373–96.

Rappaport, R. 1977: Maladaptation in Social Systems. In J. Friedman and M. Rowlands (eds), *The Evolution of Social Systems*, London: Duckworth, 79–87.

Rees, A. 1961: *Life in a Welsh Countryside*. Cardiff: University of Wales Press.

Rees, G. 1994: The Guardian Angels: making space and finding time on the London underground. *Cambridge Anthropology*, 17, 1, 27–48.

Richards, A. 1935: A modern movement of witchfinders. *Africa*, 8, 4, 448–61.

Rosenbaum, H. and Sederberg, P. (eds) 1976: *Vigilante Politics*. Philadelphia, PA: University of Pennsylvania Press.

Sabasaba, M. and Rweyemamu, N. 1986: Exercise of punitive powers outside the judicial process in Tanzania. Unpublished LLB dissertation, University of Dar es Salaam.

Schurmann, F. 1968: *Ideology and Organization in Communist China*. Berkeley, CA: University of California Press.

Senkewicz, R. 1985: *Vigilantes in Goldrush San Francisco*. Stanford, CA: Stanford University Press.

Slapper, G. 1993: The perils of putting justice out to tender. *Guardian*, 4 September, 22.

1996: Criminal statistics and white lies. *New Law Journal*, 19 April, 570.

Smurr, J. 1958: Afterthoughts on the vigilantes. *Montana Magazine of Western History*, 8, 2, 8–20.

Southall, A. 1956: *Alur Society*. Cambridge: Heffer.

Starn, O. 1992: I dreamed of foxes and hawks: reflections on peasant protest, new social movements, and the *rondas campesinas* of northern Peru. In A. Escobar and S. Alvarez (eds), *The Making of Social Movements in Latin America*, Boulder, CO: Westview, 89–111.

Stewart, G. 1964: *Committee of Vigilance: revolution in San Francisco, 1851*. Boston, MA: Houghton Mifflin.

Strathern, M. 1991: *Partial Connections*. Savage, MD: Rowman and Littlefield.

Stuart, G. 1925: *Forty Years on the Frontier* (2 vols). Cleveland, OH: Arthur H. Clark.

Stuart, J. 1833: *Three Years in North America*. Edinburgh: Robert Cadell.

Tanner, R. 1970: *The Witch Murders in Sukumaland: a sociological commentary*. Uppsala, Sweden: Scandinavian Institute of African Studies.

Thompson, E. P. 1971: Anthropology and the discipline of historical context. *Midland History*, i, 3, 1971–2.

1972: 'Rough music': le charivari anglais. *Annales*, ESC, xxvii, 285–312.

1981: Rough music et charivari: quelques réflexions complémentaires. In J. Le Goff and J.-C. Schmitt (eds), *Le Charivari*, Paris: École des Hautes Études en Sciences Sociales, 273–83.

1991: *Customs in Common*. London: Merlin.

Towle, V. 1966: *Vigilante Woman*. London: T. Yoseloff.

Trelease, A. 1972: *White Terror: the Ku Klux Klan conspiracy and southern reconstruction*. London: Secker and Warburg.

Wade, W. 1987: *The Fiery Cross: the Ku Klux Klan in America*. New York: Simon and Schuster.

Webb, W. 1936: *The Great Plains*. Boston, MA: Houghton Mifflin.

Weber, M. 1947: *The Theory of Social and Economic Organization*. London: W. Hodge.

White, J. and Kowalski, R. 1994: Deconstructing the myth of the nonaggressive woman. *Psychology of Women Quarterly*, 18, 487–508.

Willis, R. 1968: Kamcape: an anti-sorcery movement in south-west Tanzania. *Africa*, 38, 7, 1–15.

Wister, O. 1902: *The Virginian*. New York: Macmillan.

Woodcock, G. 1986: *Anarchism: a history of libertarian ideas and movements*. Harmondsworth: Penguin.

Writers' Program 1941: *Wyoming*. New York: Oxford University Press.

Yarwood, R. and Edwards, B. 1995: Voluntary action in rural areas: the case of Neighbourhood Watch. *Journal of Rural Studies*, 11, 4, 447–59.

Index